OFFICE PROCEDURES FOR THE LEGAL PROFESSIONAL RESOURCE BOOK

The West Legal Studies Series

Your options keep growing with West Legal Studies

Each year our list continues to offer you more options for every area of the law to meet your course or on-the-job reference requirements. We now have over 140 titles from which to choose in the following areas:

Administrative Law	Family Law
Alternative Dispute Resolution	Federal Taxation
Bankruptcy	Intellectual Property
Business Organizations/Corporations	Introduction to Law
Civil Litigation and Procedure	Introduction to Paralegalism
CLA Exam Preparation	Law Office Management
Client Accounting	Law Office Procedures
Computer in the Law Office	Legal Research, Writing, and Analysis
Constitutional Law	Legal Terminology
Contract Law	Paralegal Employment
Criminal Law and Procedure	Real Estate Law
Document Preparation	Reference Materials
Environmental Law	Torts and Personal Injury Law
Ethics	Will, Trusts, and Estate Administration

You will find unparalleled, practical support

Each book is augmented by instructor and student supplements to ensure the best learning experience possible. We also offer custom publishing and other benefits such as West's Student Achievement Award. In addition, our sales representatives are ready to provide you with dependable service.

We want to hear from you

Our best contributions for improving the quality of our books and instructional materials is feedback from the people who use them. if you have a question, concern, or observation about any of our materials, or you have a product proposal or manuscript, we want to hear from you. Please contact your local representative or write us at the following address:

West Legal studies, 5 Maxwell Drive, P. O. Box 8007, Clifton Park, New York 12065

For additional information point your browser at
www.westlegal studies.com

OFFICE PROCEDURES FOR THE LEGAL PROFESSIONAL RESOURCE BOOK

Judy A. Long, J.D.

THOMSON

DELMAR LEARNING

Australia   Canada   Mexico   Singapore   Spain   United Kingdom   United States

WEST LEGAL STUDIES

OFFICE PROCEDURES FOR THE LEGAL PROFESSIONAL
RESOURCE BOOK
Judy A. Long

Career Education Strategic Business Unit:

Vice President:
Dawn Gerrain

Director of Editorial:
Sherry Gomoll

Editorial Assistant:
Sarah Duncan

Director of Production:
Wendy A. Troeger

Production Manager:
Carolyn Miller

Production Editor:
Betty L. Dickson

Director of Marketing:
Wendy Mapstone

Cover Design:
Dutton and Sherman Design

NOTICE TO THE READER

CONTENTS IN BRIEF

CONTENTS

INTRODUCTION

Although the textbook that accompanies this manual contains several forms for legal pleadings and other documents, different states vary considerably in the extent of their use of forms and their requirements for office-typed pleadings. This manual contains forms and documents from many states. It is impossible to include every form from every state. Therefore, it is advisable to access your own state's Web page to determine whether there are downloadable forms available there. If you do not have your own state's Web page address, you can access **http://www.westlegalstudies.com** and then go to your state's page under "state sources" in the Student Section. Federal sources are also available at this site.

The legal forms in this manual are divided by subject matter. Only the legal forms are included herein. The administrative forms are included in the textbook. Most law offices have a system in place for their administrative functions, including their own forms or computer software packages.

The format of each section shows the directions for completing the forms followed by the specific form. Some of the forms are left blank so that the student or reader can tear out or photocopy the form and complete it for submission to the instructor or to the court. Since states usually update their forms every year, it is advisable to confirm whether the forms included herein are those currently in use in your state. Courts will not accept an outdated form for filing.

Note that it is not feasible to include every state's forms for every type of action in this *Resource Book*. Therefore, the author has attempted to include as many specific state forms as possible, as well as the format required for most states. Each state's Web site should be consulted for specific forms or documents for that state.

Finally, please note that Internet resources and Web addresses are of a time-sensitive nature and URL addresses may often change or be deleted.

This section consists of sample pages from the state courts of Texas and Hawaii, as well as the appellate procedures for Alaska.

The Texas Web page (Exhibit 1-1) shows the Northern District of Texas District Court and may be found at

http://www.txnd.uscourts.gov/

The top frame has links to the information listed therein, including:

1. *Directories.* Links to the directories of the various, courts, court reporters, directories of the divisions by county, directories of legal resources such as legal services and law libraries, and the directory of attorneys who serve on the Criminal Justice Act Voluntary Panel.

2. *Rules.* Local rules, federal rules, special orders, and appellate rules.

3. *Court Records.* Copy services, docket sheets, federal records center, electronic noticing, local rules, case filings, and transcript requests.

4. *Forms and Publications.* Links to downloadable forms and publications available from the Web page.

5. *Filing Information.* Explains how to file documents with the courts.

6. *Jury information.* Includes the Jury Handbook and jury information for the various courts.

7. *Judges.* Notable cases and opinions of the various judges, and specific rules of different judges for their courtrooms.

8. *Links and Employment.* Provides further links as well as employment opportunities.

EXHIBIT 1-1 Northern Texas United States District Court Screen Shot

Courtesy: **http://www.txnd.uscourts.gov** Reprinted with permission.

UNITED STATES DISTRICT COURT
Northern District of Texas

| Directories | Rules | Court Records | Forms | Publications | Filing Info | Jury Info | Judges | Links | Employment | FAQ | About Us |

Honorable A. Joe Fish, Chief Judge
Karen Mitchell, Clerk of Court

Search: [   ] GO!

INFO CENTER

Message from the Clerk:

It is my honor to serve the judges of the U. S. District Court for the Northern District of Texas, the bar of this court, and members of the public who use our services. The mission of the U.S. District Clerk's Office is to make our system of justice possible. We do this by maintaining court records, providing case information, explaining and publicizing court procedures, providing courtroom and case management support, and administratively supporting the court through our financial, purchasing and facilities, information technology, human resources, and quality assurance departments.

The U.S. District Clerk's Office employs professional staff in seven divisions across Texas. These employees are committed to doing quality work and providing excellent customer service.

We are genuinely interested in your ideas about how we can improve our services. If you have questions, comments, or suggestions, feel free to <u>contact us</u> at any time.

We appreciate having the opportunity to serve you.

United States District Clerk
1100 Commerce, 1452 Floor
Dallas, TX 75242
214-753-2200
Office Hours:
Monday - Friday
8:30 a.m. - 4:30 p.m.

<u>Drop Box Hours:</u>

All information provided in this document is for informational purposes only and does not constitute a contract with any person or entity unless otherwise specified. Information on this web site is subject to change without prior notice. Although every reasonable effort is made to ensure the accuracy of the information presented the content of this site is in no way guaranteed. Any links to any external web sites are provided as a courtesy and should not be construed as an endorsement of the content or views of linked materials.

PHOTO ID REQUIRED
Any visitor to a Northern District of Texas court facility must be prepared to present a photo ID to security personnel.

Amended local civil rules 7.1(c), 7.1(h), 7.1(i), 9.1(a), 56.6(b)(1), and 83.8(e), and local criminal rule 57.8(e). Repeal of local civil rules 4.2, 80.1, 83.5, 83.8 (c), and 83.15, and local criminal rules 57.5, 57.6, 57.8(c), and 57.15. Effective September 1, 2004, unless modified after receipt of public comment. <u>See Special Order 2-56.</u>

Electronic Notice for Attorneys!
Instructions on signing up to receive notice of case activity via e-mail.

New: <u>Instructions</u> for attorneys on accessing criminal document images.

<u>New Fee Schedule:</u> Effective November 1, 2003.

Quickly access docket sheets on the <u>PACER Case Management system.</u>

The Hawaii state judiciary Web page (Exhibit 1-2) is located at

http://www.courts.state.hi.us/

Subpages of this page include the different court districts. The pages illustrated herein are from the Third Judicial Circuit District Court.

This page provides a link to the various forms available in Hawaii, including the forms for the Circuit Court and the District Court. The pages illustrated here show the list of links to the District Court Forms for Hawaii's Third Judicial Circuit Court. Each form listed is a link to the form itself.

EXHIBIT 1-2   Hawaii State Judiciary Screen Shot

Courtesy: **http://www.state.courts.hi.us.** Copyright © 2002.

Hawai'i State **Judiciary**

Forms | **Search Court Records** | **Opinions** | **Rules** | **Pay Fines** | **Jury Service** | Search

Home > Self-Help > Court Forms > Hawai`i

District Court Forms for Hawai`i (Third Judicial Circuit)

- Circuit Court
- District Court

When filing a form or other documents in the District Court, please be sure to provide one copy for each plaintiff or petitioner and one copy for each defendant or respondent in addition to the original document.

Short Name	Title of Document	Form #
PLEADINGS		
Complaint (Assumpsit)	Complaint (Assumpsit-Money Owed); Declaration; Exhibit(s); Summons	3D07
Complaint (Assumpsit & Summary Possession)	Complaint (Assumpsit, Summary Possession/Landlord-Tenant, Damages); Declaration; Exhibit(s); Summons	3DC08
Complaint (Personal Injury)	Complaint (Personal Injury/Property Damages); Summons	3DC09
Complaint (Replevin)	Complaint (Replevin); Summons	3DC10
Statement of Claim (Security Deposit)	Statement of Claim and Notice (Disagreement About Security Deposit-Residential)	3DC48A
Statement of Claim (General Form)	Statement of Claim and Notice (General Form)	3DC48B
Counterclaim	Counterclaim; Certificate of Service; Declaration	3DC14
Cost Relief From Filing Fees	Ex Parte Application for Relief From Costs; Declaration; Order	3DC13
MOTIONS, PRE-TRIAL PROCEDURE		
Continuance (Non-Hearing Motion)	Non-Hearing Motion for Continuance; Declaration; Notice of Motion; Certificate of Service;	3DC11
Continuance (Stipulation)	Stipulation for Continuance	3DC12
Motion for Default Judgment (Default)	Ex Parte Motion for Default Judgment; Declaration; Exhibit(s); Affidavit of Counsel Re: Attorney's Fees; Order Granting Ex Parte Motion for Default Judgment	3DC17
Motion for Default Judgment (Non-hearing) (Default)	Non-Hearing Motion for Default Judgment; Declaration; Exhibit(s); Affidavit of Counsel Re: Attorney's Fees; Notice of Motion; Certificate of Service; Order	3DC18
Motion To Dismiss	Motion to Dismiss; Declaration; Notice of Motion; Certificate of Service	3DC36
Dismissal	Notice of Dismissal	3DC20
Dismissal (by Stipulation)	Stipulation for Dismissal	3DC21
Motion for Discovery	Motion for Discovery; Declaration; Notice of Motion; Certificate of Service	3DC37
Motion (Hearing)	Plaintiff(s)' /Defendant(s)' Motion; Declaration; Notice of Motion; Certificate of Service	3DC38
Motion (Non-Hearing)	Plaintiff(s)' /Defendant(s)' Non-Hearing Motion; Declaration; Notice of Motion; Certificate of Service	3DC39

continued

Exhibit 1-2   *continued*

Subpoena/Duces Tecum	Subpoena or Subpoena Duces Tecum; Exhibit A	3DC49
Summons	Summons	3DC50
TRIAL		
Exhibit List	Exhibit List	3DC23
Exhibit List - Continuation Sheet	Exhibit List Continuation Sheet	3DC24
Return of Exhibits	Request for Return of Exhibits	3DC46
MISCELLANEOUS		
Certificate of Service	Certificate of Service	3DC04
Return of Service	Return of Service; Acknowledgment of Service	3DC47
JUDGMENT/POST-JUDGMENT		
Judgment	Judgment	3DC34
Judgment for Possession	Judgment for Possession	3DC35
Notice of Entry of Judgment	Notice of Entry of Judgment or Order	3DC43
Motion for Reconsideration or New Trial	Motion for Reconsideration, or New Trial; Declaration; Notice of Motion; Certificate of Service	3DC41
Order for Exam Individual and Person with Knowledge	Ex Parte Motion for Examination of Judgment Debtor(s) or Person Having Knowledge of Judgment Debtor(s); Declaration; Order for Examination; Exhibit(s)	3DC44
AFDC Notice	Notice to Recipients of Aid to Families With Dependent Children (AFDC); Notice of Funds Exempt From Garnishment Under Law	3DC01
Affidavit Re: Attorney's Fees	Affidavit of Counsel Re: Attorney's Fees and Costs; Appendix	3DC02
Bench Warrant	Bench Warrant	3DC03
Discontinuance of OE	Ex Parte Motion for Discontinuance of Order for Examination and Recall of Bench Warrant; Order; Certificate of Service	3DC19
Exemplification	Exemplification	3DC22
Garnishee by Migs	Ex Parte Motion for Issuance of Garnishee Summons After Judgment; Declaration; Non-Conclusory Declaration; Order; Exhibit(s); Garnishee Summons; Garnishee Information;	3DC29
Garnishee Order	Garnishee Order	3DC30
Garnishee OSC	Motion for Order to Show Cause on Garnishee; Declaration and Order;	3DC31
Garnishee Summons	Garnishee Summons	3DC32
Garnishee Transfer	Affidavit of Garnishee Transfer; Exhibit(s) Notice to Employer of Judgment Debtor(s); Garnishee Information	3DC33
Garnishee by Affidavit	Affidavit of Judgment Creditor(s) for Garnishment of Wages; Exhibit(s); Notice to Employer of Judgment Debtor; Garnishee Information	3DC25
Garnishee Disclosure	Garnishee Disclosure	3DC26

continued

Exhibit 1-2 *continued*

Garnishee Information	Garnishee Information	3DC27
Garnishee Calculation	Garnishee Calculation Worksheet	3DC27C
Garnishee Notice	Garnishee Notice	3DC27A
Garnishee Return of Wages	Judgment Debtor(s)'s Motion Return / Release of Wages Exempt from Garnishment; Notice of Motion; Certificate of Service; Garnishment Calculation Worksheet; Exihibit "A"	3DC27B
Release of Garnishee	Release of Garnishee; Certificate of Service	3DC45
Satisfaction of Judgment	Satisfaction of Judgment/Release of Garnishee(s)	3DC48
TEMPORARY RESTRAINING ORDERS		
Petition for TRO (TRO)	Petition for Ex Parte Temporary Restraining Order and for Injunction Against Harassment; Declaration of Petitioner; Temporary Restraining Order Against Harassment; and Notice of Hearing	3DC51
Order Granting Injunction Against Harassment (TRO)	Order Granting Petition for Injunction Against Harassment	3DC52
WRITS		
Writ of Execution	Writ of Execution; Exhibit A (Hawai'i Revised Statutes 651-32)	3DC53
Writ of Possession	Writ of Possession	3DC54
Writ of Replevin	Writ of Replevin	3DC55

Search | Contact Info | Privacy Statement

The Alaska court system's appellate cases are described in the pages from the Alaska courts. Descriptions for how to complete an appeal for the Alaska Court of Appeals and the Alaska Supreme Court are supplied in Exhibit 1-3.

EXHIBIT 1-3   Alaska Court System Docketing Statement Forms

Courtesy: **http://www.appellate.courts.state.ak.us**

ALASKA COURT SYSTEM

DOCKETING STATEMENT FORMS
for

ALASKA SUPREME COURT
ALASKA COURT OF APPEALS

CLERK'S INSTRUCTIONS FOR PREPARATION OF THE EXCERPT OF RECORD

JANUARY 1998

continued

Exhibit 1-3   *continued*

TABLE OF CONTENTS

CLERK'S INSTRUCTIONS FOR PREPARATION OF EXCERPTS

A.   APPELLANT'S EXCERPT OF RECORD

1.   An excerpt of record must be bound on the left-hand side in the same manner as a brief. All excerpts, whether submitted by appellant or appellee, must have a <u>pink</u> cover. The cover must be the same weight and quality as the cover of a brief. The cover must contain the same information that appears on the front cover of the brief, but must be labeled "APPELLANT'S EXCERPT OF RECORD" instead of "BRIEF OF APPELLANT." It must also contain the volume number, e.g., "Volume 1 of 1."

EXAMPLE:

```
              IN THE SUPREME COURT OF THE STATE OF ALASKA

JANE A. DOE,            )
                       )
        Appellant,     )
                       )
    vs.                )
                       )
JOHN B. DOE,           )
                       )   Supreme Court No. S-5741
        Appellee.      )
_____)   Superior Court No. 3AN-92-4375 CI

            APPEAL FROM THE SUPERIOR COURT,
        THIRD JUDICIAL DISTRICT AT ANCHORAGE,
       THE HONORABLE J. WILLIAM JONES, PRESIDING

              APPELLANT'S EXCERPT OF RECORD
                     VOLUME 1 OF 1

                        JAMES SMITH (1234567)
                        100 A Street, Suite 100
                        Anchorage, Alaska 99000
                        (907) 333-3333

                        Attorney for Appellant
                        Jane A. Doe

Filed in the Supreme Court of
the State of Alaska, this ____
day of _____, 1994.

Jan Hansen, Clerk

By: _____
      Deputy Clerk
```

continued

Exhibit 1-3 *continued*

2. Documents in the excerpt of record must be arranged in chronological order by document execution date, with the document with the earliest date on top.

See Section E on confidential documents.

3. Documents in the excerpt must be copied on <u>both</u> sides of the paper (i.e., double-sided copies).

4. Pages must be numbered in a single consecutive sequence throughout all volumes (e.g., if volume 1 contains pages 1 through 200, then volume 2 would begin with page 201). Page numbers must appear at the bottom of the page.

5. Each excerpt must contain a table of contents at the beginning of the first volume. The table of contents must be prepared as follows:

a. Each document in the excerpt must be listed by title, execution date, document creator's name (unless the creator is obvious), and the page on which the document begins.

EXAMPLE (multi-defendant case):

Complaint, November 12, 1990 1

Smith's Answer, December 8, 1990 38

Johnson's Answer, December 10, 1990 . . . . 55)

b. When there is more than one volume of the excerpt, each document filed in a particular volume must be listed under the volume heading.

EXAMPLE:

Affidavit of Mary Smith, March 15, 1991 197

<u>Volume 2</u>

Affidavit of William Johnson, April 3, 1991 . . . . 199)

c. See Section E on confidential documents.

B. **APPELLEE'S EXCERPT OF RECORD**

The rules outlined above for Appellant's Excerpt of Record apply except that the first page of the first document in Appellee's excerpt must begin with the number immediately following the number of the last page in Appellant's excerpt (e.g., if Appellant's excerpt ends with page 237, then Appellee's excerpt would begin with page 238).

See Section E on confidential documents.

C. **SUPPLEMENTAL EXCERPT OF RECORD**

The rules outlined above apply except that the title of the file should be "Appellant's Supplemental Excerpt of Record" or "Appellee's Supplemental Excerpt of Record." In addition, the first page of the first document in a supplemental excerpt must begin with the number immediately following the number of the last page of the last excerpt filed in the case (e.g., if the last volume of Appellee's excerpt of record ends with page 225, then a supplemental excerpt filed with Appellant's reply brief would begin with page 226).

D. **CITATION GUIDELINES**

1. DOCUMENTS IN AN EXCERPT OF RECORD: (Exc. 126).

2. TRANSCRIPT: (Tr. 109).

3. DOCUMENTS IN THE RECORD, BUT NOT IN AN EXCERPT: (R. 78).

Note: When citing testimony presented by deposition, do not cite to the deposition. Instead, include the relevant pages of the deposition in the excerpt and cite to the excerpt.

E. **CONFIDENTIAL DOCUMENTS**

1. Confidential documents must be arranged in chronological order by document execution date, with the document with the earliest date on top.

2. Pages must be numbered consecutively, beginning with the number immediately following the number of the last page of the last non-confidential document in Appellant's excerpt. Page numbers must appear at the bottom of the page.

(7/94)   -2-

continued

Exhibit 1-3 *continued*

3.   Confidential documents must be placed in a manila envelope marked "APPELLANT'S EXCERPT -- CONFIDENTIAL." The case name and the appellate case number must be written on the front of the envelope. The envelope must be placed at the end of the last volume of the party's excerpt.

4.   Confidential documents must be listed at the end of the table of contents under the heading "Confidential Envelope."

EXAMPLE:

Judgment and Commitment, November 2, 1992 67

Confidential Envelope

Presentence Report, August 30, 1992 68

Updated Presentence Report,
   September 15, 1993 76

5.   The first page of the first document in Appellee's excerpt begins with the number immediately following the number of the last page of the last document in Appellant's confidential envelope (e.g., if the last confidential document in Appellant's confidential envelope ends with page 95, then Appellee's excerpt would begin with page 96).

Docketing Statements

Appellate Rule 204(b)[1] requires that the appellant file a docketing statement with the notice of appeal. Appellants may use the docketing statement forms provided by the court system or make their own statements. Appellants who make their own statements must include all of the information that appears on the court system forms in the same order that it appears on the forms.

Example:

Court System Form:

2. PARTY FILING APPEAL (Appellant)

a. Name	b. Status in the Trial Court
	☐ Plaintiff ☐ Defendant
c. Party Mailing Address	☐ Other. Specify: _____
City State Zip Code	d. Telephone

Appellant's Version:

2.   Party Filing Appeal (Appellant)

   a.   Name: Joe Party
   b.   Status in the Trial Court: **Plaintiff**
   c.   Party Mailing Address: **200 South Street**
                                  Anchorage, Alaska 99506
   d.   Telephone: **(907) 444-5555**

Court system forms may be typed or handwritten in black ink.

Final Judgments Attached to Docketing Statements

Each docketing statement must be accompanied by a copy of the final order or judgment from which the appeal is taken. Appellate Rule 204(b)[2]. If the order or judgment includes confidential information, the appellant should black out this information before filing the order or judgment. In a CINA or delinquency case, for example, the appellant should black out all of the child's name except the intitials.

Questions should be directed to the Clerk of the Appellate Courts.

Civil litigation is one of the busiest areas of law. More paralegals are employed in civil law offices than in any other major practice area. Five different states' civil forms are displayed here: Arizona, California, Hawaii, New York, and Texas.

Since California civil practice is very forms-intensive, a number of these forms are included. California Judicial Council forms may be purchased from West, a Thomson Business, at their online store at **http://www.westgroup.com**. The forms are also available in a two-volume set from West.

Section 2-A. Arizona Civil Documents

In order to commence a civil action in Arizona, the plaintiff must file a Complaint with the appropriate court. The Statute of Limitations starts to run when the complaint is filed with the court and not when it is served on the defendant. The court acquires jurisdiction over the case on the date the complaint is filed.

The purpose of the complaint is to state the claim that the plaintiff has against the defendant. The defendant is served with a Summons that states that the court has jurisdiction over the lawsuit.

The plaintiff must serve the Summons, accompanied by a copy of the Complaint, on the defendant to preserve the lawsuit itself. Service must be made on the defendant within 120 days of the filing of the Complaint with the court. Practically speaking, this 120 days may be used by the parties to settle their claims out of court.

Although the complaint does not have to be excessively detailed to be valid, the court requires that the complaint set forth enough facts to present a valid claim for relief. Special rules govern lawsuits against public entities and should be researched in those cases.

Many counties in Arizona require that a civil cover sheet accompany the complaint for filing. Always check with your county court to determine whether this sheet is required. Many other states also require cover sheets, which are provided by the courts and must be completed by the attorney. Those cases that are subject to mandatory arbitration must also be accompanied by a certificate that is filed with the Complaint and Civil Cover Sheet. The civil cover sheet may be obtained from the appropriate court clerk's office in your state. The complaint's format is similar to that of other states. It should always be prepared on ruled and numbered pleading paper. A brief description of the parts of the complaint follows:

1. *Court Caption.* This includes the name of the court and the location. It will vary depending on which county court has jurisdiction over the case.

2. *Case Caption.* The parties' names and designations are included. Some states also require that this caption include the name of the document and the case number.

3. *Body.* The body of the complaint describes the designations of the parties and their residences. It describes the nature of the action.

4. *Prayer for Damages.* The WHEREFORE clause at the end of the complaint lists the damages that are being requested by the plaintiff.

5. *Signature Clause.* The date and attorney signature appear in the signature clause. In the case of a verified complaint, a verification clause below the attorney's signature is signed by the plaintiff.

Complaint

A sample complaint using the Arizona format is shown in Exhibit 2-1.

EXHIBIT 2-1   Arizona Complaint

```
 1 │ JOHN B. GOOD
   │ 2433 Yavapai Boulevard
 2 │ Scottsdale, AZ 23456
   │ Telephone:  (444) 123-4567
 3 │
   │ Attorney for Plaintiff
 4 │

 5 │           Superior Court of Mariposa County State of Arizona

 6 │

 7 │ THE GOOD GUYS COMPANY,              Case No.: No. 12-3-456789-1

 8 │         Plaintiff,                  COMPLAINT

 9 │     vs.

10 │ JOHN AND JILL DEFENSE,

11 │         Defendant

12 │

13 │      Plaintiff THE GOOD GUYS COMPANY, allege as follows against the

14 │ defendant:

15 │

16 │                               I.

17 │      Plaintiff is a corporation organized according to the laws of the state

18 │ of Arizona and has a principal place of business in Mariposa County.  The

19 │ plaintiff is in the construction business and is licensed by the state of

20 │ Arizona to perform these services with respect to business or residential

21 │ property.

22 │                              II.

23 │      The defendants JOHN and JILL DEFENSE are husband and wife and reside in

24 │ Mariposa County, Arizona.

25 │                              III.
```

-1-

continued

Exhibit 2-1 *continued*

1   On approximately September 6, 2003, the plaintiffs and defendants

2 entered into a contract for the construction of a patio and gazebo at the

3 rear of defendants' residence in Scottsdale for the total amount of Sixty-

4 five Thousand Dollars and No/Cents ($65,000). The defendants agreed to pay

5 this amount upon the plaintiff's completion of the building project.

6   IV.

7   Plaintiff has completed the patio and gazebo in a superior and

8 workmanlike manner.

9   V.

10   Plaintiff has made demand on the defendants for the amount due under

11 the contract but the defendants have refused to pay this amount due.

12   VI.

13   The plaintiff is entitled to recover reasonable attorneys' fees since

14 this action arises out of a contract.

15   WHEREFORE, plaintiff prays for judgment against the defendants for the

16 sum of Sixty-five Thousand Dollars and No/Cents ($65,000) with interest

17 thereon from the due date until the sum is paid, for attorneys' fees and

18 for costs of suit incurred herein, and for such other and further relief as

19 the court deems proper.

20   Dated this ____ day of _____, 2003

21

22

23   JOHN B. GOOD
                         2433 Yavapai Boulevard

24   Scottsdale, AZ 23456
                         Telephone: (444) 123-4567

25

                         Attorney for Plaintiff

-2-

continued

Exhibit 2-1   *continued*

```
 1 | JOHN B. GOOD
   | 2433 Yavapai Boulevard
 2 | Scottsdale, AZ 23456
   | Telephone:  (444) 123-4567
 3 |
 4 |              Superior Court of Mariposa County State of Arizona
 5 |
 6 | THE GOOD GUYS COMPANY,            Case No.: No. 12-3-456789-1
 7 |           Plaintiff,             CERTIFICATE OF COMPULSORY ARBITRATION
 8 |      vs.
 9 | JOHN DEFENSE,
10 |           Defendant
11 |
12 |      The undersigned hereby certifies that the greatest award required by
13 | the plaintiff/complainant, excluding interest, attorneys' fees, and costs
14 | does not exceed the limits that have been set by local rule for compulsory
15 | arbitration, and hereby further certifies that this case is subject to
16 | compulsory arbitration under Rules 72 through 76 of the Arizona Rules of
17 | Civil Procedure.
18 |
19 |
20 |                                   Dated this ____ day of _____, 2003
21 |
22 |                                   JOHN B. GOOD
   |                                   2433 Yavapai Boulevard
23 |                                   Scottsdale, AZ 23456
   |                                   Telephone: (444) 123-
24 |                                   4567
25 |                                   Attorney for Plaintiff
```

-1-

continued

Exhibit 2-1 *continued*

```
 1   JOHN B. GOOD
     2433 Yavapai Boulevard
 2   Scottsdale, AZ 23456
     Telephone:  (444) 123-4567
 3

 4            Superior Court of Mariposa County State of Arizona

 5

 6   THE GOOD GUYS COMPANY,          Case No.: No. 12-3-456789-1

 7            Plaintiff,             SUMMONS

 8        vs.

 9   JOHN and JILL DEFENSE,

10            Defendant

11   THE STATE OF ARIZONA TO DEFENDANTS JOHN AND JILL DEFENSE

12   YOU ARE HEREBY SUMMONED to appear and defend, within the applicable time, in

13   the action in this court.  You are served within the state of Arizona and

14   must appear and defend within twenty (20) days after the service of the

15   Summons and Complaint upon you, exclusive of the day of service.

16   YOU ARE HEREBY NOTIFIED that in case of your failure to appear and defend

17   within the time applicable, judgment by default may be rendered against you

18   for the relief demanded in the Complaint.

19   YOU ARE CAUTIONED that to appear and defend, you must file an answer or other

20   proper response in writing with the clerk of this court, accompanied by the

21   necessary filing fee, within the time required to serve a copy of any answer

22   or other response upon the plaintiff's attorney.

23   The name and address of plaintiff's attorney is:

24   JOHN B. GOOD

25   2433 Yavapai Boulevard

     Scottsdale, AZ 23456


                                    -1-
```

continued

Exhibit 2-1 *continued*

1	REQUESTS FOR REASONABLE ACCOMMODATIONS FOR PERSONS WITH DISABILITIES MUST BE
2	MADE TO THE DIVISION ASSIGNED TO THE CASE BY PARTIES AT LEAST THREE (3)
3	JUDICIAL DAYS PRIOR TO THE SCHEDULED COURT PROCEEDING.
4	SIGNED AND SEALED THIS _____ day of _____, _____.
5	[stamp or typed clerk name]
6	Clerk
7	[signature]
8	By
9	By:_____
10	[Typed name of Clerk]
11	Deputy Clerk
12	
13	
14	
15	
16	
17	
18	
19	
20	
21	
22	
23	
24	
25	

Dated this 17th day of July, 2003

JOHN B. GOOD
2433 Yavapai Boulevard
Scottsdale, AZ 23456
Telephone: (444) 123-4567

-2-

The Summons notifies the defendant that the plaintiff has filed a lawsuit against him. It is served with a copy of the complaint. The defendant must appear and defend within 20 days of the date of service if served within the state. The summons must contain the names of the parties and the court and be directed to the person to be served. It must be under the court's seal and contain the name and address of the plaintiff's attorney.

California Summons

A sample summons for California is shown in Exhibit 2-2. The summons format is similar for all states.

EXHIBIT 2-2 California Summons

982(a)(9)

SUMMONS
(CITACION JUDICIAL)

NOTICE TO DEFENDANT: *(Aviso a Acusado)*

FOR COURT USE ONLY
(SOLO PARA USO DE LA CORTE)

YOU ARE BEING SUED BY PLAINTIFF:
(A Ud. le está demandando)

You have *30 CALENDAR DAYS* after this summons is served on you to file a typewritten response at this court. A letter or phone call will not protect you; your typewritten response must be in proper legal form if you want the court to hear your case. If you do not file your response on time, you may lose the case, and your wages, money and property may be taken without further warning from the court. There are other legal requirements. You may want to call an attorney right away. If you do not know an attorney, you may call an attorney referral service or a legal aid office (listed in the phone book).	*Después de que le entreguen esta citación judicial usted tiene un plazo de 30 DIAS CALENDARIOS para presentar una respuesta escrita a máquina en esta corte.* *Una carta o una llamada telefónica no le ofrecerá protección; su respuesta escrita a máquina tiene que cumplir con las formalidades legales apropiadas si usted quiere que la corte escuche su caso.* *Si usted no presenta su respuesta a tiempo, puede perder el caso, y le pueden quitar su salario, su dinero y otras cosasde su propiedad sin aviso adicional por parte de la corte.* *Existen otros requisitos legales. Puede que usted quiera llamar a un abogado inmediatamente. Si no conoce a un abogado, puede llamar a un servicio de referencia de abogados o a una oficina de ayuda legal (vea el directorio telefónico).*

The name and address of the court is: *(El nombre y dirección de la corte es)*

CASE NUMBER: *(Número del Caso)*

The name, address, and telephone number of plaintiff's attorney, or plaintiff without an attorney, is:
(El nombre, la dirección y el número de teléfono del abogado del demandante, o del demandante que no tiene abogado, es)

DATE: _____ Clerk, by _____, Deputy
(Fecha) _____ *(Actuario)* _____ *(Delegado)*

[SEAL]

NOTICE TO THE PERSON SERVED: You are served

1. ☐ as an individual defendant.
2. ☐ as the person sued under the fictitious name of *(specify)*:

3. ☐ on behalf of *(specify)*:

    under: ☐ CCP 416.10 (corporation)   ☐ CCP 416.60 (minor)
             ☐ CCP 416.20 (defunct corporation)   ☐ CCP 416.70 (conservatee)
             ☐ CCP 416.40 (association or partnership) ☐ CCP 416.90 (individual)
             ☐ other:
4. ☐ by personal delivery on *(date)*:

continued

Exhibit 2-2　*continued*

PROOF OF SERVICE — SUMMONS
(Use separate proof of service for each person served)

1. I served the
   a. ☐ summons ☐ complaint ☐ amended summons ☐ amended complaint
      ☐ completed and blank Case Questionnaires ☐ Other *(specify):*
   b. on defendant *(name):*

   c. by serving ☐ defendant ☐ other *(name and title or relationship to person served):*

   d. ☐ by delivery ☐ at home ☐ at business
      (1) date:
      (2) time:
      (3) address:

   e. ☐ by mailing
      (1) date:
      (2) place:

2. Manner of service *(check proper box):*
   a. ☐ **Personal service.** By personally delivering copies. (CCP 415.10)
   b. ☐ **Substituted service on corporation, unincorporated association (including partnership), or public entity.** By leaving, during usual office hours copies in the office of the person served with the person who apparently was in charge and thereafter mailing (by first-class mail, postage prepaid) copies to the person served at the place where the copies were left. (CCP 415.20(a))
   c. ☐ **Substituted service on natural person, minor, conservatee, or candidate.** By leaving copies at the dwelling house, usual place of abode, or usual place of business of the person served in the presence of a competent member of the household or a person apparently in charge of the office or place of business, at least 18 years of age, who was informed of the general nature of the papers, and thereafter mailing (by first-class mail, postage prepaid) copies to the person served at the place where the copies were left. (CCP 415.20(b)) *(Attach separate declaration or affidavit stating acts relied on to establish reasonable diligence in first attempting personal service.)*
   d. ☐ **Mail and acknowledgment service.** By mailing (by first-class mail or airmail, postage prepaid) copies to the person served, together with two copies of the form of notice and acknowledgment and a return envelope, postage prepaid, addressed to the sender. (CCP 415.30) *(Attach completed acknowledgment of receipt.)*
   e. ☐ **Certified or registered mail serivce.** By mailing to an address outside California (by first-class mail postage prepaid, requiring a return receipt) copies to the person served. (CCP 415.40) *(Attach signed return receipt or other evidence of actual delivery to the person served.)*
   f. ☐ Other *(specify code section):*
      ☐ additional page is attached.

3. The "Notice to the Person Served" (on the summons) was completed as follows (CCP 412.30, 415.10, and 474):
   a. ☐ as an individual defendant.
   b. ☐ as the person sued under the fictitious name of *(specify):*
   c. ☐ on behalf of *(specify):*
      under: ☐ CCP 416.10 (corporation) ☐ CCP 416.60 (minor) ☐ other:
      ☐ CCP 416.20 (defunct corporation) ☐ CCP 416.70 (conservatee)
      ☐ CCP 416.40 (association or partnership) ☐ CCP 416.90 (individual)
   d. ☐ by personal delivery on *(date):*
4. At the time of service I was at least 18 years of age and not a party to this action.
5. Fee for service: $
6. Person serving:
   a. ☐ California sheriff, marshal, or constable.
   b. ☐ Registered California process server.
   c. ☐ Employee or independent contractor of a registered California process server.
   d. ☐ Not a registered California process server.
   e. ☐ Exempt from registration under Bus. & Prof. Code 22350(b).

   f. Name, address and telephone number and, if applicable, county of registration and number:

I declare under penalty of perjury under the laws of the State of California that the foregoing is true and correct.

(For California sheriff, marshal, or constable use only)
I certify that the foregoing is true and correct.

Date:

▶ _____
　　　　(SIGNATURE)

Date:

▶ _____
　　　　(SIGNATURE)

982(a)(9) [Rev. January 1, 1984]

Section 2-B. Hawaii

The state of Hawaii requires a Civil Information Sheet, a Complaint, and a Summons to commence a legal action. See Exhibit 2-3. The Instructions from the court's Web page are included herein, as well as a sample of the Civil Information Sheet. A Complaint form is also included, along with the form required for the inclusion of exhibits.

EXHIBIT 2-3   Hawaii Civil Information Sheet

INSTRUCTIONS FOR ATTORNEYS COMPLETING
THE CIVIL INFORMATION SHEET

The civil information sheet and the information contained herein neither replaces nor supplements the filings, the service pleadings or other papers as required by law, except as provided by the rules of court.

This form is required by the Clerk of Court for the purpose of initiating the civil docket sheet.

Consequently, a civil information sheet is submitted to the Clerk of Court for each civil complaint filed.

The attorney filing a civil complaint is to complete the form as follows:

I. PLAINTIFFS-DEFENDANTS
List names: last, first, middle initial.
If the plaintiff or defendant is a government agency, use only the full name.
If the plaintiff or defendant is an official within a government agency, first identify the agency and then the official's name and title.
If there are several plaintiffs-defendants, list them on an attachment noting in this section, "(see attachment)".

1(a). ATTORNEYS
List the attorney's name and license number.
If there are several attorneys, list them on an attachment noting in this section, "(see attachment".

II. NATURE OF SUIT
Place an "✓" in the appropriate box.
If the cause fits more than one nature of suit, select the most definitive.

III. ORIGIN
A. Original Proceedings: cases originating in the circuit district.
B. Transfer from District Court: cases transferred from district court under Hawaii Rev. Stat. §604-5, 633-31 (1985).
C. Transfer from another Circuit: cases transferred from another circuit under Hawaii Rev. Stat §603-37-37.5 (1985).

IV. DEMAND
Indicate the remedy being demanded such as a monetary sum or preliminary injunction.

V. JURY DEMAND
Indicate whether or not a jury is being demanded.

VI. CLASS ACTION
Indicate whether or not a class action is being filed.

VII. REQUEST TO EXEMPT FROM ARBITRATION
Indicate whether or not the form, "Request to Exempt from Arbitration" is being filed.

VIII. RELATED CASES
List the docket number(s) and the corresponding judge for related pending cases.

IX. DATE AND ATTORNEY SIGNATURE
Date and sign the civil information sheet.

continued

Exhibit 2-3 *continued*

CIVIL INFORMATION SHEET

I. PLAINTIFF(S)	I. (a) PLAINTIFF ATTORNEY (NAME & NUMBER)
	DEFENDANT ATTORNEY (IF KNOWN)

II. NATURE OF SUIT

- ☐ (101) Contract
- ☐ (201) Motor Vehicle Tort
- ☐ (301) Assault & Battery
- ☐ (302) Construction Defects
- ☐ (303) Medical Malpractice
- ☐ (304) Legal Malpractice
- ☐ (306) Product Liability
- ☐ (399) Other Non-Vehicle Tort
- ☐ (401) Condemnation
- ☐ (501) Foreclosure
- ☐ (511) Agreement of Sale Foreclosure
- ☐ (503) Agency Appeal
- ☐ (504) Declaratory Judgment
- ☐ (599) Other Civil Action

DEFENDANT(S)

III. ORIGIN
- ☐ A. Original Proceeding
- ☐ B. Transfer from District Court
- ☐ C. Transfer from another Circuit

IV. DEMAND

$ _____

V. JURY DEMAND	VI. CLASS ACTION	VII. REQUEST TO EXEMPT FROM ARBITRATION
☐ YES ☐ NO	☐ YES ☐ NO	☐ YES ☐ NO

VIII. RELATED CASE(S)

JUDGE _____

DOCKET _____

RESERVED FOR COURT USE	IX. SIGNATURE OF ATTORNEY OF RECORD
CIV NO _____	_____

1C-P-167

continued

Exhibit 2-3   *continued*

COMPLAINT (PERSONAL INJURY/
PROPERTY DAMAGES); SUMMONS   Form #3DC09

IN THE DISTRICT COURT OF THE THIRD CIRCUIT _____ DIVISION STATE OF HAWAI'I	
Plaintiff(s)	
	Reserved for Court Use
	Civil No.
Defendant(s)	Plaintiff(s)/Plaintiff(s)' Attorney (Name, Attorney Number, Firm Name (if applicable), Address, Telephone and Facsimile Numbers)
	Date of Injury/Damage:

COMPLAINT

1.   This Court has jurisdiction over this matter and venue is proper.

2.   On or about the date of injury/damage stated above, Defendant(s) intentionally and/or negligently injured Plaintiff(s) and/or damaged Plaintiff(s)' property by: (state location of incident and briefly explain what happened)

3.   As a result of the incident, Defendant(s) caused the following damages:
     ☐   Physical Injury (Do not state the dollar amount, but give a brief description of the damage):

     ☐   Property Damage in the amount of $_____ (Explain the type of damage):

4.   Defendant(s) has refused to pay for Plaintiff(s)' damages.

5.   Plaintiff(s) asks for judgment against Defendant(s) for the damages proved. In addition, the Court may award court costs, interest and reasonable attorney's fees.

	Signature of Plaintiff(s)/Plaintiff(s)' Attorney:
Date:	Print/Type Name:

In accordance with the **Americans with Disabilities Act** if you require an accommodation for your disability, please contact the ADA Coordinator at PHONE NO. 934-5792, FAX 935-1959, or TTY 961-7525 at least ten (10) working days in advance of your hearing or appointment date.

COMPPI.X (Amended 4/18/97)v

> I certify that this is a full, true, and correct
> copy of the original on file in this office.
>
> _____
> Clerk, District Court of the above Circuit, State of Hawai'i

continued

Exhibit 2-3 *continued*

STATE OF HAWAI'I CIRCUIT COURT OF THE _____ CIRCUIT	EXHIBIT LIST	CASE NUMBER

PLAINTIFF	PLAINTIFF ATTORNEY (Name, Address and Tel. No.)

DEFENDANT	DEFENDANT ATTORNEY (Name, Address, and Tel. No.)

DATE OF TRIAL OR HEARING	DATE JUDGMENT FILED	PREPARING CLERK	DIVISION

EXHIBIT NO. IDENTIFY NO. CODE __ PLAINTIFF __ DEFENDANT	OFFERED FOR IDENTIFI-CATION	RECEIVED IN EVIDENCE	WITHDRAWN	DESCRIPTION OF EXHIBIT	DATE R = RETURNED D = DESTROYED OTHER COMMENTS

FOR OFFICE USE ONLY

LOCATION OF EXHIBITS

☐ Attached

☐ Shelf No. _____

☐ Code No. _____

☐ Other_____

_____

DATE	RECEIVED	PAGE _____ OF _____ PAGES

FORM NO. 000120 R6/95

EXHIBIT LIST 1C-P-053

Section 2-C. California Civil Documents

California Judicial Council forms may be purchased at the local court clerk's office of the Superior Court, from West, a Thomson business, or from different sites on the Internet. Only a few of the many forms available are shown herein.

In civil proceedings in which one of the parties is a minor, an incapacitated person, or a person for whom a conservator has been appointed, a special guardian ad litem must be appointed to represent the party in a civil action. The form shown in Exhibit 2-4 is called Application and Order for Appointment of Guardian Ad Litem. The completed form must be submitted to the court, and the judicial officer must approve the appointment.

The standard caption must be completed, indicating the attorney information, court information, parties, and case number. The applicant's name must be included in No. 1 indicating the name and designation. No. 2 requires the name of the guardian ad litem along with the address and telephone number.

No. 3 requires the name, address, and telephone number of the party who requires a guardian ad litem. No. 4 must indicate whether the individual is a minor, incompetent, or person with a conservator. If a minor, the date of birth should be included.

No. 5 should indicate the reason for appointment of the guardian ad litem. For instance, perhaps the minor was involved in an automobile accident and sustained personal injuries. No. 6 requires the guardian's relationship to the person being represented.

The form must be signed by the attorney and the applicant. The proposed guardian ad litem must also sign under "Consent to Act as Guardian Ad Litem."

The form is submitted to the court and signed by the judicial officer if this guardian ad litem is approved.

EXHIBIT 2-4   California Guardian Ad Litem Form

Courtesy: Reprinted from *West's California Judicial Council Form 2003*, with permission of West, a Thomson business. For more information about this publication please visit **http://west.thomson.com**.

982(a)(27)

ATTORNEY *(Name, state bar number, and address):*

FOR COURT USE ONLY

TELEPHONE NO.:   FAX NO. *(Optional)*:

E–MAIL ADDRESS *(Optional)*:

ATTORNEY FOR *(Name)*:

SUPERIOR COURT OF CALIFORNIA, COUNTY OF

STREET ADDRESS:

MAILING ADDRESS:

CITY AND ZIP CODE:

BRANCH NAME:

PLAINTIFF/PETITIONER:

DEFENDANT/RESPONDENT:

APPLICATION AND ORDER FOR APPOINTMENT OF GUARDIAN AD LITEM—CIVIL
☐ **EX PARTE**

CASE NUMBER:

NOTE: This form is for use in civil proceedings in which a party is a minor, an incapacitated person, or a person for whom a conservator has been appointed. A party who seeks the appointment of a guardian ad litem in a family law or juvenile proceeding should use Form FJ-200. A party who seeks the appointment of a guardian ad litem in a probate proceeding should use Form DE-350, GC-100. An individual cannot act as a guardian ad litem unless he or she is represented by an attorney or is an attorney.

1. Applicant *(name):*   is
   a. ☐ the parent of *(name):*
   b. ☐ the guardian of *(name):*
   c. ☐ the conservator of *(name):*
   d. ☐ a party to the suit.
   e. ☐ the minor to be represented *(if the minor is 14 years of age or older).*
   f. ☐ another interested person *(specify capacity):*

2. This application seeks the appointment of the following person as guardian ad litem *(state name, address, and telephone number):*

3. The guardian ad litem is to represent the interests of the following person *(state name, address, and telephone number):*

4. The person to be represented is:
   a. ☐ a minor *(date of birth):*
   b. ☐ an incompetent person.
   c. ☐ a person for whom a conservator has been appointed.

5. The court should appoint a guardian ad litem because:
   a. ☐ the person named in item 3 has a cause or causes of action on which suit should be brought *(describe):*

☐ Continued on Attachment 5a.

(Continued on reverse)

Form Adopted for Mandatory Use
Judicial Council of California

APPLICATION AND ORDER FOR APPOINTMENT OF GUARDIAN AD LITEM—CIVIL

THOMSON   Code of Civil Procedure,

continued

Exhibit 2-4 *continued*

PLAINTIFF/PETITIONER:	CASE NUMBER:
DEFENDANT/RESPONDENT:	

5. b. ☐ more than 10 days have elapsed since the summons in the above-entitled matter was served on the person named in item 3, and no application for the appointment of a guardian ad litem has been made by the person identified in item 3 or any other person.

   c. ☐ the person named in item 3 has no guardian or conservator of his or her estate.

   d. ☐ the appointment of a guardian ad litem is necessary for the following reasons *(specify):*

      ☐ Continued on Attachment 5d.

6. The proposed guardian ad litem's relationship to the person he or she will be representing is:
   a. ☐ related *(state relationship):*
   b. ☐ not related *(specify capacity):*

7. The proposed guardian ad litem is fully competent and qualified to understand and protect the rights of the person he or she will represent and has no interests adverse to the interests of that person. *(If there are any issues of competency or qualification or any possible adverse interests, describe and explain why the proposed guardian should nevertheless be appointed):*

      ☐ Continued on Attachment 7.

▶

_____	_____
(TYPE OR PRINT NAME)	(SIGNATURE OF ATTORNEY)

I declare under penalty of perjury under the laws of the State of California that the foregoing is true and correct.
Date:

▶

_____	_____
(TYPE OR PRINT NAME)	(SIGNATURE OF APPLICANT)

CONSENT TO ACT AS GUARDIAN AD LITEM

I consent to the appointment as guardian ad litem under the above petition.
Date:

▶

_____	_____
(TYPE OR PRINT NAME)	(SIGNATURE OF PROPOSED GUARDIAN AD LITEM)

ORDER ☐ EX PARTE

THE COURT FINDS that it is reasonable and necessary to appoint a guardian ad litem for the person named in item 3 of the application, as requested.

THE COURT ORDERS that *(name):*
is hereby appointed as the guardian ad litem for *(name):*
for the reasons set forth in item 5 of the application.
Date:

_____
JUDICIAL OFFICER

☐ SIGNATURE FOLLOWS LAST ATTACHMENT

APPLICATION AND ORDER FOR APPOINTMENT OF GUARDIAN AD LITEM—CIVIL

California Request for Admissions

The Request for Admissions form requests that the adverse party admit to facts that are in controversy to avoid having to litigate these particular matters. The form, shown in Exhibit 2-5 also asks the party to verify the authenticity of documents. The standard caption is used. One or both of the boxes indicating "Truth of Facts" and "Genuineness of Documents" must be checked. If the genuineness of documents is at issue, copies of the documents must be included with the Request. The attorney should sign the form, a sample of which follows.

EXHIBIT 2-5 California Request for Admissions

Courtesy: Reprinted from *West's California Judicial Council Form 2003,* with permission of West, a Thomson business. For more information about this publication please visit **http://west.thomson.com.**

FI-100

ATTORNEY OR PARTY WITHOUT ATTORNEY *(Name and Address):*	TELEPHONE NO.:	FOR COURT USE ONLY

ATTORNEY FOR *(Name)*:

NAME OF COURT:
STREET ADDRESS:
MAILING ADDRESS:
CITY AND ZIP CODE:
BRANCH NAME:

SHORT TITLE:

REQUEST FOR ADMISSIONS

☐ **Truth of Facts**   ☐ **Genuineness of Documents**

Requesting Party:
Responding Party:
Set No.:

CASE NUMBER:

You are requested to admit within thirty days after service of this Request for Admissions that

A. ☐ each of the following facts is true *(number each fact consecutively)*:

☐ continued on Attachment A.

B. ☐ the original of each of the following documents, copies of which are attached, is genuine *(number each document consecutively)*:

☐ continued on Attachment B.

▶

....
(TYPE OR PRINT NAME)   (SIGNATURE OF PARTY OR ATTORNEY)

Form Approved by the
REQUEST FOR ADMISSIONS   THOMSON   Code Civ. Proc., §§ 2033, 2033.5

California Form Interrogatories

Interrogatories are written questions propounded to the adverse party in a civil action. The first page of the form gives detailed instructions on its preparation. In most cases, the answering party must respond within 30 days after service. Often the Form Interrogatories (Exhibit 2-6) and Request for Admission are served simultaneously.

The form questions consist of eight pages. All pertinent questions should be checked for answer by the other party. The last section (Section 50) shows questions to ask in contract actions and should not be used unless there is a contract between the parties in controversy.

EXHIBIT 2-6 California Form Interrogatories

Courtesy: Reprinted from *West's California Judicial Council Form 2003*, with permission of West, a Thomson business. For more information about this publication please visit **http://west.thomson.com**.

FI-120

ATTORNEY OR PARTY WITHOUT ATTORNEY *(Name, state bar number, and address):*	TELEPHONE NO.:
	FAX NO. *(Optional):*
	E-MAIL ADDRESS *(Optional):*
ATTORNEY FOR *(Name):*	

SUPERIOR COURT OF CALIFORNIA, COUNTY OF

BRANCH, IF ANY:

SHORT TITLE OF CASE:

FORM INTERROGATORIES

Asking Party:

Answering Party:
Set No.:

CASE NUMBER:

Sec. 1. Instructions to All Parties

(a) Interrogatories are written questions prepared by a party to an action that are sent to any other party in the action to be answered under oath. The interrogatories below are form interrogatories approved for use in civil cases.

(b) For time limitations, requirements for service on other parties, and other details, see Code of Civil Procedure section 2030 and the cases construing it.

(c) These form interrogatories do not change existing law relating to interrogatories nor do they affect an answering party's right to assert any privilege or make any objection.

Sec. 2. Instructions to the Asking Party

(a) These interrogatories are designed for optional use by parties in unlimited civil cases where the amount demanded exceeds $25,000. Separate interrogatories, *Form Interrogatories—Economic Litigation* (form FI-129), which have no subparts, are designed for use in limited civil cases where the amount demanded is $25,000 or less; however, those interrogatories may also be used in unlimited civil cases.

(b) Check the box next to each interrogatory that you want the answering party to answer. Use care in choosing those interrogatories that are applicable to the case.

(c) You may insert your own definition of **INCIDENT** in Section 4, but only where the action arises from a course of conduct or a series of events occurring over a period of time.

(d) The interrogatories in section 16.0, Defendant's Contentions—Personal Injury, should not be used until the defendant has had a reasonable opportunity to conduct an investigation or discovery of plaintiff's injuries and damages.

(e) Additional interrogatories may be attached.

Sec. 3. Instructions to the Answering Party

(a) An answer or other appropriate response must be given to each interrogatory checked by the asking party.

(b) As a general rule, within 30 days after you are served with these interrogatories, you must serve your responses on the asking party and serve copies of your responses on all other parties to the action who have appeared. See Code of Civil Procedure section 2030 for details.

(c) Each answer must be as complete and straightforward as the information reasonably available to you, including the information possessed by your attorneys or agents, permits. If an interrogatory cannot be answered completely, answer it to the extent possible.

(d) If you do not have enough personal knowledge to fully answer an interrogatory, say so, but make a reasonable and good faith effort to get the information by asking other persons or organizations, unless the information is equally available to the asking party.

(e) Whenever an interrogatory may be answered by referring to a document, the document may be attached as an exhibit to the response and referred to in the response. If the document has more than one page, refer to the page and section where the answer to the interrogatory can be found.

(f) Whenever an address and telephone number for the same person are requested in more than one interrogatory, you are required to furnish them in answering only the first interrogatory asking for that information.

(g) If you are asserting a privilege or making an objection to an interrogatory, you must specifically assert the privilege or state the objection in your written response.

(h) Your answers to these interrogatories must be verified, dated, and signed. You may wish to use the following form at the end of your answers:

I declare under penalty of perjury under the laws of the State of California that the foregoing answers are true and correct.

_____   _____
(DATE)   *(SIGNATURE)*

Sec. 4. Definitions

Words in **BOLDFACE CAPITALS** in these interrogatories are defined as follows:

(a) *(Check one of the following):*

☐ (1) **INCIDENT** includes the circumstances and events surrounding the alleged accident, injury, or other occurrence or breach of contract giving rise to this action or proceeding.

Form Approved for Optional Use
Judicial Council of California

FORM INTERROGATORIES

THOMSON

Code of Civil Procedure, §§ 2030, 2033.5

continued

Exhibit 2-6 *continued*

☐ (2) **INCIDENT** means *(insert your definition here or on a separate, attached sheet labeled "Sec. 4(a)(2)"):*

(b) **YOU OR ANYONE ACTING ON YOUR BEHALF** includes you, your agents, your employees, your insurance companies, their agents, their employees, your attorneys, your accountants, your investigators, and anyone else acting on your behalf.

(c) **PERSON** includes a natural person, firm, association, organization, partnership, business, trust, limited liability company, corporation, or public entity.

(d) **DOCUMENT** means a writing, as defined in Evidence Code section 250, and includes the original or a copy of handwriting, typewriting, printing, photostats, photographs, electronically stored information, and every other means of recording upon any tangible thing and form of communicating or representation, including letters, words, pictures, sounds, or symbols, or combinations of them.

(e) **HEALTH CARE PROVIDER** includes any **PERSON** referred to in Code of Civil Procedure section 667.7(e)(3).

(f) **ADDRESS** means the street address, including the city, state, and zip code.

Sec. 5. Interrogatories

The following interrogatories have been approved by the Judicial Council under Code of Civil Procedure section 2033.5:

CONTENTS

1.0 Identity of Persons Answering These Interrogatories
2.0 General Background Information—Individual
3.0 General Background Information—Business Entity
4.0 Insurance
5.0 *[Reserved]*
6.0 Physical, Mental, or Emotional Injuries
7.0 Property Damage
8.0 Loss of Income or Earning Capacity
9.0 Other Damages
10.0 Medical History
11.0 Other Claims and Previous Claims
12.0 Investigation—General
13.0 Investigation—Surveillance
14.0 Statutory or Regulatory Violations
15.0 Denials and Special or Affirmative Defenses
16.0 Defendant's Contentions—Personal Injury
17.0 Responses to Request for Admissions
18.0 *[Reserved]*
19.0 *[Reserved]*
20.0 How the Incident Occurred—Motor Vehicle
25.0 *[Reserved]*
30.0 *[Reserved]*
40.0 *[Reserved]*
50.0 Contract
60.0 *[Reserved]*
70.0 Unlawful Detainer *[See separate form FI-128]*
101.0 Economic Litigation *[See separate form FI-129]*
200.0 Employment Law *[See separate form FI-130]*
Family Law *[See separate form 1292.10]*

1.0 Identity of Persons Answering These Interrogatories

☐ 1.1 State the name, **ADDRESS**, telephone number, and relationship to you of each **PERSON** who prepared or assisted in the preparation of the responses to these interrogatories. *(Do not identify anyone who simply typed or reproduced the responses.)*

2.0 General Background Information—Individual

☐ 2.1 State:
(a) your name;
(b) every name you have used in the past; and
(c) the dates you used each name.

☐ 2.2 State the date and place of your birth.

☐ 2.3 At the time of the **INCIDENT**, did you have a driver's license? If so state:
(a) the state or other issuing entity;
(b) the license number and type;
(c) the date of issuance; and
(d) all restrictions.

☐ 2.4 At the time of the **INCIDENT**, did you have any other permit or license for the operation of a motor vehicle? If so, state:
(a) the state or other issuing entity;
(b) the license number and type;
(c) the date of issuance; and
(d) all restrictions.

☐ 2.5 State:
(a) your present residence **ADDRESS**;
(b) your residence **ADDRESSES** for the past five years; and
(c) the dates you lived at each **ADDRESS**.

☐ 2.6 State:
(a) the name, **ADDRESS**, and telephone number of your present employer or place of self-employment; and
(b) the name, **ADDRESS**, dates of employment, job title, and nature of work for each employer or self-employment you have had from five years before the **INCIDENT** until today.

☐ 2.7 State:
(a) the name and **ADDRESS** of each school or other academic or vocational institution you have attended, beginning with high school;
(b) the dates you attended;
(c) the highest grade level you have completed; and
(d) the degrees received.

☐ 2.8 Have you ever been convicted of a felony? If so, for each conviction state:
(a) the city and state where you were convicted;
(b) the date of conviction;
(c) the offense; and
(d) the court and case number.

☐ 2.9 Can you speak English with ease? If not, what language and dialect do you normally use?

☐ 2.10 Can you read and write English with ease? If not, what language and dialect do you normally use?

continued

Exhibit 2-6 *continued*

☐ 2.11 At the time of the **INCIDENT** were you acting as an agent or employee for any **PERSON**? If so, state:
(a) the name, **ADDRESS**, and telephone number of that **PERSON**: and
(b) a description of your duties.

☐ 2.12 At the time of the **INCIDENT** did you or any other person have any physical, emotional, or mental disability or condition that may have contributed to the occurrence of the **INCIDENT**? If so, for each person state:
(a) the name, **ADDRESS**, and telephone number;
(b) the nature of the disability or condition; and
(c) the manner in which the disability or condition contributed to the occurrence of the **INCIDENT**.

☐ 2.13 Within 24 hours before the **INCIDENT** did you or any person involved in the **INCIDENT** use or take any of the following substances: alcoholic beverage, marijuana, or other drug or medication of any kind (prescription or not)? If so, for each person state:
(a) the name, **ADDRESS**, and telephone number;
(b) the nature or description of each substance;
(c) the quantity of each substance used or taken;
(d) the date and time of day when each substance was used or taken;
(e) the **ADDRESS** where each substance was used or taken;
(f) the name, **ADDRESS**, and telephone number of each person who was present when each substance was used or taken; and
(g) the name, **ADDRESS**, and telephone number of any **HEALTH CARE PROVIDER** who prescribed or furnished the substance and the condition for which it was prescribed or furnished.

3.0 General Background Information—Business Entity

☐ 3.1 Are you a corporation? If so, state:
(a) the name stated in the current articles of incorporation;
(b) all other names used by the corporation during the past 10 years and the dates each was used;
(c) the date and place of incorporation;
(d) the **ADDRESS** of the principal place of business; and
(e) whether you are qualified to do business in California.

☐ 3.2 Are you a partnership? If so, state:
(a) the current partnership name;
(b) all other names used by the partnership during the past 10 years and the dates each was used;
(c) whether you are a limited partnership and, if so, under the laws of what jurisdiction;
(d) the name and **ADDRESS** of each general partner; and
(e) the **ADDRESS** of the principal place of business.

☐ 3.3 Are you a limited liability company? If so, state:
(a) the name stated in the current articles of organization;
(b) all other names used by the company during the past 10 years and the date each was used;
(c) the date and place of filing of the articles of organization;
(d) the **ADDRESS** of the principal place of business; and
(e) whether you are qualified to do business in California.

☐ 3.4 Are you a joint venture? If so, state:
(a) the current joint venture name;
(b) all other names used by the joint venture during the past 10 years and the dates each was used;
(c) the name and **ADDRESS** of each joint venturer; and
(d) the **ADDRESS** of the principal place of business.

☐ 3.5 Are you an unincorporated association?
If so, state:
(a) the current unincorporated association name;
(b) all other names used by the unincorporated association during the past 10 years and the dates each was used; and
(c) the **ADDRESS** of the principal place of business.

☐ 3.6 Have you done business under a fictitious name during the past 10 years? If so, for each fictitious name state:
(a) the name;
(b) the dates each was used;
(c) the state and county of each fictitious name filing; and
(d) the **ADDRESS** of the principal place of business.

☐ 3.7 Within the past five years has any public entity registered or licensed your business? If so, for each license or registration:
(a) identify the license or registration;
(b) state the name of the public entity; and
(c) state the dates of issuance and expiration.

4.0 Insurance

☐ 4.1 At the time of the **INCIDENT**, was there in effect any policy of insurance through which you were or might be insured in any manner (for example, primary, pro-rata, or excess liability coverage or medical expense coverage) for the damages, claims, or actions that have arisen out of the **INCIDENT**? If so, for each policy state:
(a) the kind of coverage;
(b) the name and **ADDRESS** of the insurance company;
(c) the name, **ADDRESS**, and telephone number of each named insured;
(d) the policy number;
(e) the limits of coverage for each type of coverage contained in the policy;
(f) whether any reservation of rights or controversy or coverage dispute exists between you and the insurance company; and
(g) the name, **ADDRESS**, and telephone number of the custodian of the policy.

☐ 4.2 Are you self-insured under any statute for the damages, claims, or actions that have arisen out of the **INCIDENT**? If so, specify the statute.

5.0 [Reserved]

6.0 Physical, Mental, or Emotional Injuries

☐ 6.1 Do you attribute any physical, mental, or emotional injuries to the **INCIDENT**? *(If your answer is "no," do not answer interrogatories 6.2 through 6.7).*

☐ 6.2 Identify each injury you attribute to the **INCIDENT** and the area of your body affected.

continued

Exhibit 2-6 *continued*

☐ 6.3 Do you still have any complaints that you attribute to the **INCIDENT**? If so, for each complaint state:
(a) a description;
(b) whether the complaint is subsiding, remaining the same, or becoming worse; and
(c) the frequency and duration.

☐ 6.4 Did you receive any consultation or examination (except from expert witnesses covered by Code of Civil Procedure section 2034) or treatment from a **HEALTH CARE PROVIDER** for any injury you attribute to the **INCIDENT**? If so, for each **HEALTH CARE PROVIDER** state:

(a) the name, **ADDRESS**, and telephone number;
(b) the type of consultation, examination, or treatment provided;
(c) the dates you received consultation, examination, or treatment; and
(d) the charges to date.

☐ 6.5 Have you taken any medication, prescribed or not, as a result of injuries that you attribute to the **INCIDENT**? If so, for each medication state:
(a) the name;
(b) the **PERSON** who prescribed or furnished it;
(c) the date it was prescribed or furnished;
(d) the dates you began and stopped taking it; and
(e) the cost to date.

☐ 6.6 Are there any other medical services necessitated by the injuries that you attribute to the **INCIDENT** that were not previously listed (for example, ambulance, nursing, prosthetics)? If so, for each service state:
(a) the nature;
(b) the date;
(c) the cost; and
(d) the name, **ADDRESS**, and telephone number of each provider.

☐ 6.7 Has any **HEALTH CARE PROVIDER** advised that you may require future or additional treatment for any injuries that you attribute to the **INCIDENT**? If so, for each injury state:
(a) the name and **ADDRESS** of each **HEALTH CARE PROVIDER**;
(b) the complaints for which the treatment was advised; and
(c) the nature, duration, and estimated cost of the treatment.

7.0 Property Damage

☐ 7.1 Do you attribute any loss of or damage to a vehicle or other property to the **INCIDENT**? If so, for each item of property:
(a) describe the property;
(b) describe the nature and location of the damage to the property;

(c) state the amount of damage you are claiming for each item of property and how the amount was calculated; and
(d) if the property was sold, state the name, **ADDRESS**, and telephone number of the seller, the date of sale, and the sale price.

☐ 7.2 Has a written estimate or evaluation been made for any item of property referred to in your answer to the preceding interrogatory? If so, for each estimate or evaluation state:
(a) the name, **ADDRESS**, and telephone number of the **PERSON** who prepared it and the date prepared;
(b) the name, **ADDRESS**, and telephone number of each **PERSON** who has a copy of it; and
(c) the amount of damage stated.

☐ 7.3 Has any item of property referred to in your answer to interrogatory 7.1 been repaired? If so, for each item state:
(a) the date repaired;
(b) a description of the repair;
(c) the repair cost;
(d) the name, **ADDRESS**, and telephone number of the **PERSON** who repaired it;
(e) the name, **ADDRESS**, and telephone number of the **PERSON** who paid for the repair.

8.0 Loss of Income or Earning Capacity

☐ 8.1 Do you attribute any loss of income or earning capacity to the **INCIDENT**? *(If your answer is "no," do not answer interrogatories 8.2 through 8.8).*

☐ 8.2 State:
(a) the nature of your work;
(b) your job title at the time of the **INCIDENT**; and
(c) the date your employment began.

☐ 8.3 State the last date before the **INCIDENT** that you worked for compensation.

☐ 8.4 State your monthly income at the time of the **INCIDENT** and how the amount was calculated.

☐ 8.5 State the date you returned to work at each place of employment following the **INCIDENT**.

☐ 8.6 State the dates you did not work and for which you lost income as a result of the **INCIDENT**.

☐ 8.7 State the total income you have lost to date as a result of the **INCIDENT** and how the amount was calculated.

☐ 8.8 Will you lose income in the future as a result of the **INCIDENT**? If so, state:
(a) the facts upon which you base this contention;
(b) an estimate of the amount;
(c) an estimate of how long you will be unable to work; and
(d) how the claim for future income is calculated.

continued

Exhibit 2-6   *continued*

9.0 Other Damages

☐ 9.1 Are there any other damages that you attribute to the **INCIDENT**? If so, *for each item of damage state*:
(a) the nature;
(b) the date it occurred;
(c) the amount; and
(d) the name, **ADDRESS**, and telephone number of each **PERSON** to whom an obligation was incurred.

☐ 9.2 Do any **DOCUMENTS** support the existence or amount of any item of damages claimed in interrogatory 9.1? If so, describe each document and state the name, **ADDRESS**, and telephone number of the **PERSON** who has each **DOCUMENT**.

10.0 Medical History

☐ 10.1 At any time before the **INCIDENT** did you have complaints or injuries that involved the same part of your body claimed to have been injured in the **INCIDENT**? If so, for each state:
(a) a description of the complaint or injury;
(b) the dates it began and ended; and
(c) the name, **ADDRESS**, and telephone number of each **HEALTH CARE PROVIDER** whom you consulted or who examined or treated you.

☐ 10.2 List all physical, mental, and emotional disabilities you had immediately before the **INCIDENT**. *(You may omit mental or emotional disabilities unless you attribute any mental or emotional injury to the INCIDENT.)*

☐ 10.3 At any time after the **INCIDENT**, did you sustain injuries of the kind for which you are now claiming damages? If so, for each incident giving rise to an injury state:
(a) the date and the place it occurred;
(b) the name, **ADDRESS**, and telephone number of any other **PERSON** involved;
(c) the nature of any injuries you sustained;
(d) the name, **ADDRESS**, and telephone number of each **HEALTH CARE PROVIDER** who you consulted or who examined or treated you; and
(e) the nature of the treatment and its duration.

11.0 Other Claims and Previous Claims

☐ 11.1 Except for this action, in the past 10 years have you filed an action or made a written claim or demand for compensation for your personal injuries? If so, for each action, claim, or demand state:
(a) the date, time, and place and location (closest street **ADDRESS** or intersection) of the **INCIDENT** giving rise to the action, claim, or demand;
(b) the name, **ADDRESS**, and telephone number of each **PERSON** against whom the claim or demand was made or the action filed;

(c) the court, names of the parties, and case number of any action filed;
(d) the name, **ADDRESS**, and telephone number of any attorney representing you;
(e) whether the claim or action has been resolved or is pending; and
(f) a description of the injury.

☐ 11.2 In the past 10 years have you made a written claim or demand for workers' compensation benefits? If so, for each claim or demand state:
(a) the date, time, and place of the **INCIDENT** giving rise to the claim;
(b) the name, **ADDRESS**, and telephone number of your employer at the time of the injury;
(c) the name, **ADDRESS**, and telephone number of the workers' compensation insurer and the claim number;
(d) the period of time during which you received workers' compensation benefits;
(e) a description of the injury;
(f) the name, **ADDRESS**, and telephone number of any **HEALTH CARE PROVIDER** who provided services; and
(g) the case number at the Workers' Compensation Appeals Board.

12.0 Investigation—General

☐ 12.1 State the name, **ADDRESS**, and telephone number of each individual:
(a) who witnessed the **INCIDENT** or the events occurring immediately before or after the **INCIDENT**;
(b) who made any statement at the scene of the **INCIDENT**;
(c) who heard any statements made about the **INCIDENT** by any individual at the scene; and
(d) who **YOU OR ANYONE ACTING ON YOUR BEHALF** claim has knowledge of the **INCIDENT** (except for expert witnesses covered by Code of Civil Procedure section 2034).

☐ 12.2 Have **YOU OR ANYONE ACTING ON YOUR BEHALF** interviewed any individual concerning the **INCIDENT**? If so, for each individual state:
(a) the name, **ADDRESS**, and telephone number of the individual interviewed;
(b) the date of the interview; and
(c) the name, **ADDRESS**, and telephone number of the **PERSON** who conducted the interview.

☐ 12.3 Have **YOU OR ANYONE ACTING ON YOUR BEHALF** obtained a written or recorded statement from any individual concerning the **INCIDENT**? If so, for each statement state:
(a) the name, **ADDRESS**, and telephone number of the individual from whom the statement was obtained;
(b) the name, **ADDRESS**, and telephone number of the individual who obtained the statement;
(c) the date the statement was obtained; and
(d) the name, **ADDRESS**, and telephone number of each **PERSON** who has the original statement or a copy.

continued

Exhibit 2-6 *continued*

☐ **12.4 Do YOU OR ANYONE ACTING ON YOUR BEHALF** know of any photographs, films, or videotapes depicting any place, object, or individual concerning the **INCIDENT** or plaintiff's injuries? If so, state:

(a) the number of photographs or feet of film or videotape;

(b) the places, objects, or persons photographed, filmed, or videotaped;

(c) the date the photographs, films, or videotapes were taken;

(d) the name, **ADDRESS**, and telephone number of the individual taking the photographs, films, or videotapes; and

(e) the name, **ADDRESS**, and telephone number of each **PERSON** who has the original or a copy of the photographs, films, or videotapes.

☐ **12.5 Do YOU OR ANYONE ACTING ON YOUR BEHALF** know of any diagram, reproduction, or model of any place or thing (except for items developed by expert witnesses covered by Code of Civil Procedure section 2034) concerning the **INCIDENT**? If so, for each item state:

(a) the type (i.e., diagram, reproduction, or model);

(b) the subject matter; and

(c) the name, **ADDRESS**, and telephone number of each **PERSON** who has it.

☐ **12.6** Was a report made by any **PERSON** concerning the **INCIDENT**? If so, state:

(a) the name, title, identification number, and employer of the **PERSON** who made the report;

(b) the date and type of report made;

(c) the name, **ADDRESS**, and telephone number of the **PERSON** for whom the report was made; and

(d) the name, **ADDRESS**, and telephone number of each **PERSON** who has the original or a copy of the report.

☐ **12.7 Have YOU OR ANYONE ACTING ON YOUR BEHALF** inspected the scene of the **INCIDENT**? If so, for each inspection state:

(a) the name, **ADDRESS**, and telephone number of the individual making the inspection (except for expert witnesses covered by Code of Civil Procedure section 2034); and

(b) the date of the inspection.

13.0 Investigation—Surveillance

☐ **13.1 Have YOU OR ANYONE ACTING ON YOUR BEHALF** conducted surveillance of any individual involved in the **INCIDENT** or any party to this action? If so, for each surveillance state:

(a) the name, **ADDRESS**, and telephone number of the individual or party;

(b) the time, date, and place of the surveillance;

(c) the name, **ADDRESS**, and telephone number of the individual who conducted the surveillance; and

(d) the name, **ADDRESS**, and telephone number of each **PERSON** who has the original or a copy of any surveillance photograph, film, or videotape.

☐ **13.2** Has a written report been prepared on the surveillance? If so, for each written report state:

(a) the title;

(b) the date;

(c) the name, **ADDRESS**, and telephone number of the individual who prepared the report; and

(d) the name, **ADDRESS**, and telephone number of each **PERSON** who has the original or a copy.

14.0 Statutory or Regulatory Violations

☐ **14.1 Do YOU OR ANYONE ACTING ON YOUR BEHALF** contend that any **PERSON** involved in the **INCIDENT** violated any statute, ordinance, or regulation and that the violation was a legal (proximate) cause of the **INCIDENT**? If so, identify the name, **ADDRESS**, and telephone number of each **PERSON** and the statute, ordinance, or regulation that was violated.

☐ **14.2** Was any **PERSON** cited or charged with a violation of any statute, ordinance, or regulation as a result of this **INCIDENT**? If so, for each **PERSON** state:

(a) the name, **ADDRESS**, and telephone number of the **PERSON**;

(b) the statute, ordinance, or regulation allegedly violated;

(c) whether the **PERSON** entered a plea in response to the citation or charge and, if so, the plea entered; and

(d) the name and **ADDRESS** of the court or administrative agency, names of the parties, and case number.

15.0 Denials and Special or Affirmative Defenses

☐ **15.1** Identify each denial of a material allegation and each special or affirmative defense in your pleadings and for each:

(a) state all facts upon which you base the denial or special or affirmative defense;

(b) state the names, **ADDRESSES**, and telephone numbers of all **PERSONS** who have knowledge of those facts; and

(c) identify all **DOCUMENTS** and other tangible things that support your denial or special or affirmative defense, and state the name, **ADDRESS**, and telephone number of the **PERSON** who has each **DOCUMENT**.

16.0 Defendant's Contentions—Personal Injury

☐ **16.1** Do you contend that any **PERSON**, other than you or plaintiff, contributed to the occurrence of the **INCIDENT** or the injuries or damages claimed by plaintiff? If so, for each **PERSON**:

(a) state the name, **ADDRESS**, and telephone number of the **PERSON**;

(b) state all facts upon which you base your contention;

(c) state the names, **ADDRESSES**, and telephone numbers of all **PERSONS** who have knowledge of the facts; and

(d) identify all **DOCUMENTS** and other tangible things that support your contention and state the name, **ADDRESS**, and telephone number of the **PERSON** who has each **DOCUMENT** or thing.

☐ **16.2** Do you contend that plaintiff was not injured in the **INCIDENT**? If so:

(a) state all facts upon which you base your contention;

(b) state the names, **ADDRESSES**, and telephone numbers of all **PERSONS** who have knowledge of the facts; and

(c) identify all **DOCUMENTS** and other tangible things that support your contention and state the name, **ADDRESS**, and telephone number of the **PERSON** who has each **DOCUMENT** or thing.

continued

Exhibit 2-6 *continued*

☐ 16.3 Do you contend that the injuries or the extent of the injuries claimed by plaintiff as disclosed in discovery proceedings thus far in this case were not caused by the **INCIDENT**? If so, for each injury:

(a) identify it;

(b) state all facts upon which you base your contention;

(c) state the names, **ADDRESSES**, and telephone numbers of all **PERSONS** who have knowledge of the facts; and

(d) identify all **DOCUMENTS** and other tangible things that support your contention and state the name, **ADDRESS**, and telephone number of the **PERSON** who has each **DOCUMENT** or thing.

☐ 16.4 Do you contend that any of the services furnished by any **HEALTH CARE PROVIDER** claimed by plaintiff in discovery proceedings thus far in this case were not due to the **INCIDENT**? If so:

(a) identify each service;

(b) state all facts upon which you base your contention;

(c) state the names, **ADDRESSES**, and telephone numbers of all **PERSONS** who have knowledge of the facts; and

(d) identify all **DOCUMENTS** and other tangible things that support your contention and state the name, **ADDRESS**, and telephone number of the **PERSON** who has each **DOCUMENT** or thing.

☐ 16.5 Do you contend that any of the costs of services furnished by any **HEALTH CARE PROVIDER** claimed as damages by plaintiff in discovery proceedings thus far in this case were not necessary or unreasonable? If so:

(a) identify each cost;

(b) state all facts upon which you base your contention;

(c) state the names, **ADDRESSES**, and telephone numbers of all **PERSONS** who have knowledge of the facts; and

(d) identify all **DOCUMENTS** and other tangible things that support your contention and state the name, **ADDRESS**, and telephone number of the **PERSON** who has each **DOCUMENT** or thing.

☐ 16.6 Do you contend that any part of the loss of earnings or income claimed by plaintiff in discovery proceedings thus far in this case was unreasonable or was not caused by the **INCIDENT**? If so:

(a) identify each part of the loss;

(b) state all facts upon which you base your contention;

(c) state the names, **ADDRESSES**, and telephone numbers of all **PERSONS** who have knowledge of the facts; and

(d) identify all **DOCUMENTS** and other tangible things that support your contention and state the name, **ADDRESS**, and telephone number of the **PERSON** who has each **DOCUMENT** or thing.

☐ 16.7 Do you contend that any of the property damage claimed by plaintiff in discovery proceedings thus far in this case was not caused by the **INCIDENT**? If so:

(a) identify each item of property damage;

(b) state all facts upon which you base your contention;

(c) state the names, **ADDRESSES**, and telephone numbers of all **PERSONS** who have knowledge of the facts; and

(d) identify all **DOCUMENTS** and other tangible things that support your contention and state the name, **ADDRESS**, and telephone number of the **PERSON** who has each **DOCUMENT** or thing.

☐ 16.8 Do you contend that any of the costs of repairing the property damage claimed by plaintiff in discovery proceedings thus far in this case were unreasonable? If so:

(a) identify each cost item;

(b) state all facts upon which you base your contention;

(c) state the names, **ADDRESSES**, and telephone numbers of all **PERSONS** who have knowledge of the facts; and

(d) identify all **DOCUMENTS** and other tangible things that support your contention and state the name, **ADDRESS**, and telephone number of the **PERSON** who has each **DOCUMENT** or thing.

☐ 16.9 Do **YOU OR ANYONE ACTING ON YOUR BEHALF** have any **DOCUMENT** (for example, insurance bureau index reports) concerning claims for personal injuries made before or after the **INCIDENT** by a plaintiff in this case? If so, for each plaintiff state:

(a) the source of each **DOCUMENT**;

(b) the date each claim arose;

(c) the nature of each claim; and

(d) the name, **ADDRESS**, and telephone number of the **PERSON** who has each **DOCUMENT**.

☐ 16.10 Do **YOU OR ANYONE ACTING ON YOUR BEHALF** have any **DOCUMENT** concerning the past or present physical, mental, or emotional condition of any plaintiff in this case from a **HEALTH CARE PROVIDER** not previously identified (except for expert witnesses covered by Code of Civil Procedure section 2034)? If so, for each plaintiff state:

(a) the name, **ADDRESS**, and telephone number of each **HEALTH CARE PROVIDER**;

(b) a description of each **DOCUMENT**; and

(c) the name, **ADDRESS**, and telephone number of the **PERSON** who has each **DOCUMENT**.

17.0 Responses to Request for Admissions

☐ 17.1 Is your response to each request for admission served with these interrogatories an unqualified admission? If not, for each response that is not an unqualified admission:

(a) state the number of the request;

(b) state all facts upon which you base your response;

(c) state the names, **ADDRESSES**, and telephone numbers of all **PERSONS** who have knowledge of those facts; and

(d) identify all **DOCUMENTS** and other tangible things that support your response and state the name, **ADDRESS**, and telephone number of the **PERSON** who has each **DOCUMENT** or thing.

18.0 *[Reserved]*

19.0 *[Reserved]*

20.0 How the Incident Occurred—Motor Vehicle

☐ 20.1 State the date, time, and place of the **INCIDENT** (closest street **ADDRESS** or intersection).

☐ 20.2 For each vehicle involved in the **INCIDENT**, state:

(a) the year, make, model, and license number;

(b) the name, **ADDRESS**, and telephone number of the driver;

---

continued

Exhibit 2-6 *continued*

(c) the name, **ADDRESS**, and telephone number of each occupant other than the driver;

(d) the name, **ADDRESS**, and telephone number of each registered owner;

(e) the name, **ADDRESS**, and telephone number of each lessee;

(f) the name, **ADDRESS**, and telephone number of each owner other than the registered owner or lien holder; and

(g) the name of each owner who gave permission or consent to the driver to operate the vehicle.

☐ 20.3 State the **ADDRESS** and location where your trip began and the **ADDRESS** and location of your destination.

☐ 20.4 Describe the route that you followed from the beginning of your trip to the location of the **INCIDENT**, and state the location of each stop, other than routine traffic stops, during the trip leading up to the **INCIDENT**.

☐ 20.5 State the name of the street or roadway, the lane of travel, and the direction of travel of each vehicle involved in the **INCIDENT** for the 500 feet of travel before the **INCIDENT**.

☐ 20.6 Did the **INCIDENT** occur at an intersection? If so, describe all traffic control devices, signals, or signs at the intersection.

☐ 20.7 Was there a traffic signal facing you at the time of the **INCIDENT**? If so, state:

(a) your location when you first saw it;

(b) the color;

(c) the number of seconds it had been that color; and

(d) whether the color changed between the time you first saw it and the **INCIDENT**.

☐ 20.8 State how the **INCIDENT** occurred, giving the speed, direction, and location of each vehicle involved:

(a) just before the **INCIDENT**;

(b) at the time of the **INCIDENT**; and

(c) just after the **INCIDENT**.

☐ 20.9 Do you have information that a malfunction or defect in a vehicle caused the **INCIDENT**? If so:

(a) identify the vehicle;

(b) identify each malfunction or defect;

(c) state the name, **ADDRESS**, and telephone number of each **PERSON** who is a witness to or has information about each malfunction or defect; and

(d) state the name, **ADDRESS**, and telephone number of each **PERSON** who has custody of each defective part.

☐ 20.10 Do you have information that any malfunction or defect in a vehicle contributed to the injuries sustained in the **INCIDENT**? If so:

(a) identify the vehicle;

(b) identify each malfunction or defect;

(c) state the name, **ADDRESS**, and telephone number of each **PERSON** who is a witness to or has information about each malfunction or defect; and

(d) state the name, **ADDRESS**, and telephone number of each **PERSON** who has custody of each defective part.

☐ 20.11 State the name, **ADDRESS**, and telephone number of each owner and each **PERSON** who has had possession since the **INCIDENT** of each vehicle involved in the **INCIDENT**.

25.0 *[Reserved]*

30.0 *[Reserved]*

40.0 *[Reserved]*

50.0 Contract

☐ 50.1 For each agreement alleged in the pleadings:

(a) identify each **DOCUMENT** that is part of the agreement and for each state the name, **ADDRESS**, and telephone number of each **PERSON** who has the **DOCUMENT**;

(b) state each part of the agreement not in writing, the name, **ADDRESS**, and telephone number of each **PERSON** agreeing to that provision, and the date that part of the agreement was made;

(c) identify all **DOCUMENTS** that evidence any part of the agreement not in writing and for each state the name, **ADDRESS**, and telephone number of each **PERSON** who has the **DOCUMENT**;

(d) identify all **DOCUMENTS** that are part of any modification to the agreement, and for each state the name, **ADDRESS**, and telephone number of each **PERSON** who has the **DOCUMENT**;

(e) state each modification not in writing, the date, and the name, **ADDRESS**, and telephone number of each **PERSON** agreeing to the modification, and the date the modification was made;

(f) identify all **DOCUMENTS** that evidence any modification of the agreement not in writing and for each state the name, **ADDRESS**, and telephone number of each **PERSON** who has the **DOCUMENT**.

☐ 50.2 Was there a breach of any agreement alleged in the pleadings? If so, for each breach describe and give the date of every act or omission that you claim is the breach of the agreement.

☐ 50.3 Was performance of any agreement alleged in the pleadings excused? If so, identify each agreement excused and state why performance was excused.

☐ 50.4 Was any agreement alleged in the pleadings terminated by mutual agreement, release, accord and satisfaction, or novation? If so, identify each agreement terminated, the date of termination, and the basis of the termination.

☐ 50.5 Is any agreement alleged in the pleadings unenforceable? If so, identify each unenforceable agreement and state why it is unenforceable.

☐ 50.6 Is any agreement alleged in the pleadings ambiguous? If so, identify each ambiguous agreement and state why it is ambiguous.

60.0 *[Reserved]*

California Form Answer

The defendant has 30 days from the date of service to answer the plaintiff's complaint. The answer may be in the form of an answer denying all of plaintiff's allegations, an answer denying some allegations and admitting others, a complaint of his own against the plaintiff in the same set of circumstances, or a cross-complaint against another defendant indicating that the other defendant is liable for the plaintiff's damages.

The form answer must indicate whether it is a/an

1. Answer
2. Complaint
3. Cross-complaint

Check the appropriate box under the Answer.

The form included (Exhibit 2-7) is used for personal injury, property damage, or wrongful death actions. The defendant may deny all allegations in the complaint or deny allegations in certain paragraphs and admit others.

Affirmative defenses are indicated in Nos. 4 through 6. Examples include:

1. The plaintiff or cross-complainant was at fault, or partially at fault.
2. The Statute of Limitations has run.

The Answer must be signed by the attorney or party responding.

EXHIBIT 2-7 California Form Answer

Courtesy: Reprinted from *West's California Judicial Council Form 2003*, with permission of West, a Thomson business. For more information about this publication please visit **http://west.thomson.com.**

982.1(15)

ATTORNEY OR PARTY WITHOUT ATTORNEY (NAME AND ADDRESS):	TELEPHONE:	FOR COURT USE ONLY
ATTORNEY FOR (NAME):		
Insert name of court, judicial district or branch court, if any, and post office and street address:		
PLAINTIFF:		
DEFENDANT:		

ANSWER—Personal Injury, Property Damage, Wrongful Death ☐ COMPLAINT OF *(name)*: ☐ CROSS-COMPLAINT OF *(name)*:	CASE NUMBER:

1. This pleading, including attachments and exhibits, consists of the following number of pages: _____

DEFENDANT OR CROSS-DEFENDANT *(name)*:

2. ☐ Generally **denies** each allegation of the **unverified** complaint or cross-complaint.

3. a. ☐ DENIES each allegation of the following numbered paragraphs:

b. ☐ ADMITS each allegation of the following numbered paragraphs:

c. ☐ DENIES, ON INFORMATION AND BELIEF, each allegation of the following numbered paragraphs:

d. ☐ DENIES, BECAUSE OF LACK OF SUFFICIENT INFORMATION OR BELIEF TO ANSWER, each allegation of the following numbered paragraphs:

e. ☐ ADMITS the following allegations and generally denies all other allegations:

(Continued)

Form Approved by the
Judicial Council of California
Effective January 1, 1982

ANSWER—Personal Injury, Property Damage, Wrongful Death

THOMSON
WEST   CCP 425.12

continued

Exhibit 2-7 *continued*

SHORT TITLE:	CASE NUMBER:

ANSWER—Personal Injury, Property Damage, Wrongful Death   Page two

f. ☐ DENIES the following allegations and admits all other allegations:

g. ☐ Other *(specify):*

AFFIRMATIVELY ALLEGES AS A DEFENSE

4. ☐ The comparative fault of plaintiff or cross-complainant *(name):*
as follows:

5. ☐ The expiration of the Statute of Limitations as follows:

6. ☐ Other *(specify):*

7. DEFENDANT OR CROSS-DEFENDANT PRAYS
For costs of suit and that plaintiff or cross-complainant take nothing.
☐ Other *(specify):*

. . . .   _____
(Type or print name)   (Signature of party or attorney)

[982.1(15)]

Page two

Section 2-D. New York Summons and Complaint

The summons for New York is a standard format typed on pleading paper. A sample is shown in Exhibit 2-8. The attorney's name and address are indicated, as well as the court in which the action is being filed. Standard wording is provided.

EXHIBIT 2-8 New York Summons

Courtesy: Reprinted from *West's California Judicial Council Form 2003*, with permission of West, a Thomson business. For more information about this publication please visit **http://west.thomson.com**.

```
 1   JOHN B. GOOD
     2433 Main Street
 2   White Plains, New York 11111
     Telephone:  (444) 123-4567
 3

 4             SUPREME COURT OF THE STATE OF NEW YORK

 5                     COUNTY OF WESTCHESTER

 6

 7   DANIELLE GALLO,            )  Index No.: xxx
                                )
 8          Plaintiff,          )  SUMMONS
                                )
 9      vs.                     )
                                )
10   CURTIS BATES,              )
                                )
11          Defendant           )
                                )
     _____)
12

13   TO THE ABOVE-NAMED DEFENDANT:

14        You are hereby summoned and required to serve on plaintiff's attorney

15   an answer to the complaint in this action within twenty days after service of

16   this summons, exclusive of the day of service, or within thirty days after

17   service is complete if this summons is not personally delivered to you within

18   the State of New York.  In case of your failure to answer, judgment will be

19   taken against you by default for the relief demanded in the complaint.

20

21   ///

22   ///

23   ///

24   ///

25   ///
```

-1-

continued

Exhibit 2-8 *continued*

1	
2	The basis of the venue designated is the residence of plaintiff, which
3	is 435 Sunset Drive, White Plains, New York.
4	
5	
6	Dated this 11th day of December, 2004
7	
8	JOHN B. GOOD Attorney for Plaintiff
9	2433 Main Street White Plains, NY 11111 Telephone: (444) 123-4567
10	
11	
12	
13	
14	
15	
16	
17	
18	
19	
20	
21	
22	
23	
24	
25	

-2-

The complaint, which accompanies the summons, is typed on pleading paper. A general format for the complaint is shown in Exhibit 2-9.

EXHIBIT 2-9 New York Complaint

```
 1  JOHN B. GOOD
    2433 Main Street
 2  White Plains, NY 1111
    Telephone:  (444) 123-4567
 3

 4               SUPREME COURT OF THE STATE OF NEW YORK

 5                        COUNTY OF WESTCHESTER

 6

 7  DANIELLE GALLO,                 ) Case No.: No. 12-3-456789-1
                                    )
 8            Plaintiff,            ) COMPLAINT
                                    )
 9       vs.                        )
                                    )
10  CURTIS BATES,                   )
                                    )
11            Defendant             )
    _____)
12

13  Plaintiff DANIELLE GALLO by her attorney JOHN B. GOOD complains of the

14  defendant CURTIS BATES and alleges as follows:

15                       FIRST CAUSE OF ACTION

16       1.    At all times relevant to the action, plaintiff and defendants

17  were, and are, residents of Westchester County.

18       2.    On September 9, 2004, plaintiff was proceeding in her 2003

19  Ferrari coupe in a northerly direction on Main Street in White Plains, New

20  York, when defendant proceeded to run into the rear of her vehicle with his

21  1999 Hummer at an excessive speed of approximately fifty miles per hour.

22       3.    Upon information and belief, defendant's actions were purposeful

23  and with the knowledge that he would cause a harmful or offensive contact

24  with plaintiff.

25       4.    Upon information and belief, defendant's actions were malicious

    and with the desire to cause injury to plaintiff.

                                 -1-
```

continued

Exhibit 2-9 *continued*

1	5. As a result of defendant's actions, plaintiff suffered severe
2	physical and emotional injury, resulting in, among other things, excruciating
3	pain, a four-week hospitalization, the inability to carry on her profession
4	as a surgeon for three months, and severe emotional distress.
5	6. Accordingly, the plaintiff has suffered damages in the amount of
6	Two Million Dollars ($2,000,000.)
7	SECOND CAUSE OF ACTION
8	7. Plaintiff repeats and realleges each and every allegation
9	contained in paragraphs 1 through 5 above as though set forth fully and at
10	length herein.
11	{**Note**: Since paragraph 6 is relevant to the first cause of action
12	only, it is not realleged.}
13	8. {**Note**: The second cause of action should be given here.}
14	WHEREFORE, plaintiff demands judgment as follows:
15	1. On the first cause of action, judgment in favor of Plaintiff
16	DANIELLE GALLO and against Defendant CURTIS BATES in the sum of Two Million
17	Dollars ($2,000,000) compensatory damages and Two Million Dollars
18	($2,000,000) punitive damages;
19	2. On the second cause of action, judgment in favor of Plaintiff
20	DANIELLE GALLO and against Defendant CURTIS BATES in the sum of $_____.
21	
22	{**Note**: List all damages demanded as to other causes of action, and conclude
23	
24	
25	

-2-

continued

Exhibit 2-9 *continued*

1	with a general request for relief. In general, "and such other and further
2	relief as this court may deem just and proper."}
3	
4	
5	
6	Dated this 11th day of December, 2004
7	
8	JOHN B. GOOD 2433 Main Street White Plains, NY 1111
9	Telephone: (444) 123-4567

1
2
3
4
5
6
7
8
9
10
11
12
13
14
15
16
17
18
19
20
21
22
23
24
25

with a general request for relief. In general, "and such other and further

relief as this court may deem just and proper."}

Dated this 11th day of December, 2004

JOHN B. GOOD
2433 Main Street
White Plains, NY 1111
Telephone: (444) 123-4567

–3–

Section 2-E. Texas

In the Federal District Court in the Northern District of Texas, the plaintiff's attorney may submit a notice of the lawsuit (Exhibit 2-10) to the defendant or through her attorney for the purpose of requesting a waiver for service of the summons in the case. The form for this Notice is included herein.

The form requires insertion of the division of the court as well as the name of the defendants or officer of the corporation being sued, the title of the individual representing the corporate defendant, and the name of the corporate defendant. The addressee must be given at least 30 days in which to return the waiver.

If the defendant signs the waiver, it is filed with the court and no summons will be served. If the defendant refuses to sign the waiver, the plaintiff must effect formal service and may require the defendant to pay the full costs of such service.

EXHIBIT 2-10 Texes Notice of Lawsuit

IN THE UNITED STATES DISTRICT COURT
FOR THE NORTHERN DISTRICT OF TEXAS
_____ DIVISION

NOTICE OF LAWSUIT AND REQUEST FOR
WAIVER OF SERVICE FOR SUMMONS

A - Name of individual defendant (or name of officer or agent of corporate defendant).
B - Title, or other relationship of individual to corporate defendant.
C - Name of corporate defendant, if any.
* - Addressee must be given at least 30 days (60 days if located in a foreign country) in which to return waiver.

TO: (A) _____
as (B) _____ of (C) _____

    A lawsuit has been commenced against you for the entity on whose behalf you are addressed. A copy of the complaint is attached to this notice. It has been filed in the United States District Court for the Northern District of Texas, and has been assigned docket number _____.

    This is not a formal summons or notification from the court, but rather my request that you sign and return the enclosed waiver of service in order to save the cost of serving you with a judicial summons and an additional copy of the complaint. The cost of service will be avoided if I receive a signed copy of the waiver within _____ days* after the date designated below as the date on which this Notice and Request is sent. I am enclosing a stamped and addressed envelope (or other means of cost-free return) for your use. An extra copy of the waiver is also attached for your records.

    If you comply with this request and return the signed waiver, it will be filed with the Court and no summons will be served on you. The action will then proceed as if you had been served on the date the waiver is filed, except you will not be obligated to answer the complaint before 60 days from the date designated below as the date on which this notice is sent (or before 90 days from that date if your address is not in any judicial district of the United States).

    If you do not return the signed waiver within the time indicated, I will take appropriate steps to effect formal service in a manner authorized by the Federal Rules of Civil Procedure and will then, to the extent authorized by those Rules, ask the court to require you (or the party on whose behalf you are addressed) to pay the full costs of such service. In that connection, please read the statement concerning the duty of parties to waive the service of the summons, which is set forth on the bottom of the Waiver of Service of Summons form.

    I affirm that this request is being sent to you on behalf of the plaintiff, this _____ day of _____, _____.

_____
Signature of Plaintiff's Attorney
or Unrepresented Plaintiff

If all of the parties consent, cases may be heard before a United States magistrate judge. The procedure for disposing of a civil case in this manner is provided, (Exhibit 2-11), along with the form giving consent to proceed before the United States magistrate judge. After all parties sign the Consent form, Exhibit 2-12, it is submitted to the district clerk and the United States district judge reassigns the case to a magistrate judge.

EXHIBIT 2-11 Texas Notice of Right to Consent

NOTICE OF RIGHT TO CONSENT TO DISPOSITION OF A CIVIL CASE BY A UNITED STATES MAGISTRATE JUDGE

In accordance with the provisions of 28 U.S.C. § 636(c), you are hereby notified that the United States Magistrate Judges of this district court, in addition to their other duties, may, upon the consent of all the parties in a civil case, conduct any or all proceedings in a civil case, including a jury or non-jury trial, and order the entry of a final judgment. Copies of appropriate consent forms for this purpose are available from the clerk of the court.

You should be aware that your decision to consent, or not to consent, to the reassignment of your case to a United States Magistrate Judge for disposition is entirely voluntary and should be communicated solely to the clerk of the district court. No Judge or Magistrate Judge will be informed of a party's refusal to consent to trial of a case before a Magistrate Judge. If a consent form is not filed within twenty (20) days of the date that all parties have filed an answer or otherwise responded, the court will deem that failure as evidence that the parties wish that the cause of action proceed before the district judge to whom the case was assigned at the time it was originally filed. Should all the parties subsequently consent to trial by a magistrate judge, however, the district judge may in his/her discretion so order.

Pursuant to 28 U.S.C. § 636(c), appeal to the United States Court of Appeals for the Fifth Circuit from a judgment of a Magistrate Judge is permitted in the same manner as an appeal from any other judgment of the Court.

EXHIBIT 2-12 Texas Consent to Proceed

**IN THE UNITED STATES DISTRICT COURT
FOR THE NORTHERN DISTRICT OF TEXAS**

_____ DIVISION

_____
Plaintiff

v.   Docket No._____

_____
Defendant

CONSENT TO PROCEED BEFORE A UNITED STATES MAGISTRATE JUDGE

In accordance with the provisions of 28 U.S.C. § 636(c), the parties to the above captioned civil matter hereby waive their right to proceed before a Judge of the United States District Court and consent to have a United States Magistrate Judge conduct any and all further proceedings in the above styled case (including the trial) and order entry of a final judgment.

<u>Party or Counsel of Record</u>   <u>Date</u>

_____   _____

_____   _____

_____   _____

NOTE: Return this form to the District Clerk only if it has been executed by all parties to the case.

ORDER OF REASSIGNMENT

IT IS HEREBY ORDERED that the above captioned matter be reassigned to the United States Magistrate Judge _____ for the conduct of all further proceedings and the entry of judgment in accordance with 28 U.S.C. § 636(c) and the foregoing consent of the parties.

DATED:_____   _____

UNITED STATES DISTRICT JUDGE

Abstract of Judgment

After the judgment is rendered by the court, the deputy clerk issues an Abstract of Judgment indicating in whose favor the case was decided and any damages that must be paid. A sample abstract is included as Exhibit 2-13.

EXHIBIT 2-13 Texas Abstract of Judgment

IN THE UNITED STATES DISTRICT COURT
FOR THE NORTHERN DISTRICT OF TEXAS
_____ DIVISION

(Name All Plaintiffs and Defendants)

CIVIL NUMBER _____

Complete the following if judgment
was rendered in another District:

vs.

District: _____
Docket Number: _____
Date Entered: _____

ABSTRACT OF JUDGMENT

In the above entitled and numbered cause a judgment was rendered in this Court, or other United States District

Court as indicated above and registered herein, on the _____ day of _____,_____, in favor of

_____ against

_____

_____

in the sum of $ _____ with interest at the rate of

_____ per cent per annum from the _____ day of _____, _____.

Costs have been taxed by the Clerk of Court in the sum of $ _____.

Credits reflected by returns on execution in the sum of $_____.

The birth date and driver's license number of the defendant available to the Clerk are: _____

_____.

The address of the defendant shown in this suit in which said judgment was rendered:_____

_____or nature of

citation and date and place citation served: _____

_____.

I certify that the above and foregoing is a true and correct abstract of judgment rendered or registered in this Court.

Witness my hand and seal of the Court this _____ day of _____, 20____.

KAREN MITCHELL, CLERK

By _____
Deputy Clerk

Writ of Execution

In some cases after a judgment is rendered, the judgment debtor does not pay the amount awarded to the judgment creditor. In that case, the judgment creditor (usually the plaintiff) may file a Writ of Execution with the court stating that the judgment has not been paid, along with the amount, interest, and costs.

The debtor's property may be sold at a public sale in order to satisfy the judgment if it is not paid. The form for a Writ of Execution is shown in Exhibit 2-14.

EXHIBIT 2-14   Texas Writ of Execution

United States District Court
Northern District of Texas

Writ of Execution

Case No _____

(Complete the following if judgment
was rendered in another district)

v.

District _____
Docket No _____
Date Entered _____

TO ANY UNITED STATES MARSHAL IN THE STATE OF TEXAS:

WHEREAS, on the ____ day of _____, A.D., _____ in a cause styled as above, judgment was rendered in this Court, or other United States District Court as indicated above and registered herein, in favor of

_____

_____

against _____ ,
hereinafter called judgment debtor, for the sum of $_____ with interest thereon at the rate of ____ percent per annum from the ____ day of _____, A.D. , _____ until paid, together with costs which have been taxed to date by the Clerk of Court in the sum of $_____ ;

AND WHEREAS, according to an affidavit on the reverse side hereof, executed by or in behalf of the judgment creditor, there remains due and unpaid the following sums:

$ _____   Unpaid balance of costs specified hereinabove taxed by the Clerk of Court

$ _____   Judgment

$ _____   Interest on Judgment

and further interest will accrue on the unsatisfied judgment in the sum of $ _____ per day from date of the aforesaid affidavit;

THEREFORE YOU ARE COMMANDED, that of the goods and chattels, lands and tenements of the said judgment debtor you cause to be made the full amount of said judgment, interest, and costs, with the further costs of executing this writ.

HEREIN FAIL NOT, and have you the said monies, together with this writ, before this Court within ninety (90) days from the date of this writ.

WITNESS my hand and the seal of this Court at _____, Texas, this ____ day of _____, _____.

KAREN MITCHELL, CLERK

By _____

Deputy Clerk

continued

Exhibit 2-14 *continued*

AFFIDAVIT AND REQUEST FOR ISSUANCE OF WRIT OF EXECUTION

I, _____, judgment creditor or duly authorized agent or attorney acting in the capacity specified under my signature, do hereby swear or affirm that all of the recitals on the reverse side of this instrument relating to the entry of judgment and costs are true and correct; and, after application of all credits, first against costs, second against accrued interest, and third against the judgment as entered, there remains unpaid and unsatisfied the sums specified, and that further interest will accrue as shown.

Dated this _____ day of _____, A.D., _____.

Signature and capacity in which signed: _____

_____

Address: _____

_____

Telephone Number: _____

STATE OF   _____

COUNTY OF   _____

On this date there appeared before me, the undersigned authority, the person whose name is subscribed to the foregoing instrument and on his oath did swear or affirm that he has knowledge of the facts stated therein, that such facts are true and correct, and that he has authority to execute the instrument in the capacity stated therein.

Date: _____   _____

(SEAL)   _____

Title

MARSHAL'S RETURN

Received this writ at _____ , on _____
and executed as follows:

_____

UNITED STATES MARSHAL

By   _____

Deputy Marshal

Most states require prepared pleadings for documents filed in criminal cases. Very few forms exist in this area because a considerable number of the attorney's motions are made in open court. Whenever a document is filed with the court, use the format for your own state's captions.

Criminal subpoenas vary by state and may be obtained from the court in which the action is filed. A subpoena in a criminal case in the United States District Court is provided as Exhibit 3-1. The proper district must be inserted, as well as the names of the parties and the case number. Under "TO:" at the top of the subpoena, insert the name of the person who is being subpoenaed to appear. Under "**PLACE**" indicate the name and address of the court. Under "**COURTROOM**" indicate the courtroom number. Under "**DATE AND TIME**" indicate the date and time of the proceeding for which the subpoena is being issued. If the individual should bring any documents or objects with him, they should be listed under that section. The attorney must sign at the bottom right and indicate the name, address, and telephone number of the law firm. The magistrate judge or clerk of the court must sign at the lower left in order for the subpoena to be official.

The Proof of Service on the second page must be signed by the server. If the witness is given fees and mileage for appearing, that amount must be indicated. The server should sign the declaration under penalty of perjury that the information contained in the Proof of Service is true and correct.

EXHIBIT 3-1   United States District Court Subpoena

OAO89 (Rev. 7/95) Subpoena in a Criminal Case

UNITED STATES DISTRICT COURT

DISTRICT OF _____

V.

**SUBPOENA IN A
CRIMINAL CASE**

Case Number:

TO:

G   YOU ARE COMMANDED to appear in the United States District Court at the place, date, and time specified below, or any subsequent place, date and time set by the court, to testify in the above referenced case. This subpoena shall remain in effect until you are granted leave to depart by the court or by an officer acting on behalf of the court.

PLACE   COURTROOM

                                                                                                       DATE AND TIME

G   YOU ARE ALSO COMMANDED to bring with you the following document(s) or object(s):

U.S. MAGISTRATE JUDGE OR CLERK OF COURT   DATE

(By) Deputy Clerk

ATTORNEY=S NAME, ADDRESS AND PHONE NUMBER:

continued

Exhibit 3-1 *continued*

AO89 (Rev. 7/95) Subpoena in a Criminal Case (Reverse)

PROOF OF SERVICE

	DATE	PLACE
RECEIVED BY SERVER		
SERVED	DATE	PLACE

SERVED ON (PRINT NAME)   FEES AND MILEAGE TENDERED TO WITNESS

G YES   G NO   AMOUNT $ _____

SERVED BY (PRINT NAME)   TITLE

_____

DECLARATION OF SERVER

I declare under penalty of perjury under the laws of the United States of America that the foregoing information contained in the Proof of Service is true and correct.

Executed on

DATE   SIGNATURE OF SERVER

ADDRESS OF SERVER

_____

ADDITIONAL INFORMATION

Hawaii—Plea Document

The defendant in a criminal case may plead guilty or no contest. The form must indicate the charge or charges against the defendant as well as the maximum imprisonment and/or fine for the charged offense. (See Exhibit 3-2.) A separate section indicates the extended term of imprisonment and the mandatory minimum term of imprisonment.

The defendant must read this document and sign it in her attorney's presence. She must check the appropriate boxes, sign, and date the form. The defendant's attorney must read the plea and explain its contents to the defendant. The attorney must sign verifying that the defendant's plea is made voluntarily and with an intelligent understanding of the nature of the charges and possible consequences.

EXHIBIT 3-2 Hawaii Plea Document

STATE OF HAWAI'I CIRCUIT COURT OF THE FIRST CIRCUIT	[ ] GUILTY PLEA [ ] NO CONTEST PLEA [ ] MOTION TO DEFER	CASE NUMBER:

STATE OF HAWAI'I vs. (Defendant)

Date of Birth:	Defendant's Age:	Education (Last Grade Completed):

CHARGE(S)/HRS:	MAXIMUM IMPRISONMENT/FINE:	REPORT NUMBER(S):

Extended Term of Imprisonment:	Mandatory Minimum Term of Imprisonment:

1. My mind is clear. I have not taken any medication, alcohol, or illegal drugs within the last 48 hours. I am not sick. I speak, read, write, and understand the English language or this document has been read to me or has been interpreted for me.

2. I have received a written copy of the original charge(s) in this case. The charge(s) has/have been explained to me. I understand the original charge(s) against me. I told my lawyer all of the facts I know about the case. My lawyer explained the government's evidence against me, my possible defense(s), and the facts which the government must prove in order to convict me.

3. I understand the reduced charge(s) with which the government has agreed to charge me, instead of the original charge(s). (Applicable only if original charge has been reduced.)

4. I plead of my own free will. No one is pressuring me or threatening me or any other person to force me to plead. I am not taking the blame or pleading to protect another person from prosecution.

5. I know I have the right to plead not guilty and have a speedy and public trial by jury or by the court. I know in a trial the government is required to prove my guilt beyond a reasonable doubt. I know I can see, hear, and question witnesses who testify against me, and that I may call my own witnesses to testify for me at trial. I understand I have the right to take the stand to testify and I have the right not to testify at trial. I know by pleading I give up the right to file any pre-trial motions, and I give up the right to a trial and may be found guilty and sentenced without a trial of any kind. I also give up the right to appeal anything that has happened in this case to date.

6. I understand that the court may impose any of the following penalties for the offense(s) to which I now plead: the maximum term of imprisonment, any extended term of imprisonment, and any mandatory minimum term of imprisonment specified above; consecutive terms of imprisonment (if more than one charge); restitution; a fine; a fee and/or assessment; community service; probation with up to one year of imprisonment and other terms and conditions.

[ ] Prosecutor [ ] Defendant [ ] Defense Counsel [ ] Adult Probation Division

continued

Exhibit 3-2   *continued*

GUILTY/NO CONTEST PLEA (Continued)	CASE NUMBER:

7. [ ] I plead no contest because, after discussing all the evidence and receiving advice on the law from my lawyer, I do not want to contest the charge(s) against me.

    [ ] I plead guilty because, after discussing all the evidence and receiving advice on the law from my lawyer, I believe that I am guilty. (Give a brief statement of the facts that establish the defendant's guilt as to each offense to which the defendant is entering a plea pursuant to the requirements of HRS §§ 701-114, 701-115, 702-205, and 702-206, as amended.)

    [ ] I move to defer acceptance of my plea. I understand that if the Court denies my motion, the Court will then find and adjudge me guilty upon this plea, and impose sentence.

8. I have not been promised any kind of deal or favor or leniency by anyone for my plea, except that I have been told that the government has agreed as follows (if none, write "None"):

    [ ] I know that the court is not required to follow any deal or agreement between the Government and me. I know that the court has not promised me leniency.

    [ ] The court has agreed to follow the plea agreement pursuant to Rule 11, Hawai'i Rules of Penal Procedure.

9. I further state that (if none, write "None"):

10. I know that, if I am not a citizen of the United States, a conviction or a plea of guilty or no contest, whether acceptance of my plea is deferred or not, may have the consequences of deportation, exclusion from admission to the United States, or denial of naturalization under the laws of the United States.

11. I am signing this Guilty/No Contest Plea form after I have gone over all of it with my lawyer. I know I will not be permitted to withdraw my plea. I am signing this form in the presence of my lawyer. I have no complaints about my lawyer and I am satisfied with what he/she has done for me.

DATE	DEFENDANT'S SIGNATURE

CERTIFICATE OF COUNSEL

I certify that I have read and explained fully this Guilty/No Contest Plea document to the defendant and believe he/she understands this document in its entirety. The statements contained in this document conform with my understanding of the defendant's position. I believe the defendant's plea is made voluntarily and with an intelligent understanding of the nature of the charge(s) and possible consequences. The defendant signed this Guilty/No Contest Plea form in my presence.

DATE	ATTORNEY FOR DEFENDANT	SIGNATURE

I acknowledge that the Judge questioned me personally in open court to make sure that I knew what I was doing in pleading guilty or no contest and understood this form before I signed it.

DATE	SIGNATURE OF DEFENDANT (signed in open court after questioning)	
NAME OF JUDGE		

Indiana—Violent Crime Compensation Fund

Several states provide financial assistance to victims of crimes. Indiana enacted a law in 1978 that provides for this assistance. Funds are provided for a victim, surviving spouse, or a dependent child of a victim of violent crime. Certain conditions are required and are listed in the document provided. The application form requires information about the victim, the injuries to the victim, and the circumstances of the crime.

This form is typical of the forms used by other states that have this program. Many states have established departments within their criminal divisions for administering these victim compensation programs. The Indiana documents are included as Exhibit 3-3.

EXHIBIT 3-3 Indiana Violent Crime Compensation Fund

INDIANA CRIMINAL JUSTICE INSTITUTE
VIOLENT CRIME COMPENSATION FUND
302 W. Washington St., Rm. E209
Indianapolis, Indiana 46204-2767
Telephone: (317) 232-7103

In 1978, the Indiana General Assembly enacted a law which, for the first time in Indiana, provided for financial assistance to victims of violent crimes.

1   The claimant must be a victim, surviving spouse or a dependent child of a victim of violent crime, including cases where there is evidence of drunk driving.

2   The crime must have occurred within the State of Indiana.

3   The crime must have been reported to police within forty eight (48) hours after its occurrence and the victim and/or claimant must cooperate with the law enforcement officials in connection with the crime.

4   The victim must have incurred a minimum of $100.00 in medical expenses as a result of the crime. Such expenses as counseling, lost income and funeral expenses may be considered after the minimum has been met. (*The maximum benefit available is $10,000.00*)

5   The victim must not have contributed to the crime.

6   Where special circumstances arise, claimants are advised to contact the Division or their attorneys for information as to eligibility.

1 The application for benefits must be filed with this agency no later than 180 days after the date crime occurred. It is necessary that the victim/claimant fill out the application and include their signature.

2 The application must be filed either in person or by certified mail with return receipt requested. The return receipt is your evidence of filing your application.

3 In the event the claimant is a minor child (*under 18 years of age*), a parent or legal guardian must sign. For a minor, a certified copy of the guardianship order must be attached.

4 Send original application to the Division at the address listed above.

5 **PLEASE NOTIFY THE DIVISION OF ALL CHANGES IN NAMES, ADDRESS OR TELEPHONE NUMBER.**

For more information please contact the office at the above listed telephone

continued

Exhibit 3-3   *continued*

APPLICATION FOR BENEFITS
FROM VIOLENT CRIMES COMPENSATION FUND
State Form 23776 (R9 / 3-97)

* This state agency is requesting disclosure of Social Security numbers that are necessary to accomplish the statutory purpose of this state agency according to IC 4-1-8.
** This information is for statistical purposes only and will not effect the eligibility of the claimant.

VICTIM INFORMATION

Name of victim (last, first, middle initial)

Marital status

*Social Security number

Sex   ☐ Male   ☐ Female

Date of birth

**Race   ☐ White   ☐ Black   ☐ Hispanic   ☐ Asian   ☐ American Indian   ☐ Other

Name of victim's dependents

CLAIMANT INFORMATION

Name of claimant (if different from the victim/last, first, middle initial)

* Social Security number

Address of victim or claimant (number and street)

Work telephone number ( )

City, state, ZIP code

Home telephone number ( )

Claimant's relationship to victim

INJURIES TO VICTIM

What injuries did the victim sustain as a result of the victimization?

Hospital for medical treatment

Address (number and street, city, state, ZIP code)

Name attending physician

Address (number and street, city, state, ZIP code)

CRIME AND PROSECUTION

Date of crime

Location of crime (city, state, county)

Briefly give a description of the crime

Date and time police report was filed   ☐ AM   ☐ PM

Name of law enforcement agency

Name of detective

Case number (if known)

Name of suspect (s)

Victim's relationship to suspect

Has suspect been arrested?   ☐ Yes   ☐ No

Were you willing to pursue prosecution?   ☐ Yes   ☐ No

If "No", please explain:

Cause number (if known)

continued

Exhibit 3-3 *continued*

INSURANCE

Were the injuries you sustained covered by any of the following?

☐ Medicare ☐ Medicaid ☐ Worker's Compensation ☐ County Trustee

Medical and / or car insurance amount $ _____

Carrier(s) _____

Health Maintenance Organization carrier: _____ Coverage _____

Are you receiving any of the following as a result of the victimization:

Social Security disability $_____ Per Month

Social Security survivors benefit $_____ Per Month

Life insurance death benefits $_____ TOTAL

Were you the beneficiary ? ☐ Yes ☐ No

Worker's compensation benefits $_____ Per Week

Employer disability benefits $_____ Per Week / Month

EMPLOYMENT INFORMATION

Victim's employment name	Telephone number ( )

Address (number and street, city, state, ZIP code)

RELEASE
I do hereby release the State of Indiana and the Violent Crimes Compensation Division from any and all liability which might be connected with the processing and payment of this claim. In the event the fund from which the award is paid, if the claim is allowed, is such that it is necessary to prorate the payment of the claim, I do hereby release and discharge the State of Indiana and the Violent Crimes Compensation Division from any and all liability beyond the amount actually paid to me from the fund.

SUBROGATIONS
The claimant hereby certifies that no release has been or will be given in settlement or for compromise with any third party who may be liable in damages to the claimant; and the claimant, in consideration of any payment and/or award by the Violent Crime Compensation Division in accordance with IC 5-2-6.1-22, here subrogates the State of Indiana to the extent of any such payment and/or award to any right or cause of action occurring to the claimant against any third person, and agrees to accept any such payment and/or award pursuant to the provisions of the statute. The claimant hereby authorizes the State of Indiana to sue in his/her name, but at the cost of the State of Indiana, pledging full cooperation in such action, to execute and deliver all papers and instruments, and do all things necessary to secure such right to a cause of action.

CONSENT TO PAY PROVIDERS
I do hereby consent and agree that if an award is made, money due and owing to any provider of medical services and due to any other qualified person or entity, including any attorney's fees allowed to my attorney, may be paid direct to said provider, entity or attorney by the agency and need not be paid to me.

AUTHORIZATION TO RELEASE INFORMATION
I hereby authorize any hospital, physician, or other person, who attended or examined _____
any undertaker or other person who rendered services; any employers of the victim; any police or other municipal authority or agency, or public authority; any insurance company or organization, or its representative, to release any and all information with respect to the incident resulting in the victim's personal injury or death, and the claim made herewith for benefits. A photocopy of this authorization will be considered as effective and valid as the original.

I the undersigned Claimant, hereby certify under the penalties of perjury that the statements made herein are true to the best of my knowledge and belief and were made for the purpose of inducing the State of Indiana to award benefits to me for losses incurred as described above through the Violent Crime Victims Compensation Fund as prescribed in IC 5-2-6.1-40.

Signature of claimant	Date

The primary function of an estate planning practice is advising the client of the best way to distribute her estate upon her death. In most cases, the attorney will prepare either a will or a trust, or both, for the client. Included herein is a simple will checklist along with a sample will form. The trust instrument may be found in the textbook.

The Simple Formal Will is provided in the textbook as Exhibit 8-1. The Simple Will Checklist is provided here as Exhibit 4-1 to assist in the preparation of the multiple-page Will provided in Exhibit 4-2. The checklist should include the name of the testator (maker of the will), spouse, and address. On the first page, the various parts of the will are listed, along with whether or not they are required or recommended additions. This checklist may be modified for the individual client. List the bequests specifically or generally, depending on the type of bequest. For example, listing "all the cars I own at my death" would be a general bequest, while "my 1999 red Ferrari couple" is a specific bequest. Most attorneys advise clients to only make specific bequests of items they are sure to have upon their death.

While interviewing the client, the checklist should be completed. After all items are discussed, the actual will can be prepared.

EXHIBIT 4-1 Will Checklist

Courtesy: Reprinted from **www.LegalLawForms.com.** Copyright © 2001.

SIMPLE WILL CHECKLIST

NAME OF TESTATOR: _____
(person making will)

NAME OF SPOUSE: _____

TOWN/CITY: _____

COUNTY: _____

	Description	Required	Recommended	or	Optional
W. 1.10	Heading and Introduction	X			
W. 1.11	Heading and Introduction a/k/a _____		X		
W. 2.10	Simple Direction to Pay Debts		X		
W. 2.10.01	Simple Direction to Pay Debts Discretionary		X		
W. 3.10	Pay all Taxes from Residue		X		
W. 33.10.01	Taxes from Residue; alternate source if inadequate Alternate Source _____		X		
W. 4.10	Specific Bequest of Specific Item of Personal Effects Item _____ Devisee _____ Contingent Devisee _____		X		
W. 4.20	General Bequest of Personal and Household Effects with Precatory Separate Writing		X		
W. 4.21	General Bequest of Personal and Household Effects with Mandatory Separate Writing	X			
W. 6.10	Cash Legacy Amount _____ Legatee _____		X		
W. 6.11	Cash Legacy with Contingent Takes Contingent Takes _____		X		
W. 6.20	Specific Bequest of Stock Devisee ____, Corp. ____, Shares ____	X			
W. 7.10	Specific Devise of Residence Devisee _____ Address of Residence _____		X		

continued

Exhibit 4-1 *continued*

	Description	Required	Recommended	or	Optional
W. 7.12	Other Devise of Real Estate Devisee _____ Legal Description or address _____ _____		X		
W.10.10	Residue to Spouse, Contingent to Issue; Is Spouse and Issue deceased to _____		X		
W.10.20	Pour-over Residue to Testator's Intervivos Trust		X		
W.10.30	Residue to Issue, Contingent to _____		X		

W.10.32	Residue to other(s)
	Name _____
	  % or Share _____
	Name _____
	  % or Share _____
			X		

W.13. 71	Personal Representative to act as Trustee for Beneficiaries under age 21 (other age _____)	X			
W.13.93	Trustee Discretion to Terminate Small Trust Amount $_____	X			

[choose one of these]

	Description	Required	Recommended	or	Optional
W.13.10	Naming Corporate Executor Name _____		X		
W.13.11	Naming Individual Executor with Corporate Alternate Name (Individual) _____ Name (Corp. Alt.) _____				X
W.13.11.01	Naming Individual Executor - No Alternate Name _____				X
W.13.20	Naming Corporate Executor & Trustee Name _____		X		
W.13.40	Change in Corporate Fiduciary	X			
W.13.45	Definition of Executor		X		
W.13.46	Definition of Executor and Trustee		X		
W.13.48	Executor's Fee - Standard Schedule or Reasonable		X		

continued

Exhibit 4-1   *continued*

	Description	Required	Recommended	or	Optional
W.13.49	Executor's and Trustees - Standard Schedule or Reasonable		X		
W.13.50	Short Form Powers - Executor	X			
W.13.51	Short Form Powers - Executor & Trustee		X		
W.13.90	Executor Discretion in Tax Matters	X			
W.13.94	Appointment of Ancillary Personal Representative		X		
W.14.10	Definition of Children		X		
W.14.11	Definition of IRC Terms		X		
W.14.20	Naming Testamentary Guardian Name _____		X		
W.14.20.01	Naming Testamentary Guardian and Alternate Name (Primary) _____ Name (Alternate) _____				X
W.14.40	Simultaneous Death Provision	X			
W.15.10	Spendthrift Provision		X		
W.16.00	Testimonium Clause	X			
W.16.01	Attestation Clause - 2 witnesses	X			
W.16.01.02	Attestation Clause - 3 witnesses		X		
W.16.03	Self-Proof Affidavit - 2 witnesses	X			
W.16.04	Self-Proof Affidavit - 3 witnesses		X		

Last Will and Testament

The will form included consists of 11 pages and is shown in Exhibit 4-2. It may be modified to fit a particular situation or to comply with the laws of a particular state. For instance, this will provides a form for the signature of a notary public. However, many states require that the testator sign the will in the presence of two witnesses, who also sign at the same time.

The first five items are standard clauses for paying bills and taxes. Item 6 begins the actual disposal of the estate. Several paragraphs may be used to bequeath specific estate items.

Item 7 represents the residue of the testator's personal property. Items 9 and 10 provide for the distribution of sums of money. These clauses may be omitted if all property is divided among named individuals. Read through the will form to determine which clauses are appropriate for your particular client. For instance, if the client owns no stock, then Item 11 is not required.

Item 37 provides for the appointment of a testamentary guardian for minor children. The client should be advised to discuss this appointment with the prospective guardian before indicating the name in the will. Item 38 is a substitute for Item 37 in the event an alternate guardian is named.

Although this will form does not include a "One Dollar Clause," the will shown in Chapter 8 of the textbook includes this clause stating that anyone contesting the will receives $1 from it. This may be included if the client desires.

EXHIBIT 4-2 Last Will and Testament

Courtesy: Reprinted with permission from **www.LegalLawForms.com**.

LAST WILL AND TESTAMENT
OF

_____

I, _____, a resident of and domiciled in the County of _____, and State of _____, do hereby make, publish, and declare this to be my Last Will and Testament, hereby revoking all Wills and Codicils at any time heretofore made by me.

ITEM 1

I direct that all my legally enforceable debts, secured and unsecured, be paid as soon as practicable after my death. If at the time of my death any of the real property herein devised is subject to a mortgage, I direct that the devisee taking such mortgaged property shall take it subject to such mortgage and that the devisee shall not be entitled to have the obligation secured thereby paid out of my general estate.

ITEM 2

I direct that all estate, inheritance, succession, death, or similar taxes (except generation-skipping transfer taxes) assessed with respect to my estate herein disposed of, or any part thereof, or on any bequest or devise contained in this my Last Will (which term wherever used herein shall include any Codicil hereto), or on any insurance upon my life or on any property held jointly by me with another or on any transfer made by me during my lifetime or on any other property or interests in property included in my estate for such tax purposes be paid out of my residuary estate and shall not be charged to or against any recipient, beneficiary, transferee or owner of any such property or interests in property included in my estate for such tax purposes.

ITEM 3

I direct that all estate, inheritance, succession, death, or similar taxes (except generation-skipping transfer taxes) assessed with respect to my estate herein disposed of, or any part thereof, or on any bequest or devise contained in this my Last Will (which term wherever used herein shall include any Codicil hereto), or on any insurance upon my life or on any property held jointly by me with another or on any transfer made by me during my lifetime or on any other property or interests in property included in my estate for such tax purposes be paid out of my residuary estate and shall not be charged to or against any recipient, beneficiary, transferee, or owner of any such property or interests in property included in my estate for such tax purposes. If my residuary estate is inadequate to pay such taxes, they shall be paid from the assets of _____ [alternate source of payment of taxes]_____.

ITEM 4

(1) Except as provided in (2) herein, all estate, inheritance, succession, death or similar taxes (except generation-skipping transfer taxes) assessed with respect to my estate herein disposed

continued

Exhibit 4-2 *continued*

of, or any part thereof, or on any bequest or devise contained in this my Last will (which term wherever used herein shall include any Codicil hereto), be paid out of my residuary estate and shall not be charged to or against any recipient, beneficiary, transferee or owner of any such property or interest in property included in my estate for such tax purposes.

(2) All such taxes in respect to any property or interests in property included in my gross estate under sections 2035, 2036, 2037, 2038, 2039, 2040, 2041, 2042, and 2044 of the Internal Revenue Code shall be charged against and paid by the recipient or beneficiary of such property or interest in property or from the property or interest in the property, provided, however: (a) there shall be no apportionment against any donee or recipient of any such property or interest in property which is a qualified charity under section 2055 and the property or interest in property was allowed in my federal estate tax proceedings as a charitable deduction; (b) there shall be no apportionment against my surviving husband/wife, if he/she is a donee or recipient of any such property or interest in property and the property or interest in property was allowed in my federal estate tax proceedings as a marital deduction under I.R.C. section 2056. The amount of the tax to be charged against such donee or recipient shall be determined by multiplying a fraction (the numerator of which shall be the federal estate tax value of the property to be apportioned as finally determined in my federal estate tax proceedings and the denominator of which shall be the total value of my taxable estate for such federal estate tax purposes) times the net amount of such taxes payable by my estate after the application of all credits against such taxes.

ITEM 5

I give and bequeath to _____ if he/she shall survive me the following property: _____.
If he/she shall not survive me, then I give and bequeath this described property to _____, if he/she shall survive me.

ITEM 6

I give and bequeath all [of the rest and remainder of] my personal and household effects of every kind, including, but not limited to, furniture, appliances, furnishings, pictures, silverware, china, glass, books, jewelry, wearing apparel, boats, automobiles, and other vehicles, and all policies of fire, burglary, property damage, and other insurance on or in connection with the use of this property, to my husband/wife, _____, if he/she shall survive me. If he/she shall not survive me, I give and bequeath all this property to my children surviving me in approximately equal shares; provided, however, the issue of a deceased child surviving me shall take per stirpes the share their parent would have taken had he or she survived me. If my issue do not agree to the division of the property among themselves, my Executor shall make such division among them, the decision of my Executor to be in all respects binding upon my issue. I request that my husband/wife, my Executor, and my issue abide by any memorandum by me directing the disposition of this property or any part thereof. This request is precatory and not mandatory. If any beneficiary hereunder is a minor, my Executor may distribute such minor's share to such minor or for such minor's use to any person with whom such minor is residing or who has the care or control of such minor without further responsibility and the receipt of the person to whom it is distributed shall be a complete discharge of my Executor.

continued

Exhibit 4-2 *continued*

ITEM 7

I give and bequeath all [the rest and remainder of] my personal and household effects of every kind, including, but not limited to, furniture, appliances, furnishings, pictures, silverware, china, glass, books, jewelry, wearing apparel, boats, automobiles, and other vehicles, and all policies of fire, burglary, property damage, and other insurance on or in connection with the use of this property, as follows:

1. I may leave written memoranda signed by me disposing of certain items of my tangible personal property. Any such item of tangible personal property shall pass according to the terms of such memoranda in existence at the time of my death. If no such written memoranda are found or identified by my Executor within ninety (90) days after my Executor's qualification, it shall be conclusively presumed that there are no such memoranda and any subsequent discovered memoranda shall be ineffective. Any property given and devised to a beneficiary who is not living at the time of my death and for whom no effective alternate provision has been made shall pass according to the provisions of the following paragraph, and not pursuant to any anti-lapse statute.

2. In default of such memoranda, or to the extent such memoranda do not completely or effectively dispose of such property, I give and bequeath the rest of my personal and household effects of every kind to my husband/wife, _____, if he/she shall survive me. If he/she shall not survive me, I give and bequeath all this property to my children surviving me, in approximately equal shares; provided, however, the issue of a deceased child surviving me shall take per stirpes the share their parent would have taken had he or she survived me. If my issue do not agree to the division of the property among themselves, my Executor shall make such division among them, the decision of my Executor to be in all respects binding upon my issue. If any beneficiary hereunder is a minor, my Executor may distribute such minor's share to such minor or for such minor's use to any person with whom such minor is residing or who has the care or control of such minor without further responsibility and the receipt of the person to whom it is distributed shall be a complete discharge of my Executor.

ITEM 8

I give and bequeath to _____, if he/she shall survive me, the sum of _____.

ITEM 9

I give and bequeath to _____, if he/she shall survive me, the sum of _____. If he/she shall not survive me, then I give and bequeath such sum to _____ if he/she shall survive me.

ITEM 10

I give and bequeath to _____, if he/she shall survive me, of the stock of _____ or of any successor or resulting corporation of such corporation which I own at the time of my death.

ITEM 11

I give and devise to _____, if he/ she shall survive me, any interest which I own at the time of my death in the house and lot located at _____ _____._____.

continued

Exhibit 4-2   *continued*

ITEM 12

I give and devise to _____, if he/she shall survive me, the real property described as follows:

[insert description of real property]

ITEM 13

I give, devise, and bequeath all the rest, residue, and remainder of my property of every kind and description (including lapsed legacies and devises) wherever situate and whether acquired before or after the execution of this Will, absolutely in fee simple to my husband/wife, _____, if he/she shall survive me. If he/she shall not survive me, then I give, devise, and bequeath all of said property to my [issue surviving me, in equal shares, per stirpes, or in default of such issue to _____[name of contingent residuary beneficiary]_____.] [children surviving me, in equal shares; provided, however, the issue of a deceased child surviving me shall take per stirpes the share their parent would have taken if he or she survived me.]

ITEM 14

I give, devise, and bequeath all the rest, residue, and remainder of my property of every kind and description (including lapsed legacies and devises), wherever situate and whether acquired before or after the execution of this Will, to the then acting Trustee under that certain Trust Agreement between myself as Settlor and _____ as Trustee executed prior to the execution of this Will on ___[date of trust agreement if any]___. My Trustee shall add the property bequeathed and devised by this Item to the principal of the above Trust and shall hold, administer, and distribute the property in accordance with the provisions of the Trust Agreement, including any amendments thereto made before my death.

ITEM 15

In the event for any reason the bequest and devise under Item _____ above is ineffective and invalid, then I hereby give, devise, and bequeath the rest, residue, and remainder of my property of every kind and description (including lapsed legacies and devises), wherever situate and whether acquired before or after the execution of this Will, to the then acting Trustee to be held, administered, and distributed in accordance with the provisions of that certain Trust Agreement between myself as Settlor and myself as Trustee executed prior to the execution of this Will on _____[date of trust agreement if any]_____, which Trust Agreement is hereby incorporated by reference and made apart hereof the same as if the entire Trust Agreement were set forth herein. If for any reason the Trustee or successor Trustee named in the Trust Agreement is unable or unwilling to serve, then I hereby nominate, constitute, and appoint as successor or substitute Trustee a bank or trust company qualified to do business in the State of my domicile at the time of my death, designated by the court having jurisdiction over the probate of my estate.

continued

Exhibit 4-2 *continued*

ITEM 16

I give, devise, and bequeath all the rest, residue, and remainder of my property of every kind and description, (including lapsed legacies and devises), wherever situate and whether acquired before or after the execution of this Will to my issue surviving me, in equal shares, per stirpes, or in default of such issue to <u>   [name of contingent residuary beneficiary]   </u>.

ITEM 17

I give, devise, and bequeath all the rest, residue, and remainder of my property of every kind and description (including lapsed legacies and devises) wherever situate and whether acquired before or after the execution of this Will, to <u>   [names of residuary beneficiaries]   </u>.

ITEM 18

I hereby nominate, constitute and appoint as Executor of this my Last Will and Testament _____ and direct that it shall serve without bond.

ITEM 19

I hereby nominate, constitute and appoint as Executor of this my Last Will and Testament <u>(name of individual Executor)</u> and direct that such Executor shall serve without bond. If for any reason my Executor is unable or unwilling to serve or continue to serve then I hereby nominate, constitute and appoint as substitute or successor Executor <u>   [name of corporate executor]   </u> and direct that it shall serve without bond.

ITEM 20

I hereby nominate, constitute, and appoint as Executor of this my Last Will and Testament _____ and direct that such Executor shall serve without bond. If for any reason my Executor is unable or unwilling to serve or continue to serve, then I hereby nominate, constitute, and appoint as substitute or successor Executor _____ and direct that he/she shall serve without bond.

ITEM 21

I hereby nominate, constitute, and appoint as Executor [and Trustee] of this my Last Will and Testament _____ and direct that such Executor [and Trustee] shall serve without bond. If for any reason my Executor [and Trustee] is unable or unwilling to serve or continue to serve then I hereby nominate, constitute, and appoint as substitute or successor Executor [and Trustee] _____ and direct that it shall serve without bond.

ITEM 22

I hereby nominate, constitute, and appoint as Executor and Trustee of this my Last Will and Testament _____ and direct that it shall serve without bond.

continued

Exhibit 4-2   *continued*

ITEM 23

Any corporate successor to the trust business of the corporate fiduciary designated herein or at any time acting hereunder shall succeed to the capacity of its predecessor without conveyance or transfer.

ITEM 24

Whenever the word "Executor" or any modifying or substituted pronoun therefor is used in this my Will, such words and respective pronouns shall include both the singular and the plural, the masculine, feminine, and neuter gender thereof, and shall apply equally to the Executor named herein and to any successor or substitute Executor acting hereunder, and such successor or substitute Executor shall possess all the rights, powers and duties, authority, and responsibility conferred upon the Executor originally named herein. The word "Executor", as used in this Will, is synonymous with and has the same meaning as the term "personal representative" as defined in any applicable probate code.

ITEM 25

Whenever the word "Executor" and/or the word "Trustee," or any modifying or substituted pronoun therefor are used in this my Will, such words and respective pronouns shall include both the singular and the plural, the masculine, feminine, and neuter gender thereof, and shall apply equally to the Executor and/or Trustee named herein and to any successor or substitute Executor and/or Trustee acting hereunder, and such successor or substitute Executor and/or Trustee shall possess all the rights, powers and duties, authority, and responsibility conferred upon my Executor and/or Trustee originally named herein.

ITEM 26

For its services as Executor, my Executor shall receive an amount determined by its Standard Fee Schedule in effect and applicable at the time of the performance of such services. If no such schedule shall be in effect at that time, it shall be entitled to reasonable compensation for the services rendered.

ITEM 27

For its services as Executor and Trustee, my Executor and Trustee shall receive an amount determined by its Standard Fee Schedule in effect and applicable at the time of the performance of such services. If no such schedule shall be in effect at that time, it shall be entitled to reasonable compensation for the services rendered.

ITEM 28

By way of illustration and not of limitation and in addition to any inherent, implied, or statutory powers granted to executors generally, my Executor is specifically authorized and empowered with respect to any property, real or personal, at any time held under any provision of this my Will: to allot, allocate between principal and income, assign, borrow, buy, care for, collect, compromise claims, contract with respect to, continue any business of mine,

continued

Exhibit 4-2 *continued*

convey, convert, deal with, dispose of, enter into, exchange, hold, improve, incorporate any business of mine, invest, lease, manage, mortgage, grant and exercise options with respect to, take possession of, pledge, receive, release, repair, sell, sue for, to make distributions or divisions in cash or in kind or partly in each without regard to the income tax basis of such asset, and in general, to exercise all of the powers in the management of my Estate which any individual could exercise in the management of similar property owned in his or her right, upon such terms and conditions as to my Executor may deem best, and to execute and deliver any and all instruments and to do all acts which my Executor may deem proper or necessary to carry out the purposes of this my Will, without being limited in any way by the specific grants of power made, and without the necessity of a court order.

ITEM 29

By way of illustration and not of limitation and in addition to any inherent, implied, or statutory powers granted to executors or trustees generally, my Executor and Trustee are specifically authorized and empowered with respect to any property, real or personal, at any time held under any provision of this my Will: to allot, allocate between principal and income, assign, borrow, buy, care for, collect, compromise claims, contract with respect to, continue any business of mine, convey, convert, deal with, dispose of, enter into, exchange, hold, improve, incorporate any business of mine, invest, lease, manage, mortgage, grant and exercise options with respect to, take possession of, pledge, receive, release, repair, sell, sue for, to make distributions or divisions in cash or in kind or partly in each without regard to the income tax basis of such asset and in general, to exercise all of the powers in the management of my estate of the Trust Estate which any individual could exercise in the management of similar property owned in his or her own right, upon such terms and conditions as to my Executor and Trustee may seem best, and to execute and deliver any and all instruments and to do all acts which my Executor and Trustee may deem proper or necessary to carry out the purposes of this my Will, without being limited in any way by the specific grants of power made, and without the necessity of a court order.

ITEM 30

If any share or property hereunder becomes distributable to a beneficiary who has not attained the age of Twenty-one (21) years or if any real property shall be devised to a person who has not attained the age of Twenty-one (21) years at the date of my death, then such share or property shall immediately vest in the beneficiary, but notwithstanding the provisions herein, my Executor acting as Trustee shall retain possession of the share or property in trust for the beneficiary until the beneficiary attains the age of Twenty-one (21), using so much of the net income and principal of the share or property as my Executor deems necessary to provide for the proper support, medical care, and education of the beneficiary, taking into consideration, to the extent my Executor deems advisable, any other income or resources of the beneficiary or his or her parents known to my Executor. Any income not so paid or applied shall be accumulated and added to principal. The beneficiary's share or property shall be paid over, distributed, and conveyed to the beneficiary upon attaining age Twenty-one (21), or if he or she shall sooner die, to his or

continued

Exhibit 4-2 *continued*

her executors or administrators. Whenever my Executor determines it appropriate to pay any money for the benefit of a beneficiary for whom a trust is created hereunder, then such amounts shall be paid out by my Executor in such of the following ways as my Executor deems best: (1) directly to the beneficiary; (2) to the legally appointed guardian of the beneficiary; (3) to some relative or friend for the care, support, and education of the beneficiary; (4) by my Executor using such amounts directly for the beneficiary's care, support, and education. My Executor as Trustee shall have with respect to each share or property so retained all the powers and discretions conferred upon it as Executor.

ITEM 31

My Executor, as the fiduciary of my estate, shall have the discretion, but shall not be required when allocating receipts of my estate between income and principal, to make adjustments in the rights of any beneficiaries, or among the principal and income accounts to compensate for the consequences of any tax decision or election, or of any investment or administrative decision, that my Executor believes has had the effect, directly or indirectly, of preferring one beneficiary or group of beneficiaries over others; provided, however, my Executor shall not exercise its discretion to select the valuation date and to determine whether any or all of the allowable administration expenses in my estate shall be used as state or federal estate tax deductions or as state or federal income tax deductions and shall have the discretion to file a joint income tax return with my husband/wife.

ITEM 32

If at any time any trust created hereunder has a fair market value as determined by my Trustee of Twenty-Five Thousand ($25,000.00) Dollars or less, my Trustee, in its absolute discretion if it determines that it is uneconomical to continue such trust, may terminate such trust and distribute the trust property to the person or persons then entitled to receive or have the benefit of the income therefrom or the legal representative of such person. If there is more than one income beneficiary, my Trustee shall make such distribution to such income beneficiaries in the proportion in which they are beneficiaries or if no proportion is designated in equal shares to such beneficiaries.

ITEM 33

If it becomes necessary for a representative of my estate to qualify in any jurisdiction other than the state of my domicile at the time of my death, then to the extent that I may legally do so, I hereby nominate, constitute, and appoint my Executor named in this Will as my representative in such jurisdiction and direct that such Executor shall serve without bond. If for any reason my Executor is unable or unwilling to serve as such representative or cannot qualify as such representative, then I hereby appoint my Executor named herein to designate (to the extent that it may legally do so) a person or a corporation to serve as my representative and request that such person or corporation shall serve without bond. Any representative named as provided herein (to the extent that it may legally do so) shall have in such jurisdiction all the powers and duties conferred or imposed on my Executor by the provisions of this Will.

continued

Exhibit 4-2 *continued*

ITEM 34

For purposes of this my will, "children" means the lawful blood descendants in the first degree of the parent designated; and "issue" and "descendants" mean the lawful blood descendants in any degree of the ancestor designated; provided, however, that if a person has been adopted, that person shall be considered a child of such adopting parent and such adopted child and his or her issue shall be considered as issue of the adopting parent or parents and of anyone who is by blood or adoption an ancestor of the adopting parent or either of the adopting parents. The terms "child", "children", "issue", "descendant", and "descendants" or those terms preceded by the terms "living" or "then living" shall include the lawful blood descendant in the first degree of the parent designated even though such descendant is born after the death of such parent.

ITEM 35

As used herein, the words "gross estate", "adjusted gross estate", "taxable estate", "unified credit", "state death tax credit", "maximum marital deduction", "marital deduction", "pass", "qualified terminable interest", "qualified terminable interest property", and any other word or words which from the context in which it or they are used refer to the Internal Revenue Code shall have the same meaning as such words have for the purposes of applying the Internal Revenue Code to my estate. For purposes of this Will, my "available generation-skipping transfer exemption" means the generation-skipping transfer tax exemption provided in Section 2631 of the Internal Revenue Code of 1986, as amended, in effect at the time of my death reduced by the aggregate of (1) the amount, if any, of my exemption allocated to lifetime transfers of mine by me or by operation of law, and (2) the amount, if any, I have specifically allocated to other property of my gross estate for federal estate tax purposes. For purposes of this Will, if at the time of my death I have made gifts with an inclusion ration of greater than zero for which the gift tax return due date has not expired (including extensions) and I have not yet filed a return, it shall be deemed that my generation-skipping transfer exemption has been allocated to these transfers to the extent necessary (and possible) to exempt the transfer(s) from generation-skipping transfer tax.

ITEM 36

If my husband/wife shall predecease me, of if he/she dies after my death without having appointed a testamentary guardian for any minor child or children of ours, then I hereby nominate, constitute, and appoint _____(name of Guardian)_____ as testamentary guardian of the person and the property of such minor child or children and to the extent allowed by law direct that such guardian shall serve without bond.

ITEM 37

If my husband/wife shall predecease me, or if he/she dies after my death without having appointed a testamentary guardian for any minor child or children of ours, then I hereby nominate, constitute, and appoint _____(name of Guardian)_____ as testamentary guardian of the person and the property of such minor child or children and, and to the extent

continued

Exhibit 4-2 *continued*

allowed by law, direct that such guardian shall serve without bond. If _____(name of Guardian)_____ dies, resigns, or refuses or is otherwise unable to act, then I appoint (name of Successor Guardian)_____ as testamentary guardian of the person and property of such child or children and direct that such guardian shall also serve without bond.

ITEM 38

I hereby refrain from exercising any power of appointment that I may have at the time of my death.

ITEM 39

If any beneficiary and I should die under such circumstances as would make it doubtful whether the beneficiary or I died first, then it shall be conclusively presumed for the purposes of this my Will that the beneficiary predeceased me.

ITEM 40

If any beneficiary under this Will should not survive me for more than thirty (30) days, then such beneficiary shall be conclusively presumed, for the purposes of this Will, to have predeceased me.

ITEM 41

Except as otherwise provided herein, all payments of principal and income payable, or to become payable, to the beneficiary of any trust created hereunder shall not be subject to anticipation, assignment, pledge, sale, or transfer in any manner, nor shall any beneficiary have the power to anticipate or encumber such interest, nor shall such interest, while in the possession of my Executor or Trustee, be liable for, or subject to, the debts, contracts, obligations, liabilities, or torts of any beneficiary.

IN WITNESS WHEREOF, I have hereunto set my hand and affixed my seal this _____ day of _____,20___.

_____ (Signature)
Testator/Testatrlx

The foregoing Will consisting of _____ typewritten pages, this included, was this _____ day of _____, 20___, signed, sealed, published, and declared by the Testator/Testatrix as and for his/her Last Will and Testament in our presence, and we, at his/her request and in his/her presence, and in the presence of each other, have hereunto subscribed our names as witnesses on the above date.

_____ of _____ ,_____
(signature & name of witness)   (insert city)   (insert state)

_____ of _____ ,_____
(signature & name of witness)   (insert city)   (insert state)

continued

Exhibit 4-2 *continued*

STATE OF _____

COUNTY OF _____

We, _____, and _____,
and _____, the Testator/Testatrix and the witnesses, respectively,
whose names are signed to the attached or foregoing instrument, having been sworn,
declared to the undersigned officer that the Testator/Testatrix, in the presence of witnesses,
signed the instrument as his/her Last Will and Testament, that he/she had signed (or directed
another to sign for him/her), and that each of the witnesses, in the presence of the
Testator/Testatrix, and in the presence of each other, signed the Will as witnesses.

_____ (Signature)
Testator/Testatrix

_____
Witness

_____
Witness

SUBSCRIBED, SWORN TO, and acknowledged before me by the Testator/Testatrix, and
by _____ and _____, the witnesses, on this
_____ day of _____, 20___, all of whom personally appeared before me.
_____ is personally known to me or has produced , as identification.
is personally known to me or has produced as identification. _____
is personally known to me or has produced _____ as identification.

_____
Notary Public

_____
(print name of Notary)

_____
(Serial number, if any)

My Commission Expires:

Arizona Acceptance of Guardianship

Arizona provides a special form for filing in the Superior Court whereby the guardian of the minor must formally accept their responsibilities. (See Exhibit 4-3.) The form requires either the attorney's name, address, and telephone number, or the same information for the individual appearing without an attorney. The minor's name(s) are included in the caption. The guardian(s) must sign the acceptance before a notary public or a deputy clerk of the court.

EXHIBIT 4-3   Arizona Acceptance of Guardianship

Your Name: _____

Your Address: _____

Your City, State, ZIP: _____

Your Telephone No: _____

Representing Self, Without an Attorney

IN THE SUPERIOR COURT OF ARIZONA, _____ COUNTY

In the Matter of the Guardianship of:)   Case No. _____

_____)

_____)   **ACCEPTANCE OF GUARDIANSHIP**
)   **OF MINOR(S)**
_____)

_____)

_____Minor(s)_____)   _____
                                               Judge/Commissioner

ACCEPTANCE

STATE OF ARIZONA   )
) ss.
COUNTY OF _____)

        I accept the duties of guardian of the minor(s) and swear/affirm that I will perform those duties according to law.

_____   _____
(Co-)Guardian's Signature   (Co-)Guardian's Signature

SUBSCRIBED and SWORN TO/AFFIRMED before me on _____.

My Commission Expires:_____   _____
                                               Notary Public/Deputy Clerk

A packet of forms required for probate may be purchased at the probate clerk's office in most states. Since most states' forms are similar to those provided in the textbook, only a few forms will be shown here.

Illinois Affidavit: Copy of Will

The affidavit requires that the Petitioner and the Attorney sign the form stating, under penalty of perjury, that a copy of the will attached to the affidavit is a true copy of the will filed for admission to probate. The attorney must provide her name, address, designation, and telephone number. See Exhibit 5-1.

EXHIBIT 5-1   Illinois Affidavit: Copy of Will

Affidavit - Copy of Will   (Rev. 3/30/99) CCP 0317

**IN THE CIRCUIT COURT OF COOK COUNTY, ILLINOIS
COUNTY DEPARTMENT, PROBATE DIVISION**

Estate of

No. _____

Docket

_____
                          Deceased

Page

COPY OF WILL

The undersigned states under penalties of perjury that the attached facsimile is a copy of the will filed for admission to probate.

_____
(Petitioner)

_____
(Attorney)

Atty. No.: _____

Atty. Name: _____

Firm Name: _____

Atty. for Petitioner: _____

Address: _____

City/Zip: _____

Telephone: _____

AURELIA PUCINSKI, CLERK OF THE CIRCUIT COURT OF COOK COUNTY, ILLINOIS

Illinois Petition for Letters of Administration

The caption of the form requires the name of the decedent and the case number. No. 1 requires the Petitioner to state, under penalty of perjury, that the decedent left no will. The approximate value of the estate should be provided in No. 2. Exhibit A requires the names and addresses of all of the decedent's heirs. No. 4 requires the listing of those individuals who are entitled to nominate an administrator. In No. 5, the petitioner indicates his relationship to the decedent. The attorney's information must be indicated, as well as the name and address of the Petitioner. The Petitioner must sign on the line in the bottom right side of the form. See Exhibit 5-2.

EXHIBIT 5-2 Illinois Petition for Letters of Administration

PETITION FOR LETTERS OF ADMINISTRATION   (Rev. 4/5/99) CCP-0302

IN THE CIRCUIT COURT OF COOK COUNTY, ILLINOIS

Estate of

_____
Deceased

No. _____

Docket

Page

Hearing on petition set for

_____, _____

_____ M., Room _____

Richard J. Daley Center
Chicago, Illinois 60602

PETITION FOR LETTERS OF ADMINISTRATION

_____, states under the penalties of perjury:

1. _____, whose place of residence at the time of death was

_____
(address)   (city)   (county)   (state)   (zip)

died _____, _____, at _____ leaving no will.
                                              (city)   (state)

2. The approximate value of the estate in this state is:

                                                                  Annual Income
    Personal   **Real**   **From Real Estate**
    $ _____ $ _____ $ _____

3. The names and post-office addresses of decedent's heirs are set forth on Exhibit A and made a part of this petition. (Indicate the relationship and whether an heir is a minor or disabled person.)

4. The names and post-office addresses of persons who are entitled to nominate and administrator in preference to (P) or equally with (E) petitioner are set forth on Exhibit A of this petition. If none, so state:
    _____.

5. Petitioner is a _____ of decedent and is legally qualified to act, or to nominate a resident of Illinois to act, as administrator.

*6 The name and post-office address of the personal fiduciary designated to act during independent administration for each heir, who is a minor or disabled person, are shown on Exhibit A of this petition.

    Petitioner asks that Letters of Administration issue to the following person(s), qualified and willing to act:
            Name   **Post-Office Address**

Atty. No.: _____   _____
Firm Name: _____   **Petitioner**
Atty. for Petitioner: _____   Address: _____
Address: _____   City/State/Zip: _____
City/Zip:_____   Telephone: _____
Telephone: _____   Atty. Certification _____

If a consul or consular agent is to be notified, name country: _____

*If supervised administration is requested, so state and strike Paragraph 6.

AURELIA PUCINSKI, CLERK OF THE CIRCUIT COURT OF COOK COUNTY, ILLINOIS

Illinois Final Report of Independent Representative

The administrator or executor is required to complete the Final Report (Exhibit 5-3) indicating that all responsibilities have been accomplished. The attorney's designation is typed in the lower left and the independent representative signs on the bottom right. The attorney must sign a certification to the authenticity of the claim that all duties have been completed.

EXHIBIT 5-3 Illinois Final Report of Independent Representative

Final Report of Independent Representative   (Rev. 3/17/98) CCP-1011

IN THE CIRCUIT COURT OF COOK COUNTY, ILLINOIS

Estate of _____ No._____

                                                        } Docket

_____
                                    Deceased   Page

FINAL REPORT OF INDEPENDENT REPRESENTATIVE

_____ , independent representative of this estate, states under the penalties of perjury that the administration of this estate has been completed and in accordance with 755 ILCS 5/28-11 further states as follows:

1. Notice of probate has been given in compliance with 755 ILCS 5/6-10 or 5/9-5.

2. The notice to creditors required by 755 ILCS 5/18-3 has been published, reasonable care was used to determine the creditors of the decedent and all known creditors have been given notice as required under 755 ILCS 5/18-3.

3. Copies of the inventory and accounting have been mailed or delivered to the extent required by 755 ILCS 5/28-6 and 5/28-11.

4. Each claim filed has been allowed, disallowed, compromised or dismissed or is barred; and
   *(a) all claims allowed have been paid in full.
   *(b) the estate was not sufficient to pay all of the claims in full, and all claims allowed have been paid according to their respective priorities.

5. *(a) A spouse's award has been (paid)(waived) (is barred) (is not applicable).
   *(b) A child's award (has been paid)(is not applicable).

6. *(a) All death taxes have been determined and paid or otherwise provided for.
   *(b) The estate is not subject to death taxes.

7. All administration expenses and other liabilities of the estate have been paid and administration
   *(a) has been completed;
   *(b) has not been completed but has been provided for (see attached).

8. Notice of probate and release of the estate's interest in real estate has been recorded to the extent required by 755 ILCS 5/20-24 and 5/28-10(a).

9. The remaining assets of the estate have been distributed to the persons entitled thereto.

10.*The fees paid or payable to the independent representative and attorney (have been) (have not been) approved by all interested persons.

11. Receipts have been obtained from all heirs or legatees and written approvals have been obtained from unpaid creditors and are filed with this report, except as attached.

Atty. No.: _____

Atty. Name:_____   _____
                                                              Independent Representative
Firm Name: _____

Atty. for Repesentative   _____,_____
                                                                      Date
Address: _____

City/Zip: _____   _____
                                                              Attorney Certification
Telephone: _____

*FINAL REPORT MUST BE COMPLETED BEFORE FILING. STRIKE ANY PORTION(S) NOT APPLICABLE
AURELIA PUCINSKI, CLERK OF THE CIRCUIT COURT OF COOK COUNTY, ILLINOIS

FAMILY LAW

The field of family law encompasses many different areas. Most of the family law practice involves either divorce or dissolution cases. Included therein are issues of child custody, restraining orders, and numerous procedures to follow. Different state forms are included herein. Others are available in the textbook under the Family Law chapter.

CALIFORNIA DISSOLUTION AND CHILD SUPPORT FORMS

A large number of Judicial Council forms are required for the filing of a dissolution in California. Some of the forms have been provided in the textbook; others are provided in this section.

Summons

The Summons (Exhibit 6-1) in Family Law must be served on the respondent with the Petition in a dissolution action. In the top left of the form, the names of the petitioner and respondent should be inserted. There is a box for the case number. The name and address of the court should be inserted under No. 1. No. 2 should include the name and address of the petitioner's attorney, or of the petitioner without an attorney. The appropriate box should be checked on the bottom, usually No. 1. The second page indicates restrictions on both parties.

Child Support Case Registry Form

Exhibit 6-2 provides an Informtion Sheet and a sample Child Support Case Registry Form. The information sheet explains in detail how to fill out the registry form.

EXHIBIT 6-1 California Summons

Courtesy: Reprinted from *West's California Judicial Council Form 2003,* with permission of West, a Thomson business. For more information about this publication please visit **http://west.thomson.com.**

SUMMONS (FAMILY LAW)

CITACION JUDICIAL—DERECHO DE FAMILIA

NOTICE TO RESPONDENT *(Name):*
AVISO AL DEMANDADO (Nombre):

FOR COURT USE ONLY
(SOLO PARA USO DE LA CORTE)

You are being sued. A usted lo están demandando.

PETITIONER'S NAME IS:
EL NOMBRE DEL DEMANDANTE ES :

CASE NUMBER *(Número del Caso):*

You have **30 CALENDAR DAYS** after this *Summons* and *Petition* are served on you to file a *Response* (form FL-120) at the court and have a copy served on the petitioner. A letter or phone call will not protect you.

If you do not file your *Response* on time, the court may make orders affecting your marriage, your property, and custody of your children. You may be ordered to pay support and attorney fees and costs. If you cannot pay the filing fee, ask the clerk for a fee waiver form.

If you want legal advice, contact a lawyer immediately.

Usted tiene 30 DIAS CALENDARIOS después de recibir oficialmente esta citación judicial y petición, para completar y presentar su formulario de Respuesta (Response form FL-120) ante la corte. Una carta o una llamada telefónica no le ofrecerá protección.

Si usted no presenta su Respuesta a tiempo, la corte puede expedir órdenes que afecten su matrimonio, su propiedad y que ordenen que usted pague mantención, honorarios de abogado y las costas. Si no puede pagar las costas por la presentación de la demanda, pida al actuario de la corte que le dé un formulario de exoneración de las mismas (Waiver of Court Fees and Costs).

Si desea obtener consejo legal, comuníquese de inmediato con un abogado.

NOTICE *The restraining orders on the back are effective against both husband and wife until the petition is dismissed, a judgment is entered, or the court makes further orders. These orders are enforceable anywhere in California by any law enforcement officer who has received or seen a copy of them.*

AVISO *Las prohibiciones judiciales que aparecen al reverso de esta citación son efectivas para ambos cónyuges, tanto el esposo como la esposa, hasta que la petición sea rechazada, se dicte una decisión final o la corte expida instrucciones adicionales. Dichas prohibiciones pueden hacerse cumpliren cualquier parte de California por cualquier agente del orden público que las haya recibido o que haya visto una copia de ellas.*

1. The name and address of the court is *(El nombre y dirección de la corte es):*

2. The name, address, and telephone number of petitioner's attorney, or petitioner without an attorney, is
   (El nombre, la dirección y el número de teléfono del abogado del demandante, o del demandante que no tiene abogado, es):

Date *(Fecha):*

Clerk *(Actuario),* by _____, Deputy

[SEAL]

NOTICE TO THE PERSON SERVED: You are served

1. ☐ as an individual, **or**
2. ☐ on behalf of respondent who is a
   ☐ minor   ☐ other:
   ☐ ward or conservatee

(Read the reverse for important information.)
(Lea el reverso para obtener información de importancia.)

Page 1 of 2

Form Adopted for Mandatory Use
Judicial Council of California
FL-110 [Rev. January 1, 2003]

SUMMONS
(Family Law)

Family Code, §§ 232, 233, 2040, 7700;
Code of Civil Procedure, §§ 412.20, 416.60–416.90;
www.courtinfo.ca.gov

continued

Exhibit 6-1 *continued*

WARNING—IMPORTANT INFORMATION

WARNING: California law provides that, for purposes of division of property upon dissolution of marriage or legal separation, property acquired by the parties during marriage in joint form is presumed to be community property. If either party to this action should die before the jointly held community property is divided, the language of how title is held in the deed (i.e., joint tenancy, tenants in common, or community property) will be controlling and not the community property presumption. You should consult your attorney if you want the community property presumption to be written into the recorded title to the property.

STANDARD FAMILY LAW RESTRAINING ORDERS

Starting immediately, you and your spouse are restrained from

1. removing the minor child or children of the parties, if any, from the state without the prior written consent of the other party or an order of the court;

2. cashing, borrowing against, canceling, transferring, disposing of, or changing the beneficiaries of any insurance or other coverage including life, health, automobile, and disability held for the benefit of the parties and their minor child or children;

3. transferring, encumbering, hypothecating, concealing, or in any way disposing of any property, real or personal, whether community, quasi-community, or separate, without the written consent of the other party or an order of the court, except in the usual course of business or for the necessities of life; and

4. creating a nonprobate transfer or modifying a nonprobate transfer in a manner that affects the disposition of property subject to the transfer, without the written consent of the other party or order of the court. Before revocation of a nonprobate transfer can take effect, or a right of survivorship to property can be eliminated, notice of the change must be filed and served on the other party.

You must notify each other of any proposed extraordinary expenditures at least five business days prior to incurring these extraordinary expenditures and account to the court for all extraordinary expenditures made after these restraining orders are effective. However, you may use community property, quasi-community property, or your own separate property to pay for an attorney to help you or pay for court costs.

ADVERTENCIA–INFORMACION IMPORTANTE EN ESPAÑOL

ADVERTENCIA: Para los efectos de la división de bienes al momento de una separación legal o de la disolución de un matrimonio, las leyes de California disponen que se presuman como bienes de la sociedad conyugal aquélles adquiridos en forma conjunta por las partes durante el matrimonio. Si cualquiera de las partes de esta acción muriese antes de que se dividan los bienes en tenencia conjunta de la sociedad conyugal, prevalecerá el lenguaje relativo a la tenencia de los derechos de propriedad contenido en la escritura—como, por ejemplo, copropiedad con derechos de sucesión (joint tenancy), tenencia en común (tenants in common) o bienes de la sociedad conyugal (community property)—y no la presunción de que los bienes son de la sociedad conyugal. Usted debe consultar a su abogado o abogada si desea que la presunción de que los bienes son de la sociedad conyugal se especifique en el título de propiedad inscrito.

PROHIBICIONES JUDICIALES ESTANDARES—DERECHO DE FAMILIA

A usted y a su cónyuge se les prohibe

1. *que saquen del estado al hijo o hijos menores de las partes, si los hay, sin el consentimiento previo por escrito de la otra parte o sin una orden de la corte; y*

2. *que cobren en efectivo, usen como colateral para préstamos, cancelen, transfieran, descontinúen o cambien los beneficiarios de, cualquier póliza de seguro u otras coberturas de seguro, inclusive los de vida, salud, automóvil e incapacidad mantenido para el beneficio de las partes y su hijo o hijos menores; y*

3. *que transfieran, graven, hipotequen, escondan o de cualquier otra manera enajenen cualquier propiedad mueble o inmueble, ya sean bienes de la sociedad conyugal, quasi conyugales o bienes propios de los cónyuges, sin el consentimiento por escrito de la otra parte o sin una orden de la corte, excepto en el curso normal de los negocios o para atender a las necesidades de la vida; y*

4. *crear una transferencia no incluida en el procedimiento sucesorio o modificar una transferencia no incluida en el procedimiento sucesorio de manera tal que afecte la disposición de los bienes sujetos a la transferencia, sin el consentimiento por escrito de la otra parte o una orden del tribunal. Antes de que la revocación de una transferencia no incluida en el procedimiento sucesorio pueda entrar en vigor, o de que el derecho de supervivencia a los bienes se pueda eliminar, se debe presentar un aviso del cambio al tribunal, y dicho aviso se debe entregar a la otra parte.*

Ustedes deben notificarse entre sí sobre cualquier gasto extraordinario propuesto, por lo menos con cinco días de antelación a la fecha en que se van a incurrir dichos gastos extraordinarios y responder ante la corte por todo gasto extraordinario hecho después de que estas prohibiciones judiciales entren en vigor. Sin embargo, nada de lo contenido en las prohibiciones judiciales le impedirá que use bienes de la sociedad conyugal para pagar honorarios razonables de abogados con el fin de obtener representación legal durante el proceso.

FL-110 [Rev. January 1, 2003]   **STANDARD FAMILY LAW RESTRAINING ORDERS**   Page 2 of 2
(Summons—Family Law)

EXHIBIT 6-2   California Child Support Case Registry Form

Courtesy: Reprinted from *West's California Judicial Council Form 2003,* with permission of West, a Thomson business. For more information about this publication please visit **http://west.thomson.com.**

INFORMATION SHEET FOR CHILD SUPPORT CASE REGISTRY FORM
(Do NOT deliver this Information Sheet to the court clerk.)

Please follow these instructions to complete the *Child Support Case Registry Form* (form FL-191) if you do not have an attorney to represent you. Your attorney, if you have one, should complete this form.

Both parents must complete a *Child Support Case Registry Form.* The information on this form will be included in a national database, which, among other things, is used to locate absent parents. When you file a court order, you must deliver a completed form to the court clerk along with your court order. If you did not file a court order, you must deliver a completed form to the court clerk **WITHIN 10 DAYS** of the date you received a copy of your court order. If any of the information you provide on this form changes, you must complete a new form and deliver it to the court clerk within 10 days of the change. The address of the court clerk is the same as the one shown for the Superior Court on your order. This form is confidential and will not be filed in the court file. It will be maintained in a confidential file with the State of California. **HOWEVER,** if the local child support agency is involved in this case, you must deliver this form and any updates to the form to the local child support agency, instead of delivering it to the court. It is important to keep the court or the local child support agency informed, in writing, of any changes in your address or phone number.

INSTRUCTIONS FOR COMPLETING THE *CHILD SUPPORT CASE REGISTRY FORM* **(TYPE OR PRINT IN INK):**

If the top section of the form has already been filled out, skip down to number 1 below. If the top section of the form is blank, you must provide this information.

<u>Front page, first box, top of form, left side</u>: Print your name, address, telephone number, and fax number, if any, in this box. Attorneys must include their state bar number.

<u>Front page, second box, left side</u>: Print the name of the county and the court's address in this box. Use the same address for the court that is on the court order you are filing or have received.

<u>Front page, third box, left side</u>: Print the names of the Petitioner/Plaintiff, Respondent/Defendant, and Other Parent in this box. Use the same names listed on the court order you are filing or have received.

<u>Front page, fourth box, left side</u>: Check the box indicating whether you are the mother or the father, or the attorney for either. Also, if this is the first time you have filled out this form, check the box by "first form completed." If you have filled out a form like this before, and you are changing any of the information, check the box by "change to previous information."

<u>Front page, first box, top of form, right side</u>: Leave this box blank for the court's use.

<u>Front page, second box, right side</u>: Print the court case number in this box. This number is also shown on the court papers.
<u>Instructions for numbered paragraphs:</u>

1. a. Enter the date the court order was filed. This date is shown in the "COURT PERSONNEL: STAMP DATE RECEIVED HERE" box on the front page at the top of the order on the right side. If the order has not been filed, leave this item blank for the court clerk to fill in.

    b. If the court order you filed or received is the first child or family support order for this case, check the box by "Initial child support order or family support order." If this is a change to your order, check the box by "Modification."

    c. Information regarding the amount and type of support ordered is on the court order you are filing or have received.

       (1) Check this box if your order says that child support is ordered. If there is an amount, put it in the blank provided. If the order says the amount is reserved, check the "reserved order" box. If the order says the amount is zero, check the "$0 (zero) order" box. Do not include child care, special needs, uninsured medical expenses, travel for visitation, spousal support, or court-ordered payments on past due support.

       (2) Check this box if your order says that family support is ordered. If there is an amount, put it in the blank provided. If the order says the amount is reserved, check the "reserved order" box. If the order says the amount

FL-191 [Rev. January 1, 2003]   **CHILD SUPPORT CASE REGISTRY FORM**   Page 3 of 4

continued

Exhibit 6-2   *continued*

is zero, check the "$0 (zero) order" box. Do not include child care, special needs, uninsured medical expenses, travel for visitation, spousal support, or court-ordered payments on past due support.

2. a. Write the name of the person who is supposed to pay child or family support.

    b. Write the relationship of that person to the children.

3. a. Write the name of the person or agency that is supposed to receive child or family support payments.

    b. Write the relationship of that person to the children.

4. List the full name, date of birth, and social security number for each child included in the support order. If there are more than five children included in the support order, check the box after item 4e and list the remaining children with dates of birth and social security numbers on another sheet of paper. Attach the other sheet to this form.

The local child support agency is required, under Section 466(a)(13) of the Social Security Act, to place in the records pertaining to child support the social security number of any individual who is subject to a divorce decree, support order or paternity determination or acknowledgment. This information is mandatory and will be kept on file at the local child support agency.

Top of second page, box on left side: Print the names of the Petitioner/Plaintiff, Respondent/Defendant, and Other Parent in this box. Use the same names listed on the front page.

Top of second page, box on right side: Print your court case number in this box. Use the same case number as on the front page, second box, right side.

You are required to complete information about yourself. If you know information about the other person, you may also fill in what you know about him or her.

5. If you are the father in this case, list your full name in this space. See instructions for a-g under number six below.

6. If you are the mother in this case, list your full name in this space.

    a. List your date of birth.

    b. Write in your social security number.

    c. List the street address, city, state, and zip code where you live.

    d. List the street address, city, state, and zip code where you want your mail to be sent, if different from the address where you live.

    e. Write in your driver's license number and the state where it was issued.

    f. List the telephone number where you live.

    g. Indicate whether you are employed, self-employed, or not employed by checking the appropriate box. If you are employed, write in the name, street address, city, state, zip code, country, and telephone number where you work.

7. a. If there is a restraining order, protective order, or non-disclosure order, check this box. Check the box beside each person who is being protected by the restraining order.

    b. Check the box beside the parent who is being restrained.

    c Write in the date the restraining order expires. See the restraining order, protective order, or non-disclosure order for this date.

If you are in fear of domestic violence, you may want to ask the court for a restraining order, protective order, or non-disclosure order.

You must print your name, fill in the date, and sign the *Child Support Case Registry Form* under penalty of perjury. When you sign under penalty of perjury, you are stating that the information you have provided is true and correct.

FL-191 [Rev. January 1, 2003]   **CHILD SUPPORT CASE REGISTRY FORM**   Page 4 of 4

continued

Exhibit 6-2 *continued*

FL-191

ATTORNEY OR PARTY WITHOUT ATTORNEY *(Name, state bar number, and address):*	*COURT PERSONNEL:* *STAMP DATE RECEIVED HERE* **DO NOT FILE**

TELEPHONE NO.:
E-MAIL ADDRESS *(optional)*:   FAX NO.:
ATTORNEY FOR *(Name)*:

SUPERIOR COURT OF CALIFORNIA, COUNTY OF
STREET ADDRESS:
MAILING ADDRESS:
CITY AND ZIP CODE:
BRANCH NAME:

PETITIONER/PLAINTIFF:

RESPONDENT/DEFENDANT:

OTHER PARENT:

CHILD SUPPORT CASE REGISTRY FORM ☐ Mother ☐ First form completed ☐ Father ☐ Change to previous information	CASE NUMBER:

THIS FORM WILL NOT BE FILED IN THE COURT FILE. IT WILL BE MAINTAINED IN A CONFIDENTIAL FILE WITH THE STATE OF CALIFORNIA.

Notice: Pages 1 and 2 of this form must be completed and delivered to the court along with the court order for support. Pages 3 and 4 are instructional only and do not need to be delivered to the court. If you did not file the court order, you must complete this form and deliver it to the court within 10 days of the date on which you received a copy of the support order. Any later change to the information on this form must be delivered to the court on another form within 10 days of the change. It is important that you keep the court informed in writing of any changes of your address and telephone number. HOWEVER, if the local child support agency is involved in this case, you must deliver this form, and any updates to the form, to the local child support agency instead of delivering it to the court.

1. Support order information *(this information is on the court order you are filing or have received)*.
   a. Date order filed:
   b. ☐ Initial child support or family support order   ☐ Modification
   c. Total monthly base current child or family support amount ordered for children listed below *(do not include child care, special needs, uninsured medical expenses, travel for visitation, spousal support, or court-ordered payments on past due support)*:
      (1) ☐ Child Support: $ ☐ Reserved Order   ☐ $0 (zero) order
      (2) ☐ Family Support: $ ☐ Reserved Order   ☐ $0 (zero) order

2. Person required to pay child or family support *(name)*:
   Relationship to child *(specify)*:

3.
   Relationship to child *(if applicable)*:

4. The child support order is for the following children:

Child's name	Date of birth	Social security number
a.		
b.		
c.	Person or agency to receive child or family support payments *(name):*	
d.		
e.		

   ☐ Additional children are listed on a page attached to this document.

TYPE OR PRINT IN INK

Form Adopted for Mandatory Use
Judicial Council of California
FL-191 [Rev. January 1, 2003]

CHILD SUPPORT CASE REGISTRY FORM

Page 1 of 4
Family Code, § 4014
www.courtinfo.ca.gov

Exhibit 6-2   *continued*

PETITIONER/PLAINTIFF:	CASE NUMBER:
RESPONDENT/DEFENDANT:	
OTHER PARENT:	

You are required to complete the following information about yourself. You are not required to provide information about the other person, but you are encouraged to provide as much as you can. This form is confidential and will not be filed in the court file. It will be maintained in a confidential file with the State of California.

5. Father's name:

   a. Date of birth:

   b. Social security number:

   c. Street address:

      City, State, ZIP code:

   d. Mailing address:

      City, State, ZIP code:

   e. Driver's license number:

      State:

   f. Telephone number:

   g. ☐ Employed ☐ Not Employed ☐ Self-Employed

      Employer's name:

      Street address:

      City, State, ZIP code:

   h. Telephone number:

6. Mother's name:

   a. Date of birth:

   b. Social security number:

   c. Street address:

      City, State, ZIP code:

   d. Mailing address:

      City, State, ZIP code:

   e. Driver's license number:

      State:

   f. Telephone number:

   g. ☐ Employed ☐ Not Employed ☐ Self-Employed

      Employer's name:

      Street address:

      City, State, ZIP code:

   h. Telephone number:

7. ☐ A restraining order, protective order, or non-disclosure order due to domestic violence is in effect.
     a. The order protects: ☐ Father ☐ Mother ☐ Children
     b. From: ☐ Father ☐ Mother
     c. The restraining order expires *(date):*

I declare under penalty of perjury under the laws of the State of California that the foregoing is true and correct.

Date:

▶

_____
(TYPE OR PRINT NAME)

_____
(SIGNATURE OF PERSON COMPLETING THIS FORM)

Response

The respondent must respond to the petitioner's petition with a formal response and request for dissolution, legal separation, or nullity. See Exhibit 6-3. In most cases, the respondent will check the box for dissolution. The caption must include the name and address of the attorney, the name and address of the court where the proceeding is being commenced, and the case number.

1. Residency Requirement—6 months state; 3 months county
2. Statistical Facts—date of marriage, separation, and period between marriage and separation
3. Minor children—check box a or b and list children's names, birth dates, ages, and sex. Check box d, Declaration of paternity, if children were born before themarriage.
4. List property that respondent wishes confirmed as separate property assets and debts.
5. List community and quasi-community assets and debts.
6. Check only if there is a reasonable possibility of reconciliation.
7. Check if respondent denies the grounds set forth in the petition.
8. Check the appropriate box for respondent's request.
9. Check the requests of the respondent related to child custody, visitation, determination of parentage, spousal support, attorney fees, property rights, and termination of court's jurisdiction. Other requests may be added as a separate attachment.

The respondent and his attorney must sign the form. The original is filed with the court with the proof of service of a copy served on the petitioner.

EXHIBIT 6-3   California Response

Courtesy: Reprinted from *West's California Judicial Council Form 2003*, with permission of West, a Thomson business. For more information about this publication please visit **http://west.thomson.com**.

FL-120

ATTORNEY OR PARTY WITHOUT ATTORNEY *(Name, state bar number, and address):*	FOR COURT USE ONLY

TELEPHONE NO. *(Optional):*   FAX NO. *(Optional):*

E–MAIL ADDRESS *(Optional):*

ATTORNEY FOR *(Name):*

SUPERIOR COURT OF CALIFORNIA, COUNTY OF

STREET ADDRESS:

MAILING ADDRESS:

CITY AND ZIP CODE:

BRANCH NAME:

MARRIAGE OF

PETITIONER:

RESPONDENT:

RESPONSE ☐ **and REQUEST FOR**	CASE NUMBER:
☐ **Dissolution of Marriage**	
☐ **Legal Separation**	
☐ **Nullity of Marriage** ☐ **AMENDED**	

1. RESIDENCE (Dissolution only) ☐ Petitioner ☐ Respondent   has been a resident of this state for at least six months and of this county for at least three months immediately preceding the filing of the *Petition for Dissolution of Marriage.*

2. STATISTICAL FACTS
   a. Date of marriage: c. Period between marriage and separation
   b. Date of separation: Years: Months:

3. DECLARATION REGARDING MINOR CHILDREN *(include children of this relationship born prior to or during the marriage or adopted during the marriage):*
   a. ☐ There are no minor children.
   b. ☐ The minor children are:

Child's name	Birth date	Age	Sex

   ☐ Continued on Attachment 3b.
   c. If there are minor children of the Petitioner and Respondent, a completed *Declaration Under Uniform Child Custody Jurisdiction and Enforcement Act (UCCJEA)* (form FL-105) must be attached.
   d. ☐ A completed voluntary declaration of paternity regarding minor children born to the Petitioner and Respondent prior to the marriage is attached.

4. ☐ **Respondent requests** confirmation as separate property assets and debts the items listed
   ☐ in Attachment 4 ☐ below:

Item	Confirm to

NOTICE: Any party required to pay child support must pay interest on overdue amounts at the "legal" rate, which is currently 10 percent.

Page 1 of 2

Form Adopted for Mandatory Use
Judicial Council of California
FL-120 [Rev. January 1, 2003]

RESPONSE
(Family Law)

Family Code, § 2020
www.courtinfo.ca.gov.

continued

Exhibit 6-3 *continued*

MARRIAGE OF *(last name, first name of parties):*	CASE NUMBER:

5. DECLARATION REGARDING COMMUNITY AND QUASI-COMMUNITY ASSETS AND DEBTS AS CURRENTLY KNOWN
   a. ☐ There are no such assets or debts subject to disposition by the court in this proceeding.
   b. ☐ All such assets and debts have been disposed of by written agreement.
   c. ☐ All such assets and debts are listed ☐ in Attachment 5c ☐ below *(specify):*

6. ☐ **Respondent contends** that there is a reasonable possibility of reconciliation.

7. ☐ **Respondent denies** the grounds set forth in item 6 of the petition.

8. **Respondent requests**
   a. ☐ Dissolution of the marriage based on
      (1) ☐ irreconcilable differences. Fam. Code, § 2310(a)
      (2) ☐ incurable insanity. Fam. Code, § 2310(b)
   b. ☐ Legal separation of the parties based on
      (1) ☐ irreconcilable differences. Fam. Code, § 2310(a)
      (2) ☐ incurable insanity. Fam. Code, § 2310(b)
   c. ☐ Nullity of void marriage based on
      (1) ☐ incestuous marriage. Fam. Code, § 2200
      (2) ☐ bigamous marriage. Fam. Code, § 2201

   d. ☐ Nullity of voidable marriage based on
      (1) ☐ Respondent's age at time of marriage. Fam. Code, § 2210(a)
      (2) ☐ prior existing marriage. Fam. Code, § 2210(b)
      (3) ☐ unsound mind. Fam. Code, § 2210(c)
      (4) ☐ fraud. Fam. Code, § 2210(d)
      (5) ☐ force. Fam. Code, § 2210(e)
      (6) ☐ physical incapacity. Fam. Code, § 2210(f)

9. **Respondent requests** that the court grant the above relief and make injunctive (including restraining) and other orders as follows:

	Petitioner	Respondent	Joint	Other
a. Legal custody of children to	☐	☐	☐	☐
b. Physical custody of children to	☐	☐	☐	☐
c. Child visitation be granted to	☐	☐		☐
(1) ☐ Supervised for:	☐	☐		
(2) ☐ No visitation for:	☐	☐		
(3) ☐ Continued on Attachment 9c(3).				

   d. ☐ Determination of parentage of any children born to the Petitioner and Respondent prior to the marriage.

	Petitioner	Respondent		
e. Spousal support payable to (wage assignment will be issued)	☐	☐		
f. Attorney fees and costs payable by	☐	☐		

   g. ☐ Terminate the court's jurisdiction (ability) to award spousal support to Petitioner.
   h ☐ Property rights be determined.
   i. ☐ Respondent's former name be restored *(specify):*
   j. ☐ Other *(specify):*

      ☐ Continued on Attachment 9j.

10. If there are minor children born to or adopted by the Petitioner and Respondent before or during this marriage, the court will make orders for the support of the children. An earnings assignment will be issued without further notice.

I declare under penalty of perjury under the laws of the State of California that the foregoing is true and correct.
Date:

_____   ▶ _____
        (TYPE OR PRINT NAME)   (SIGNATURE OF RESPONDENT)
Date:

_____   ▶ _____
        (TYPE OR PRINT NAME)   (SIGNATURE OF ATTORNEY FOR RESPONDENT)

> **The original response must be filed in the court with proof of service of a copy on Petitioner.**

FL-120 [Rev. January 1, 2003]   **RESPONSE**   Page 2 of 2
                                (Family Law)

Uniform Child Custody Jurisdiction Declaration

Minor children must be listed on the Declaration under Uniform Child Custody Jurisdiction and Enforcement Act form. See Exhibit 6-4. The standard caption appears at the top of the form. All children must be listed, along with their addresses and the name and address of the person(s) with whom they are living. If there is a restraining order due to an abuse issue, then the address may not be disclosed because of confidentiality. Residence information is given for the last five years.

Item 4. Indicate whether other custody proceedings have been held, as well as the court and the order.

Item 5. Indicate whether another custody proceeding is pending in another court.

Item 6. If another person, not a party to this proceeding, has physical custody or claims to have custody of or visitation rights with a child subject to this proceeding, indicate here, along with the name and address of the person and the name of each child.

Type the declarant's name on the left. The declarant must sign on the right.

EXHIBIT 6-4 California Uniform Child Custody Jurisdiction Declaration

Courtesy: Reprinted from *West's California Judicial Council Form 2003*, with permission of West, a Thomson business. For more information about this publication please visit **http://west.thomson.com.**

FL-105/GC-120

ATTORNEY OR PARTY WITHOUT ATTORNEY (Name and Mailing Address):	TELEPHONE NO.:	FOR COURT USE ONLY

ATTORNEY FOR *(Name):*

SUPERIOR COURT OF CALIFORNIA, COUNTY OF

STREET ADDRESS:

MAILING ADDRESS:

CITY AND ZIP CODE:

BRANCH NAME:

CASE NAME:

DECLARATION UNDER UNIFORM CHILD CUSTODY JURISDICTION AND ENFORCEMENT ACT (UCCJEA)	CASE NUMBER:

1. **I am a party** to this proceeding to determine custody of a child.
2. ☐ Declarant's present address is not disclosed. It is confidential under Family Code section 3429. The address of children presently residing with declarant is identified on this declaration as confidential.
3. *(Number):* _____ minor children are subject to this proceeding as follows:
   (Insert the information requested below. The residence information must be given for the last FIVE years.)

a. Child's name		Place of birth	Date of birth	Sex

Period of residence	Address	Person child lived with (name and present address)	Relationship
to present	☐ Confidential		
to			
to			
to			

b. Child's name		Place of birth	Date of birth	Sex
☐ Residence information is the same as given above for child **a.** *(If NOT the same, provide the information below.)*				

Period of residence	Address	Person child lived with (name and present address)	Relationship
to present	☐ Confidential		
to			
to			

c. ☐ Additional children are listed on Attachment 3c. *(Provide requested information for additional children on an attachment.)*

Page 1 of 2

Form Approved for Optional Use Judicial Council of California FL-105/GC-120 [Rev. January 1, 2003]	**DECLARATION UNDER UNIFORM CHILD CUSTODY JURISDICTION AND ENFORCEMENT ACT (UCCJEA)**	Family Code, § 3400 et seq. Probate Code, §§ 1510(f), 1512 www.courtinfo.ca.gov

continued

Exhibit 6-4 *continued*

SHORT TITLE:	CASE NUMBER:

4. Have you participated as a party or a witness or in some other capacity in another litigation or custody proceeding, in California or elsewhere, concerning custody of a child subject to this proceeding?

☐ No ☐ Yes *(If yes, provide the following information:)*

   a. Name of each child:

   b. Capacity of declarant: ☐ party ☐ witness ☐ other *(specify):*
   c. Court *(specify name, state, location):*

   d. Court order or judgment *(date):*

5. Do you have information about a custody proceeding pending in a California court or any other court concerning a child subject to this proceeding, other than that stated in item 4?

☐ No ☐ Yes *(If yes, provide the following information:)*

   a. Name of each child:

   b. Nature of proceeding: ☐ dissolution or divorce ☐ guardianship ☐ adoption ☐ other *(specify):*

   c. Court *(specify name, state, location):*

   d. Status of proceeding:

6. Do you know of any person who is not a party to this proceeding who has physical custody or claims to have custody of or visitation rights with any child subject to this proceeding?

☐ No ☐ Yes *(If yes, provide the following information:)*

a. Name and address of person	b. Name and address of person	c. Name and address of person
☐ Has physical custody ☐ Claims custody rights ☐ Claims visitation rights	☐ Has physical custody ☐ Claims custody rights ☐ Claims visitation rights	☐ Has physical custody ☐ Claims custody rights ☐ Claims visitation rights
Name of each child	Name of each child	Name of each child

I declare under penalty of perjury under the laws of the State of California that the foregoing is true and correct.
Date:

▶

_____   _____
(TYPE OR PRINT NAME)   (SIGNATURE OF DECLARANT)

7. ☐ Number of pages attached after this page:

NOTICE TO DECLARANT: You have a continuing duty to inform this court if you obtain any information about a custody proceeding in a California court or any other court concerning a child subject to this proceeding.

FL-105/GC-120 [Rev. January 1, 2003] **DECLARATION UNDER UNIFORM CHILD CUSTODY JURISDICTION AND ENFORCEMENT ACT (UCCJEA)** Page 2 of 2

California Declaration of Disclosure

Several schedules must be provided to the other party. The Declaration of Disclosure form (Exhibit 6-5) is served on the other party, with the following attachments:

1. Schedule of Assets and Debts
2. Income and Expense Declaration
3. Declaration Regarding Service
4. Property Declaration
   a. Valuation of community property assets
   b. Obligations for which the community is liable
   c. Income or investment opportunities presented after separation that results from investment during the marriage

The declaration is signed by the individual preparing the forms, either petitioner or respondent. The name is typed in the bottom left corner of the form.

The following items must be completed and included with the Declaration and served on the other party:

1. Schedule of Assets and Debts (Exhibit 6-6)

All assets and debts should be included. Check the box for separate property if appropriate. List real estate, household furniture and furnishings (list each item individually), jewelry, antiques, art, and coin collections (list each item separately), and all other assets. List a total value. List all debts and show to whom they are owed, including student loans, taxes, support, unsecured loans, credit cards, and other debts. A total of all the debts.

2. Income and Expense Declaration (Exhibit 6-7)

Use the standard heading. Complete all income and expense requirements on pages 2 and 3. Answer all applicable questions in step 2. List your net monthly disposable income under No. 7. This figure will be found in line 16a on page 2. If the amount in No. 8 is different from No. 7, explain. Under step 4, list the total monthly expenses from line 2q of page 3 and the amount of these expenses paid by others. Under step 5 list your estimate of the other party's gross monthly income. Type the name, sign it, and check the box for petitioner or respondent.

Exhibit 6-8 shows an attachment for Child Support Information.

3. Declaration Regarding Service (Exhibit 6-9)

This form must be filed with the court. Use the standard caption and indicate whether the Declaration of Disclosure and Income and Expense Declaration are those of the petitioner or respondent.

a. Indicate designation: attorney for petitioner or respondent.
b. Check appropriate boxes for service.
c. Check boxes for service.
d. Check this box only if the service has been waived.

Type the name of the attorney and have him sign.

4. Property Declaration (Exhibit 6-10)

Use the standard caption and indicate whether this is the petitioner or respondent completing the form. indicate whether itis community or separate property being listed. List all real estate under No. 1 with the gross fari market value, the amount of debt on the property, the net fair market value after deducting debt from gross value, and the proposal for division between petitioner and respondent. Folow the same procedures for all of the property listed. The attorney and decarant must sign.

EXHIBIT 6-5 California Declaration of Disclosure

Courtesy: Reprinted from *West's California Judicial Council Form 2003,* with permission of West, a Thomson business. For more information about this publication please visit http://west.thomson.com.

FL-140

ATTORNEY OR PARTY WITHOUT ATTORNEY *(Name and Address):*

TELEPHONE NO.:

ATTORNEY FOR *(Name):*

SUPERIOR COURT OF CALIFORNIA, COUNTY OF

STREET ADDRESS:

MAILING ADDRESS:

CITY AND ZIP CODE:

BRANCH NAME:

PETITIONER:

RESPONDENT:

DECLARATION OF DISCLOSURE

☐ **Petitioner's**   ☐ **Preliminary**

☐ **Respondent's**   ☐ **Final**

CASE NUMBER:

DO NOT FILE WITH THE COURT

Both the preliminary and the final declaration of disclosure must be served on the other party with certain exceptions. Neither disclosure is filed with the court. A declaration stating service was made of the final declaration of disclosure must be filed with the court (see form FL-141).

A preliminary declaration of disclosure but not a final declaration of disclosure is required in the case of a summary dissolution (see Family Code section 2109) or in a default judgment (see Family Code section 2110) provided the default is not a stipulated judgment or a judgment based upon a marriage settlement agreement.

A declaration of disclosure is required in a nullity or legal separation action as well as in a dissolution action.

Attached are the following:

1. ☐ A completed *Schedule of Assets and Debts* (form FL-142).

2. ☐ A completed *Income and Expense Declaration* (form FL-150 (as applicable)).

3. ☐ A statement of all material facts and information regarding valuation of all assets that are community property or in which the community has an interest *(not a form).*

4. ☐ A statement of all material facts and information regarding obligations for which the community is liable *(not a form).*

5. ☐ An accurate and complete written disclosure of any investment opportunity, business opportunity, or other income-producing opportunity presented since the date of separation that results from any investment, significant business, or other income-producing opportunity from the date of marriage to the date of separation *(not a form).*

I declare under penalty of perjury under the laws of the State of California that the foregoing is true and correct.

Date:

▶

_____
(TYPE OR PRINT NAME)

_____
(SIGNATURE)

Page 1 of 1

Form Adopted for Mandatory Use
Judicial Council of California
FL-140 [Rev. January 1, 2003]

DECLARATION OF DISCLOSURE
(Family Law)

Family Code, §§ 2102, 2104, 2105,
2106, 2112
www.courtinfo.ca.gov

EXHIBIT 6-6 California Schedule of Assets and Debts

Courtesy: Reprinted from *West's California Judicial Council Form 2003,* with permission of West, a Thomson business. For more information about this publication please visit **http://west.thomson.com.**

FL-142

ATTORNEY OR PARTY WITHOUT ATTORNEY *(Name and Address):*	TELEPHONE NO.:

ATTORNEY FOR *(Name):*

SUPERIOR COURT OF CALIFORNIA, COUNTY OF

MARRIAGE OF
PETITIONER:

RESPONDENT:

SCHEDULE OF ASSETS AND DEBTS ☐ **Petitioner's** ☐ **Respondent's**	CASE NUMBER:

— **INSTRUCTIONS** —

List all your known community and separate assets or debts. Include assets even if they are in the possession of another person, including your spouse. If you contend an asset or debt is separate, put H or W in the first column (separate property) to indicate to whom you contend it belongs.

All values should be as of the date of signing the declaration unless you specify a different valuation date with the description.

For additional space, use a continuation sheet numbered to show what item is being continued.

ITEM NO.	ASSETS—DESCRIPTION	SEP. PROP.	DATE ACQUIRED	CURRENT GROSS FAIR MARKET VALUE	AMOUNT OF MONEY OWED OR ENCUMBRANCE
1.	REAL ESTATE *(Give street addresses and attach copies of deeds with legal descriptions and latest lender's statement.)*			$	$
2.	HOUSEHOLD FURNITURE, FURNISHINGS, APPLIANCES *(Identify)*				
3.	JEWELRY, ANTIQUES, ART, COIN COLLECTIONS, etc. *(Identify)*				

Page 1 of 4

Form Approved for Optional Use
Judicial Council of California
FL-142 [Rev. January 1, 2003]

SCHEDULE OF ASSETS AND DEBTS
(Family Law)

Code of Civil Procedure, §§ 2030(c), 2033.5
www.courtinfo.ca.gov

continued

Exhibit 6-6 *continued*

ITEM NO.	ASSETS—DESCRIPTION	SEP. PROP	DATE ACQUIRED	CURRENT GROSS FAIR MARKET VALUE	AMOUNT OF MONEY OWED OR ENCUMBRANCE
				$	$
4.	VEHICLES, BOATS, TRAILERS *(Describe and attach copy of title document.)*				
5.	SAVINGS ACCOUNTS *(Account name, account number, bank, and branch. Attach copy of latest statement.)*				
6.	CHECKING ACCOUNTS *(Account name and number, bank, and branch. Attach copy of latest statement.)*				
7.	CREDIT UNION, OTHER DEPOSIT ACCOUNTS *(Account name and number, bank, and branch. Attach copy of latest statement.)*				
8.	CASH *(Give location.)*				
9.	TAX REFUND				
10.	LIFE INSURANCE WITH CASH SURRENDER OR LOAN VALUE *(Attach copy of declaration page for each policy.)*				

FL-142 [Rev. January 1, 2003]

SCHEDULE OF ASSETS AND DEBTS
(Family Law)

Page 2 of 4

continued

Exhibit 6-6   *continued*

ITEM NO.	**ASSETS**—DESCRIPTION	SEP. PROP.	DATE ACQUIRED	CURRENT GROSS FAIR MARKET VALUE	AMOUNT OF MONEY OWED OR ENCUMBRANCE
				$	$
11.	STOCKS, BONDS, SECURED NOTES, MUTUAL FUNDS *(Give certificate number and attach copy of the certificate or copy of latest statement.)*				
12.	RETIREMENT AND PENSIONS *(Attach copy of latest summary plan documents and latest benefit statement.)*				
13.	PROFIT-SHARING, ANNUITIES, IRAS, DEFERRED COMPENSATION *(Attach copy of latest statement.)*				
14.	ACCOUNTS RECEIVABLE AND UNSECURED NOTES *(Attach copy of each.)*				
15.	PARTNERSHIPS AND OTHER BUSINESS INTERESTS *(Attach copy of most current K–1 form and schedule C.)*				
16.	OTHER ASSETS				
17.	TOTAL ASSETS FROM CONTINUATION SHEET				
18.	TOTAL ASSETS			$	$

FL-142 [Rev. January 1, 2003]

SCHEDULE OF ASSETS AND DEBTS
(Family Law)

Page 3 of 4

continued

Exhibit 6-6   *continued*

ITEM NO.	DEBTS—SHOW TO WHOM OWED	SEP. PROP	TOTAL OWING	DATE INCURRED
19. STUDENT LOANS *(Give details.)*			$	
20. TAXES *(Give details.)*				
21. SUPPORT ARREARAGES *(Attach copies of orders and statements.)*				
22. LOANS—UNSECURED *(Give bank name and loan number and attach copy of latest statement.)*				
23. CREDIT CARDS *(Give creditor's name and address and the account number. Attach copy of latest statement.)*				
24. OTHER DEBTS *(specify):*				
25. TOTAL DEBTS FROM CONTINUATION SHEET				
26. TOTAL DEBTS			$	

27. ☐ _____ pages are attached as continuation sheets.

I declare under penalty of perjury under the laws of the State of California that the foregoing is true and correct.

Date:

▶

_____   _____
(TYPE OR PRINT NAME)   (SIGNATURE OF DECLARANT)

FL-142 [Rev. January 1, 2003]   **SCHEDULE OF ASSETS AND DEBTS**   Page 4 of 4
                                                                      (Family Law)

EXHIBIT 6-7   California Income and Expense Declaration

Courtesy: Reprinted from *West's California Judicial Council Form 2003,* with permission of West, a Thomson business. For more information about this publication please visit **http://west.thomson.com.**

FL-150

ATTORNEY OR PARTY WITHOUT ATTORNEY *(Name and Address):*	TELEPHONE NO.:	FOR COURT USE ONLY

ATTORNEY FOR *(Name):*

SUPERIOR COURT OF CALIFORNIA, COUNTY OF

STREET ADDRESS:

MAILING ADDRESS:

CITY AND ZIP CODE:

BRANCH NAME:

PETITIONER/PLAINTIFF:

RESPONDENT/DEFENDANT:

INCOME AND EXPENSE DECLARATION	CASE NUMBER:

Step 1
Attachments to this summary

I have completed ☐ Income (page 2)   ☐ Expense (page 3)   ☐ Child Support (page 4)   Information forms.
(If child support is not an issue, do not complete Page 4. If your only income is TANF, do not complete Page 2.)

Step 2
Answer all questions that apply to you

1. Are you receiving or have you applied for or do you intend to apply for welfare or TANF?
   ☐ Receiving   ☐ Applied for   ☐ Intend to apply for   ☐ No
2. What is your date of birth *(month/day/year)?* ....
3. What is your occupation? _____
4. Highest year of education completed: _____
5. Are you currently employed?   ☐ Yes   ☐ No
   a. If yes: (1) Where do you work? *(name and address):* _____

   (2) When did you start work there *(month/year)?* ....
   b. If no: (1) When did you last work *(month/year)?* ....
   (2) What were your gross monthly earnings? ....
6. What is the total number of minor children you are legally obligated to support? ....

Step 3
Monthly income information

7. Net monthly disposable income *(from line 16a of Page 2):* .... $ _____

8. Current net monthly disposable income *(if different from line 7, explain below or on Attachment 8):* .... $ _____

Step 4
Expense Information

9. Total monthly expenses from line 2q of Page 3: .... $ _____
10. Amount of these expenses paid by others: .... $ _____

Step 5   Other party's income

11. My estimate of the other party's gross monthly income is: .... $ _____

Step 6
Date and sign this form

I declare under penalty of perjury under the laws of the State of California that the foregoing and the attached information forms are true and correct.

Date:

▶

_____ | _____
(TYPE OR PRINT NAME) | (SIGNATURE OF DECLARANT)
| ☐ Petitioner   ☐ Respondent

Form Adopted for Mandatory Use
Judicial Council of California
FL-150 [Rev. January 1, 2003]

INCOME AND EXPENSE DECLARATION

Page 1 of 4

www.courtinfo.ca.gov

continued

Exhibit 6-7 *continued*

PETITIONER/PLAINTIFF: RESPONDENT/DEFENDANT:	CASE NUMBER:
INCOME INFORMATION OF *(name)*:	

1. Total gross salary or wages, including commissions, bonuses, and overtime paid during the last 12 months: 1. $ _____

2. All other money received during the last 12 months **except welfare, TANF,** *Specify sources below:*
   SSI, spousal support from this marriage, or any child support. _____ 2a. $ _____
   Include pensions, social security, disability, unemployment, military
   basic allowance for quarters (BAQ), spousal support from a different _____ 2b. $ _____
   marriage, dividends, interest or royalty, trust income, and annuities.
   Include income from a business, rental properties, and reimbursement _____ 2c. $ _____
   of job-related expenses
   ➤ *Prepare and attach a schedule showing gross receipts less cash* _____ 2d. $ _____
   expenses for each business or rental property

3. Add lines 1 through 2d .... 3. $ _____
   Divide line 3 by 12 and place result on line 4a.

	Average last 12 months:	Last month:
4. Gross income	4a. $ _____	4b. $ _____
5. State income tax	5a. $ _____	5b. $ _____
6. Federal income tax	6a. $ _____	6b. $ _____
7. Social Security and Hospital Tax ("FICA" and "MEDI") or self-employment tax, or the amount used to secure retirement or disability benefits	7a. $ _____	7b. $ _____
8. Health insurance for you and any children you are required to support	8a. $ _____	8b. $ _____
9. State disability insurance	9a. $ _____	9b. $ _____
10. Mandatory union dues	10a. $ _____	10b. $ _____
11. Mandatory retirement and pension fund contributions .... *Do not include any deduction claimed in item 7.*	11a. $ _____	11b. $ _____

12. Court-ordered child support, court-ordered spousal support, and voluntarily
    paid child support in an amount not more than the guideline amount,
    actually being paid for a relationship *other* **than that involved in this
    proceeding:**
	12a. $ _____	12b. $ _____

13. Necessary job-related expenses *(attach explanation)*	13a. $ _____	13b. $ _____
14. Hardship deduction (Line 4d on Page 4)	14a. $ _____	14b. $ _____
15. Add lines 5 through 14. .... **Total monthly deductions:**	15a. $	15b. $
16. Subtract line 15 from line 4. .... **Net monthly disposable income:**	16a. $	16b. $

17. TANF, welfare, spousal support from this marriage, and child support from other relationships received
    each month: .... 17. $ _____
18. Cash and checking accounts: .... 18. $ _____
19. Savings, credit union, certificates of deposit, and money market accounts: .... 19. $ _____
20. Stocks, bonds, and other liquid assets: .... 20. $ _____
21. All other property, real or personal *(specify below)*: .... 21. $ _____

➤ **Attach a copy of your three most recent pay stubs.**

FL-150 [Rev. January 1, 2003]   **INCOME INFORMATION**   Page 2 of 4

continued

Exhibit 6-7 *continued*

PETITIONER/PLAINTIFF:	CASE NUMBER:
RESPONDENT/DEFENDANT:	
EXPENSE INFORMATION OF *(name):*	

1.

		name	age	relationship	gross monthly income
a. List all persons living in your home **whose expenses are included below** and their income: ☐ Continued on Attachment 1a.	1. 2. 3. 4.				
b. List all other persons living in your home and their income: ☐ Continued on Attachment 1b.	1. 2. 3.				

2. MONTHLY EXPENSES

a. Residence payments

  (1) ☐ Rent or ☐ mortgage . . . . $_____

  (2) If mortgage, include:

    Average principal . . . . . . $_____

    Average interest . . . . $_____

    Impound for real property taxes . . . . $_____

    Impound for homeowner's insurance . . . . . $_____

  (3) Real property taxes *(if not included in item (2))* . . . . $_____

  (4) Homeowner's or renter's insurance *(if not included in item (2))* . . . . $_____

  (5) Maintenance . . . . $_____

b. Unreimbursed medical and dental expenses . . . . $_____

c. Child care . . . . $_____

d. Children's education . . . . $_____

e. Food at home and household supplies . . $_____

f. Food eating out . . . . $_____

g. Utilities . . . . $_____

h. Telephone . . . . $_____

i. Laundry and cleaning . . . . $_____

j. Clothing . . . . $_____

k. Insurance *(life, accident, etc. Do not include auto, home, or health insurance)* $_____

l. Education *(specify):* . . . . $_____

m. Entertainment . . . . $_____

n. Transportation and auto expenses *(insurance, gas, oil, repair)* . . . . $_____

o. Installment payments *(insert total and itemize below in item 3)* . . . . $_____

p. Other *(specify):* . . . . $_____

q. TOTAL EXPENSES (a-p) . . . . $_____
(do not include amounts in a(2))

3. ITEMIZATION OF INSTALLMENT PAYMENTS OR OTHER DEBTS ☐ Continued on Attachment 3.

CREDITOR'S NAME	PAYMENT FOR	MONTHLY PAYMENT	BALANCE	DATE LAST PAYMENT MADE

4. ATTORNEY FEES

a. To date I have paid my attorney for fees and costs: $ _____   The source of this money was:

b. I owe to date the following fees and costs over the amount paid:

c. My arrangement for attorney fees and costs is:

    I confirm this information and fee arrangement. ▶ _____

                                            (SIGNATURE OF ATTORNEY)

                                            (TYPE OR PRINT NAME OF ATTORNEY)

FL-150 [Rev. January 1, 2003]   **EXPENSE INFORMATION**   Page 3 of 4

continued

EXHIBIT 6-8 California Child Support Information

Courtesy: Reprinted from *West's California Judicial Council Form 2003,* with permission of West, a Thomson business. For more information about this publication please visit **http://west.thomson.com.**

PETITIONER/PLAINTIFF: RESPONDENT/DEFENDANT: CHILD SUPPORT INFORMATION OF *(name):*	CASE NUMBER:

THIS PAGE MUST BE COMPLETED IF CHILD SUPPORT IS AN ISSUE.

1. Health insurance for my children ☐ is ☐ is not   available through my employer.
   a. Monthly cost paid by me or on my behalf for the children *only* is: $ _____
   Do not include the amount paid or payable by your employer.
   b. Name of carrier:
   c. Address of carrier:

   d. Policy or group policy number:

2. Approximate percentage of time each parent has primary physical responsibility for the children:
   Mother   % Father   %

3. ☐ The court is requested to order the following as additional child support:
   a. ☐ Child care costs related to employment or to reasonably necessary education or training for employment skills
      (1) Monthly amount currently paid by mother: $
      (2) Monthly amount currently paid by father: $
   b. ☐ Uninsured health care costs for the children *(for each cost state the purpose for which the cost was incurred and the estimated monthly, yearly, or lump sum amount paid by each parent):*

   c. ☐ Educational or other special needs of the children *(for each cost state the purpose for which the cost was incurred and the estimated monthly, yearly, or lump sum amount paid by each parent):*

   d. ☐ Travel expense for visitation
      (1) Monthly amount currently paid by mother: $
      (2) Monthly amount currently paid by father: $

4. ☐ The court is requested to allow the deductions identified below, which are justifiable expenses that have caused an extreme financial hardship.

	Amount paid per month	How many months will you need to make these payments
a. ☐ Extraordinary health care expenses *(specify and attach any supporting documents):*	$ _____	_____
b. ☐ Uninsured catastrophic losses *(specify and attach supportingdocuments):*	$ _____	_____
c. ☐ Minimum basic living expenses of dependent minor children from other marriages or relationships who live with you *(specify names and ages of these children):*	$ _____	_____
d. Total hardship deductions requested *(add lines a-c):*	$ _____	

EXHIBIT 6-9 California Declaration Regarding Service

Courtesy: Reprinted from *West's California Judicial Council Form 2003,* with permission of West, a Thomson business. For more information about this publication please visit **http://west.thomson.com.**

FL-141

ATTORNEY OR PARTY WITHOUT ATTORNEY *(Name, state bar number, and address):*

FOR COURT USE ONLY

TELEPHONE NO.:   FAX NO.:

ATTORNEY FOR *(Name):*

SUPERIOR COURT OF CALIFORNIA, COUNTY OF

STREET ADDRESS:

MAILING ADDRESS:

CITY AND ZIP CODE:

BRANCH NAME:

PETITIONER:

RESPONDENT:

DECLARATION REGARDING SERVICE OF DECLARATION OF DISCLOSURE AND INCOME AND EXPENSE DECLARATION

☐ **Petitioner's**   ☐ **Preliminary**

☐ **Respondent's**   ☐ **Final**

CASE NUMBER:

1. I am the ☐ Attorney for ☐ Petitioner ☐ Respondent in this matter.

2. ☐ Petitioner's ☐ Respondent's *Preliminary Declaration of Disclosure* and *Income and Expense Declaration* was served on:
   ☐ Attorney for ☐ Petitioner ☐ Respondent by: ☐ personal service ☐ mail ☐ other *(specify):*

   on *(date):*

3. ☐ Petitioner's ☐ Respondent's *Final Declaration of Disclosure* and *Income and Expense Declaration* was served on:
   ☐ Attorney for ☐ Petitioner ☐ Respondent by: ☐ personal service ☐ mail ☐ other *(specify):*

   on *(date):*

4. ☐ Service of the *Final Declaration of Disclosure* has been waived under Family Code section 2105, subdivision (d).

I declare under penalty of perjury under the laws of the State of California that the foregoing is true and correct.

Date:

▶

_____
(TYPE OR PRINT NAME)

_____
(SIGNATURE)

> **Note:**
> **File this document with the court.**
> **Do not file a copy of either the *Preliminary* or *Final Declaration of Disclosure* with this document.**

Form Adopted for Mandatory Use
Judicial Council of California
FL-141 [Rev. January 1, 2003]

DECLARATION REGARDING SERVICE OF DECLARATION OF DISCLOSURE
(Family Law)

Page 1 of 1
Family Code, §§ 2104, 2106, 2112

www.courtinfo.ca.gov

EXHIBIT 6-10 California Property Declaration

Courtesy: Reprinted from *West's California Judicial Council Form 2003,* with permission of West, a Thomson business. For more information about this publication please visit **http://west.thomson.com**.

ITEM NO.	BRIEF DESCRIPTION	GROSS FAIR MARKET VALUE	AMOUNT OF DEBT	NET FAIR MARKET VALUE	PROPOSAL FOR DIVISION AWARD TO	
					PETITIONER	RESPONDENT
		$	$	$	$	$
6.	LIFE INSURANCE (CASH VALUE)					
7.	EQUIPMENT, MACHINERY, LIVESTOCK					
8.	STOCKS, BONDS, SECURED NOTES					
9.	RETIREMENT, PENSION, PROFIT-SHARING, ANNUITIES					
10.	ACCOUNTS RECEIVABLE, UNSECURED NOTES, TAX REFUNDS					
11.	PARTNERSHIPS, OTHER BUSINESS INTERESTS					
12.	OTHER ASSETS AND DEBTS					
13.	TOTAL FROM CONTINUATION SHEET					
14.	TOTALS					

15. ☐ A *Continuation of Property Declaration* (form FL-161) is attached and incorporated by reference.

_____   _____
(TYPE OR PRINT NAME OF ATTORNEY)   (SIGNATURE OF ATTORNEY)

I declare under penalty of perjury under the laws of the State of California that, to the best of my knowledge, the foregoing is a true and correct listing of assets and obligations and that the amounts shown are correct.

Date:

_____   _____
(TYPE OR PRINT NAME)   (SIGNATURE)

FL-160 [Rev. January 1, 2003]

PROPERTY DECLARATION (FAMILY LAW)

Page 2 of 2

continued

Exhibit 6-10 *continued*

FL-161

MARRIAGE OF (Last name—first names of parties)	CASE NUMBER

☐ **PETITIONER'S**   ☐ **RESPONDENT'S**

☐ **COMMUNITY AND QUASI-COMMUNITY PROPERTY DECLARATION**
☐ **SEPARATE PROPERTY DECLARATION**

ITEM NO.	BRIEF DESCRIPTION	GROSS FAIR MARKET VALUE	AMOUNT OF DEBT	NET FAIR MARKET VALUE	PROPOSAL FOR DIVISION AWARD TO	
					PETITIONER	RESPONDENT
		$	$	$	$	$

Page 1 of 2

Form Adopted for Mandatory Use
Judicial Council of California
FL-161 [Rev. January 1, 2003]

CONTINUATION OF PROPERTY DECLARATION
(FAMILY LAW)

Family Code, §§ 2500–2600
www.courtinfo.ca.gov

continued

Exhibit 6-10 *continued*

ITEM NO.	BRIEF DESCRIPTION	GROSS FAIR MARKET VALUE	AMOUNT OF DEBT	NET FAIR MARKET VALUE	PROPOSAL FOR DIVISION AWARD TO	
					PETITIONER	RESPONDENT
		$	$	$	$	$

FL-161 [Rev. January 1, 2003]

CONTINUATION OF PROPERTY DECLARATION
(FAMILY LAW)

Page 2 of 2

Request to Enter Default

If the respondent fails to file a response, the petitioner may enter A Request to Enter Default in the proceeding. See Exhibit 6-11 The standard caption is completed.

Item 2. Indicate what items are attached.

Date the request. The attorney or petitioner must sign.

Item 3. Check the appropriate box and sign.

Item 4. Check the proper box whether or not costs are waived or listed. Type or print the name and sign.

Item 5. Sign this section if respondent is not in the military service.

EXHIBIT 6-11 California Request to Enter Default

Courtesy: Reprinted from *West's California Judicial Council Form 2003*, with permission of West, a Thomson business. For more information about this publication please visit **http://west.thomson.com.**

FL-165

ATTORNEY OR PARTY WITHOUT ATTORNEY *(Name, state bar number, and address):*	FOR COURT USE ONLY

TELEPHONE NO.:   FAX NO.:

ATTORNEY FOR *(Name):*

SUPERIOR COURT OF CALIFORNIA, COUNTY OF
STREET ADDRESS:
MAILING ADDRESS:
CITY AND ZIP CODE:
BRANCH NAME:

PETITIONER:

RESPONDENT:

REQUEST TO ENTER DEFAULT	CASE NUMBER:

1. **TO THE CLERK: Please enter the default of the respondent who has failed to respond to the petition.**
2. A completed *Income and Expense Declaration* (form FL-150) or *Financial Statement (Simplified)* (form FL-155)
   ☐ is attached ☐ is not attached
   A completed *Property Declaration* (form FL-160) ☐ is attached ☐ is not attached
   because *(check at least one of the following):*
   (a) ☐ There have been no changes since the previous filing.
   (b) ☐ The issues subject to disposition by the court in this proceeding are the subject of a written agreement.
   (c) ☐ There are no issues of child or spousal support, or attorney fees and costs subject to determination by the court.
   (d) ☐ The petition does not request money, property, costs, or attorney fees. (Fam. Code, § 2330.5.)
   (e) ☐ There are no issues of division of community property.
   (f) ☐ This is an action to establish parental relationship.

Date:

▶

_____   _____
(TYPE OR PRINT NAME)   (SIGNATURE OF [ATTORNEY FOR] PETITIONER)

3. **DECLARATION**
   a. ☐ No mailing is required because service was by publication and the address of respondent remains unknown.
   b. ☐ A copy of this *Request to Enter Default* including any attachments and an envelope with sufficient postage was provided to the court clerk addressed as follows *(address of respondent's attorney or, if none, respondent's last known address):*

   c. I declare under penalty of perjury under the laws of the State of California that the foregoing is true and correct.

Date:

▶

_____   _____
(TYPE OR PRINT NAME)   (SIGNATURE OF DECLARANT)

FOR COURT USE ONLY
☐ *Request to Enter Default* mailed to respondent or respondent's attorney on *(date):*
☐ Default entered as requested on *(date):*
☐ Default NOT entered. Reason:
Clerk, by _____ , Deputy

Page 1 of 2

Form Adopted for Mandatory Use Judicial Council of California FL-165 [Rev. January 1, 2003]	**REQUEST TO ENTER DEFAULT** **(Family Law—Uniform Parentage)**	Code of Civil Procedure, §§ 585, 587; Family Code, § 2335.5 www.courtinfo.ca.gov

continued

Exhibit 6-11 *continued*

CASE NAME:	CASE NUMBER:

4. MEMORANDUM OF COSTS

    a. ☐ Costs and disbursements are waived.

    b. Costs and disbursements are listed as follows:

        (1) ☐ Clerk's fees . . . . $. . . . .

        (2) ☐ Process server's fees . . . . $. . . . .

        (3) ☐ Other *(specify):* . . . . $. . . . .

        . . . . $. . . . .

        . . . . $. . . . .

        . . . . $ _____

        TOTAL . . . . $. . . . .

    c. I am the attorney, agent, or party who claims these costs. To the best of my knowledge and belief the foregoing items of cost are correct and have been necessarily incurred in this cause or proceeding.

    d. I declare under penalty of perjury under the laws of the State of California that the foregoing is true and correct.

Date:

_____   ▶   _____
        (TYPE OR PRINT NAME)   (SIGNATURE OF DECLARANT)

5. DECLARATION OF NONMILITARY STATUS

    a. Respondent is not in the military service or in the military service of the United States as defined in section 101 of the Soldiers' and Sailors' Relief Act of 1940, as amended (50 U.S.C. appen. § 501 et seq.), and not entitled to the benefits of such act.

    b. I declare under penalty of perjury under the laws of the State of California that the foregoing is true and correct.

Date:

_____   ▶   _____
        (TYPE OR PRINT NAME)   (SIGNATURE OF DECLARANT)

FL-165 [Rev. January 1, 2003]

REQUEST TO ENTER DEFAULT
(Family Law—Uniform Parentage)

Page 2 of 2

Declaration for Default

Complete the caption and check whether the proceeding is a dissolution or legal separation. See Exhibit 6-12. This form is self-explanatory. Complete all sections that are applicable and include the appropriate attachments. Type the name and get the signature.

EXHIBIT 6-12   California Declaration for Default

Courtesy: Reprinted from *West's California Judicial Council Form 2003,* with permission of West, a Thomson business. For more information about this publication please visit **http://west.thomson.com.**

FL-170

ATTORNEY OR PARTY WITHOUT ATTORNEY *(Name, state bar number, and address):*

FOR COURT USE ONLY

TELEPHONE NO.:   FAX NO.:

ATTORNEY FOR *(Name):*

SUPERIOR COURT OF CALIFORNIA, COUNTY OF

STREET ADDRESS:

MAILING ADDRESS:

CITY AND ZIP CODE:

BRANCH NAME:

MARRIAGE OF

PETITIONER:

RESPONDENT:

| **DECLARATION FOR DEFAULT OR UNCONTESTED** ☐ **DISSOLUTION or** ☐ **LEGAL SEPARATION** | CASE NUMBER: |

(NOTE: Items 1 through 16 apply to both dissolution and legal separation proceedings.)

1. I declare that if I appeared in court and were sworn, I would testify to the truth of the facts in this declaration.
2. I agree that my case will be proven by this declaration and that I will not appear before the court unless I am ordered by the court to do so.
3. All the information in the ☐ Petition ☐ Response is true and correct.
4. **DEFAULT OR UNCONTESTED** *(Check a or b)*
    a. ☐ The default of the respondent was entered or is being requested, and I am not seeking any relief not requested in the petition. **OR**
    b. ☐ The parties have agreed that the matter may proceed as an uncontested matter without notice, and the agreement is attached or it is incorporated in the attached marital settlement agreement or stipulated judgment.
5. **MARITAL SETTLEMENT AGREEMENT** *(Check a or b)*
    a. ☐ The parties have entered into an ☐ AGREEMENT or ☐ STIPULATED JUDGMENT regarding their property and marital rights, including support, the original of which is or has been submitted to the court. I request the court to approve the agreement. **OR**
    b. ☐ There is NO AGREEMENT or STIPULATED JUDGMENT, and the following statements are true *(check at least one, including item (2) if a community estate exists):*
        (1) ☐ There are no community or quasi-community assets or community debts to be disposed of by the court.
        (2) ☐ The community and quasi-community assets and debts are listed on the attached **completed** current *Property Declaration* (form FL-160), which includes an estimate of the value of the assets and debts that I propose to be distributed to each party. The division in the proposed *Judgment (Family Law)* (form FL-180) is a fair and equal division of the property and debts, or if there is a negative estate, the debts are assigned fairly and equitably.
6. **DECLARATION OF DISCLOSURE** *(Check a, b, or c)*
    a. ☐ Both the petitioner and respondent have filed, or are filing concurrently, a *Declaration Regarding Service of the Declaration of Disclosure* (form FL-141) and *Income and Expense Declaration* (form FL-150).
    b. ☐ This matter is proceeding by default. I am the Petitioner in this action and have filed a proof of service of the preliminary *Declaration of Disclosure* (form FL-140) with the court. I hereby waive receipt of the final *Declaration of Disclosure* (form FL-140) from the respondent.
    c. ☐ This matter is proceeding as an uncontested action. Service of the final *Declaration of Disclosure* (form FL-140) is mutually waived by both parties. A waiver provision executed by both parties under penalty of perjury is contained in the marital settlement agreement or proposed judgment, or other separate stipulation.
7. ☐ CHILD CUSTODY should be ordered as set forth in the proposed *Judgment (Family Law)* (form FL-180).
8. ☐ CHILD VISITATION should be ordered as set forth in the proposed *Judgment (Family Law)* (form FL-180).
9. SPOUSAL AND FAMILY SUPPORT *If a support order or attorney fees are requested, submit a completed* Income and Expense Declaration *(form FL-150), unless a current form is on file. Include your best estimate of the other party's income.*
    (Check at least one of the following)
    a. ☐ I knowingly give up forever any right to receive spousal support.
    b. ☐ I ask the court to reserve jurisdiction to award spousal support in the future to *(name):*
    c. ☐ Spousal support should be ordered as set forth in the proposed *Judgment (Family Law)* (form FL-180).
    d. ☐ Family support should be ordered as set forth in the proposed *Judgment (Family Law)* (form FL-180).

Page 1 of 2

Form Adopted for Mandatory Use
Judicial Council of California
FL-170 [Rev. January 1, 2003]

**DECLARATION FOR DEFAULT OR UNCONTESTED
DISSOLUTION OR LEGAL SEPARATION**
(Family Law)

Family Code, § 2336;
Cal. Rules of Court, rule 1241
www.courtinfo.ca.gov.

continued

Exhibit 6-12 *continued*

PETITIONER:	CASE NUMBER:
RESPONDENT:	

10. ☐ CHILD SUPPORT should be ordered as set forth in the proposed *Judgment (Family Law)* (form FL-180).

11. a. I ☐ am receiving ☐ am not receiving ☐ intend to apply for public assistance for the child or children listed in the proposed order.

 b. To the best of my knowledge the other party ☐ is ☐ is not receiving public assistance.

12. ☐ Petitioner ☐ Respondent is presently receiving public assistance and all support should be made payable to the local child support agency at the address set forth in the proposed judgment. A representative of the local child support agency has signed the proposed judgment.

13. If there are minor children, check and complete item a and item b or c:

 a. My gross (before taxes) monthly income is as follows: $

 b. ☐ The estimated gross monthly income of the other party is as follows: $

 c. ☐ I have no knowledge of the estimated monthly income of the other party for the following reasons *(specify):*

 d. ☐ I request that this order be based on ☐ Petitioner's ☐ Respondent's earning ability. The facts in support of my estimate of earning ability are *(specify):*
 ☐ Continued in Attachment 13d.

14. ☐ PARENTAGE of the children of the Petitioner and Respondent born prior to their marriage should be ordered as set forth in the proposed *Judgment (Family Law)* (form FL-180). A declaration regarding parentage is attached.

15. ☐ ATTORNEY FEES should be ordered as set forth in the proposed *Judgment (Family Law)* (form FL-180).

16. There are irreconcilable differences that have led to the irremediable breakdown of the marriage and there is no possibility of saving the marriage through counseling or other means.

17. This declaration may be reviewed by a commissioner sitting as a temporary judge who may determine whether to grant this request or require my appearance under Family Code section 2336.

STATEMENTS IN THIS BOX APPLY ONLY TO DISSOLUTIONS — items 18 through 21

18. Petitioner and/or the Respondent has been a resident of this county for at least three months and of the State of California for at least six months continuously and immediately preceding the date of the filing of the petition.

19. I ask that the court grant the request for a judgment for dissolution of marriage based upon irreconcilable differences and that the court make the orders set forth in the proposed *Judgment (Family Law)* (form FL-180) submitted with this declaration.

20. ☐ This declaration is for the termination of **marital status only.** I ask the court to reserve jurisdiction over all issues whose determination is not requested in this declaration.

21. ☐ Petitioner ☐ Respondent requests restoration of his/her former name as set forth in the proposed *Judgment (Family Law)* (form FL-180).

THIS STATEMENT APPLIES ONLY TO LEGAL SEPARATIONS

22. I ask that the court grant the request for a judgment for legal separation based upon irreconcilable differences and that the court make the orders set forth in the proposed *Judgment (Family Law)* (form FL-180) submitted with this declaration.

I UNDERSTAND THAT A JUDGMENT OF LEGAL SEPARATION DOES NOT TERMINATE A MARRIAGE AND I AM STILL MARRIED.

---

23. ☐ Other *(specify):*

I declare under penalty of perjury under the laws of the State of California that the foregoing is true and correct.

Date:

▶

_____ _____
(TYPE OR PRINT NAME)   (SIGNATURE OF DECLARANT)

FL-170 [Rev. January 1, 2003]   **DECLARATION FOR DEFAULT OR UNCONTESTED DISSOLUTION OR LEGAL SEPARATION (Family Law)**   Page 2 of 2

Judgment

Use the appropriate caption and indicate whether it is a dissolution, legal separation, or nullity. See Exhibit 6-13. Indicate the date marital status ends.

1. Check the box if the judgment includes restraining orders or modifications thereto.
2. Indicate the date the case was heard, the judge's name, the department and room number of the court, whether attorneys were present and their names, and whether petitioner and respondent were present.
3. Check applicable box.
4. a. Fill in the date
   b. Check if legal separation
   c. Check if nullity
   d. Check if judgment nunc pro tunc and date
   e. Check if judgment on reserved issues
   f. Indicate if former name is restored and what it is
   g. Check if jurisdiction reserved
   h. Check if judgment contains provisions for child or family support

   Page 2. Fill in names of parties and case number.

   i. Check if marital settlement agreement is included
   j. Check if parties have written stipulation for judgment
   k. Check if child custody, visitation, other written agreements
   l. Check if child support and agreement
   m. Check if spousal support and agreement
   n. Check if children were born before marriage

Indicate number of pages attached.

EXHIBIT 6-13 California Judgment

Courtesy: Reprinted from *West's California Judicial Council Form 2003*, with permission of West, a Thomson business. For more information about this publication please visit **http://west.thomson.com**.

FL-180

ATTORNEY OR PARTY WITHOUT ATTORNEY *(Name, state bar number, and address)* :	FOR COURT USE ONLY

TELEPHONE NO.:   FAX NO.:

ATTORNEY FOR *(Name)*:

SUPERIOR COURT OF CALIFORNIA, COUNTY OF

STREET ADDRESS:

MAILING ADDRESS:

CITY AND ZIP CODE:

BRANCH NAME:

MARRIAGE OF

PETITIONER:

RESPONDENT:

JUDGMENT   CASE NUMBER:

☐ **Dissolution**   ☐ **Legal separation**   ☐ **Nullity**

☐ **Status only**

☐ **Reserving jurisdiction over termination of marital status**

☐ **Judgment on reserved issues**

Date marital status ends:

1. ☐ This judgment ☐ contains personal conduct restraining orders ☐ modifies existing restraining orders. The restraining orders are contained on page(s)   of the attachment. They expire on *(date):*

2. This proceeding was heard as follows: ☐ default or uncontested ☐ by declaration under Fam. Code, § 2336 ☐ contested
   a. Date: Dept.:   Rm.:
   b. Judicial officer *(name):*   ☐ Temporary judge
   c. ☐ Petitioner present in court   ☐ Attorney present in court *(name):*
   d. ☐ Respondent present in court   ☐ Attorney present in court *(name):*
   e. ☐ Claimant present in court *(name):*   ☐ Attorney present in court *(name):*
   f. ☐ Other *(specify name):*

3. The court acquired jurisdiction of the respondent on *(date):*
   ☐ Respondent was served with process   ☐ Respondent appeared

4. THE COURT ORDERS, GOOD CAUSE APPEARING:
   a. ☐ Judgment of dissolution be entered. Marital status is terminated and the parties are restored to the status of unmarried persons
      (1) ☐ on the following date *(specify):*
      (2) ☐ on a date to be determined on noticed motion of either party or on stipulation.
   b. ☐ Judgment of legal separation be entered.
   c. ☐ Judgment of nullity be entered. The parties are declared to be unmarried persons on the ground of *(specify):*

   d. ☐ This judgment will be entered nunc pro tunc as of *(date):*
   e. ☐ Judgment on reserved issues.
   f. ☐ Wife's ☐ Husband's former name be restored *(specify):*
   g. ☐ Jurisdiction is reserved over all other issues and all present orders remain in effect except as provided below.
   h. ☐ This judgment contains provisions for child support or family support. Both parties must complete and file with the court a *Child Support Case Registry Form* (form FL-191) within 10 days of the date of this judgment. The parents must notify the court of any change in the information submitted within 10 days of the change by filing an updated form. The form *Notice of Rights and Responsibilities and Information Sheet on Changing a Child Support Order* (form FL-192) is attached.

Page 1 of 2

Form Adopted for Mandatory Use Judicial Council of California FL-180 [Rev. January 1, 2003]	**JUDGMENT (Family Law)**	Family Code, §§ 2024, 2340, 2343, 2346 www.courtinfo.ca.gov.

continued

Exhibit 6-13 *continued*

MARRIAGE OF *(last name, first name of parties):*	CASE NUMBER:

4. i. ☐ A marital settlement agreement between the parties is attached.
   j. ☐ A written stipulation for judgment between the parties is attached.
   k. ☐ Child custody and visitation is ordered as
      set forth in the attached
          ☐ Marital settlement agreement, stipulation for judgment, or other written agreement.
          ☐ *Child Custody and Visitation Order Attachment* (form FL-341)
          ☐ Other *(specify):*

   l. ☐ Child support is ordered as set forth in
      the attached
          ☐ Marital settlement agreement, stipulation for judgment, or other written agreement.
          ☐ *Child Support Information and Order Attachment* (form FL-342)
          ☐ *Non-Guideline Child Support Findings Attachment* (form FL-342(A))
          ☐ *Stipulation to Establish or Modify Child Support and Order* (form FL-350)
          ☐ Other *(specify):*

   m. ☐ Spousal support is ordered as set forth
      in the attached
          ☐ Marital settlement agreement, stipulation for judgment, or other written agreement.
          ☐ *Spousal or Family Support Order Attachment* (form FL-343)
          ☐ Other *(specify):*

       ☐ NOTICE: It is the goal of this state that each party shall make reasonable good faith efforts to become self-supporting as provided for in Family Code section 4320. The failure to make reasonable good faith efforts may be one of the factors considered by the court as a basis for modifying or terminating spousal support.

   n. ☐ Parentage is established for children of this relationship born prior to the marriage.
   o. ☐ Other *(specify):*

Each attachment to this judgment is incorporated into this judgment, and the parties are ordered to comply with each attachment's provisions.

Jurisdiction is reserved to make other orders necessary to carry out this judgment.

Date:

                                 JUDGE OF THE SUPERIOR COURT

5. Number of pages attached: _____
    ☐ SIGNATURE FOLLOWS LAST ATTACHMENT

NOTICE:

Dissolution or legal separation may automatically cancel the rights of a spouse under the other spouse's will, trust, retirement benefit plan, power of attorney, pay on death bank account, transfer on death vehicle registration, survivorship rights to any property owned in joint tenancy, and any other similar thing. It does not automatically cancel the rights of a spouse as beneficiary of the other spouse's life insurance policy. You should review these matters, as well as any credit cards, other credit accounts, insurance polices, retirement benefit plans, and credit reports to determine whether they should be changed or whether you should take any other actions.

A debt or obligation may be assigned to one party as part of the dissolution of property and debts, but if that party does not pay the debt or obligation, the creditor may be able to collect from the other party.

An earnings assignment will automatically be issued if child support, family support, or spousal support is ordered.

Any party required to pay support must pay interest on overdue amounts at the "legal rate," which is currently 10 percent.

FL-180 [Rev. January 1, 2003]   **JUDGMENT**   Page 2 of 2
                                   (Family Law)

Notice of Entry of Judgment

Complete caption. See Exhibit 6-14. Check appropriate box under notification. Specify the effective date of termination of marital status in the box. Type in parties' names and addresses on the labels at the bottom of the form.

EXHIBIT 6-14 California Notice of Entry of Judgment

Courtesy: Reprinted from *West's California Judicial Council Form 2003*, with permission of West, a Thomson business. For more information about this publication please visit **http://west.thomson.com**.

FL-190

ATTORNEY OR PARTY WITHOUT ATTORNEY *(Name, state bar number, and address):*

FOR COURT USE ONLY

TELEPHONE NO.:   FAX NO.:
ATTORNEY FOR *(Name):*

SUPERIOR COURT OF CALIFORNIA, COUNTY OF
STREET ADDRESS:
MAILING ADDRESS:
CITY AND ZIP CODE:
BRANCH NAME:

PETITIONER:

RESPONDENT:

NOTICE OF ENTRY OF JUDGMENT

CASE NUMBER:

You are notified that the following judgment was entered on *(date):*

1. ☐ Dissolution of Marriage
2. ☐ Dissolution of Marriage — Status Only
3. ☐ Dissolution of Marriage — Reserving Jurisdiction Over Termination of Marital Status
4. ☐ Legal Separation
5. ☐ Nullity
6. ☐ Parent-Child Relationship
7. ☐ Judgment on Reserved Issues
8. ☐ Other *(specify):*

Date:

Clerk, by _____ , Deputy

— NOTICE TO ATTORNEY OF RECORD OR PARTY WITHOUT ATTORNEY —

Under the provisions of Code of Civil Procedure section 1952, if no appeal is filed the court may order the exhibits destroyed or otherwise disposed of after 60 days from the expiration of the appeal time.

STATEMENTS IN THIS BOX APPLY ONLY TO JUDGMENTS OF DISSOLUTION
Effective date of termination of marital status *(specify):*
WARNING: NEITHER PARTY MAY REMARRY UNTIL THE EFFECTIVE DATE OF THE TERMINATION OF MARITAL STATUS AS SHOWN IN THIS BOX.

CLERK'S CERTIFICATE OF MAILING

I certify that I am not a party to this cause and that a true copy of the Notice of Entry of Judgment was mailed first class, postage fully prepaid, in a sealed envelope addressed as shown below, and that the notice was mailed
at *(place):*   , California,
on *(date):*

Date:

Clerk, by _____ , Deputy

Page 1 of 1

Form Adopted for Mandatory Use
Judicial Council of California
FL-190 [Rev. January 1, 2003]

NOTICE OF ENTRY OF JUDGMENT
(Family Law—Uniform Parentage—Custody and Support)

Family Code, §§ 2338, 7636, 7637
www.courtinfo.ca.gov

NEW YORK DIVORCE

Detailed instructions for the individual seeking a divorce in New York are included on the state court Web page. The following introduction describes the basics of obtaining a divorce in New York, residency requirements, grounds for divorce, filing fees, and the papers needed to obtain an uncontested divorce in New York state.

Detailed instructions for completing the documents are provided, accompanied by the documents and individual instructions. The subsequent pages include the following documents in the order listed:

1. Introduction: What You Need to Know Before Starting Your Divorce Action and instructions for completing all forms required for a divorce (Exhibit 6-15).
2. Summons Form UD-1a, which is required with Verified Complaint form, and instructions for its completion (Exhibit 6-16).
3. Summons Form (Exhibit 6-17).
4. Instructions for completion of Verified Complaint (Exhibit 6-18).
5. Verified Complaint Action for Divorce (Exhibit 6-19).
6. Instructions for completion and Summons with Notice form required when commencing an action for divorce without a Verified Complaint (Exhibits 6-20 and 6-21).

Other states that require grounds for obtaining a divorce have similar forms to those filed in New York State.

EXHIBIT 6-15   New York Introduction and Instructions for Forms Completion

Courtesy: **http://www.courts.state.ny.us.**

INTRODUCTION:
WHAT YOU NEED TO KNOW BEFORE STARTING YOUR DIVORCE ACTION

This section will outline:

- The "basics": the important things you will need to know before starting your divorce action. (See pages 1-6)
- The schedule of filing fees for an uncontested divorce. (See page 5)
- The documents and papers needed to obtain an uncontested divorce. (See page 6)
- The instructions for starting the action. (See pages 7-10)
- The instructions for filing the action with the court and placing the case on the court's calendar. (See pages 10-12)

THE BASICS

There are two requirements that must be met before you can file for a divorce in New York State.

1. You must satisfy the *residency* requirements as set forth in Domestic Relations Law Section 230. The Domestic Relations Law is the law that governs divorces in New York State.

2. You must satisfy one of the *grounds for divorce* set forth in Domestic Relations Law Section 170.

RESIDENCY

To file for a divorce in New York you must satisfy one of the following residency requirements:

1) The marriage ceremony was performed in New York State and either spouse is a resident of the state at the time of the commencement of the action for divorce and resided in the state for a continuous period of one year immediately before the action began; **OR**

2) The couple lived as husband and wife in New York State and either spouse is a resident of the state at the time of the commencement of the action for divorce and resided in this state for a continuous period of one year immediately before the action began; **OR**

3) The grounds for divorce occurred in New York State and either spouse is a resident of the state at the time of the commencement of the action for divorce and resided in this state for a continuous period of one year immediately before the action began; **OR**

4) The grounds for divorce occurred in New York State and both spouses are New York residents at the time the action is commenced; **OR**

5) If you and your spouse were married outside of New York State and you never lived together as husband and wife in this state and the grounds for divorce did not occur in this state—either you or your spouse must presently be a resident of New York State and have resided continuously in the state for at least two years prior to bringing this action for divorce.

continued

Exhibit 6-15 *continued*

GROUNDS FOR DIVORCE

In order to file for a divorce in New York State you must have a **ground** *(a legally acceptable reason)* for the granting of a divorce by the New York courts. The legally acceptable reasons, or grounds for divorce, in New York are described in Domestic Relations Law §170. They are: **(1)** cruel and inhuman treatment; **(2)** abandonment; **(3)** imprisonment; **(4)** adultery; **(5)** living separate and apart pursuant to a separation judgment or decree; and **(6)** living separate and apart pursuant to a separation agreement.

Definition of Plaintiff and Defendant

Where you are the person seeking the divorce, you are the Plaintiff and your spouse is called the Defendant.

CRUEL AND INHUMAN TREATMENT:

- The treatment of the Plaintiff by the Defendant must rise to the level that the *physical* or *mental well being* of the Plaintiff is endangered and making it *unsafe or improper* for the Plaintiff to continue living with the Defendant.

- You cannot obtain a divorce simply because you do not get along with your spouse (**"irreconcilable differences"**) or because you have arguments or because of an isolated act in an otherwise long and peaceful marriage.

- All acts must have happened within five (5) years of the date the summons is filed with the County Clerk.

- In describing the specific acts of cruelty, you must be clear and to the point. You must supply the court with details like dates and places. If you do not remember the exact date, use the words "on or about."

- After describing the acts of cruelty you should conclude with the following language: *"The conduct of the Defendant was cruel and inhuman and so endangered the physical or mental well being of the Plaintiff as to render it unsafe or improper for the Plaintiff to cohabit with the Defendant."*

ABANDONMENT:

- An action for divorce may be maintained where the Defendant abandons the Plaintiff for a period of one year or longer prior to commencing the action and continuing to the present.

- Abandonment may take the form of your spouse *physically departing* your marital home without any intention of returning for a period of one year or longer prior to commencing the action, and continuing to the present, without any good reason for doing so and without your consent.

- Another form of abandonment is called *constructive abandonment*, which involves one spouse's refusal to engage in sexual relations with the other spouse continuously for one year or longer prior to commencing the action, and continuing to the present, without consent, good cause or justification.

- Another form of abandonment is called a *lock out*, which involves one spouse's refusal to allow the other spouse into the home continuously for more than one year prior to commencing the action and continuing to the present.

continued

Exhibit 6-15 *continued*

IMPRISONMENT:

- An action for divorce may be maintained where the Defendant is *imprisoned* for a period of at least *three consecutive years*. The imprisonment must have commenced after the date of the marriage and the Defendant must still be in prison when this divorce action is commenced. There is a five (5)- year time limit to start the action, beginning from the time of the completion of the third year of imprisonment.

ADULTERY:

- An action for divorce may be maintained based on adultery, which is an act of sexual or deviate sexual intercourse voluntarily performed by the Defendant with a person other than his or her spouse during the course of the marriage.
- The ground of adultery can be difficult and expensive to prove because the testimony of the Plaintiff is not enough and other evidentiary requirements must be satisfied (the Defendants admission is not enough). You should keep in mind that acts of adultery may qualify as acts of cruelty and entitle you to maintain a divorce action on the grounds of cruel and inhuman treatment.

CONVERSION OF A JUDGMENT OF SEPARATION:

- This ground is not used often. It involves a judgment of separation signed by a Judge or Referee of the Supreme Court.
- To maintain a divorce action the parties are required to live separate and apart. They must satisfy the terms of the judgment of separation for more than one year after the judgment was granted.

CONVERSION OF A SEPARATION AGREEMENT:

- A **separation agreement** is an agreement between the spouses that sets forth the terms and conditions by which the parties will live apart. The agreement must be signed by the parties before a notary and filed with the County Clerk in the county where one of the parties resides.
- If you and your spouse have *lived apart for more than one year* according to the terms and conditions of a properly executed separation agreement, you may maintain an action for divorce. It may be advisable to consult an attorney regarding this ground for divorce.

After you have determined that you have met the requirements for residency and grounds for divorce, you may use the forms in this packet to file for a divorce. The instructions in this packet will help you in completing these forms, starting your action, and satisfying the other requirements for obtaining a divorce.

SCHEDULE OF FILING FEES:

You will have to pay the following fees in your action for a divorce:

- Index Number $185.
- Note of Issue (New York City) $100.
- Note of Issue (Outside NYC) $25.

continued

Exhibit 6-15 *continued*

- Request for Judicial Intervention (Outside NYC) $75.
- Certificate of Dissolution Check with your local County of Marriage Clerk's Office
- Certified Copy of Judgment Approx. $4.-$10.

Check with the County Clerk's Office regarding acceptable forms of payment.

POOR PERSON STATUS:

Where an individual lacks the financial resources to pay the costs associated with a divorce action, an application may be made to have these fees **waived** or forgiven by the court. The **Supplemental Appendix of Forms** in this booklet (beginning at page 34) contains instructions on how to complete the forms that are required to apply to have the fees waived.

THE PAPERS NEEDED TO OBTAIN AN UNCONTESTED DIVORCE IN NEW YORK STATE:

1. Summons With Notice (Form UD-l) **OR** la) Summons (to be served with Verified
2. Verified Complaint (Form UD-2) Complaint) (Form UD-la)
3. Affidavit of Service (Form UD-3)
4. Sworn Statement of Removal of Barriers to Remarriage (Form UD-4) and Affidavit of Service (Form UD-4a)
5. Affirmation (Affidavit) of Regularity (Form UD-5) 6) Affidavit of Plaintiff (Form UD-6)
7. Affidavit of Defendant (Form UD-7)
8. Child Support Worksheet (Form UD-8)
8a. Support Collection Unit Information Sheet (Form UD-8a)
8b. Qualified Medical Child Support Order ("QMCSO") (Form UD-8b)
9. Note of Issue (Form UD-9)
10. Findings of Fact/Conclusions of Law (Form UD-10)
11. Judgment of Divorce (Form UD-11)
12. Part 130 Certification (Form UD-12)
13. Request for Judicial Intervention ("RJI") (Form UD-13) - Outside of New York City
14. Notice of Entry (Form UD-14)
Certificate of Dissolution of Marriage
Self-Addressed and Stamped Postcard

UCS-113 (UCS Divorce and Child Support Summary Form)
New York State Case Registry Filing Form

SUPPLEMENTAL APPENDIX OF FORMS

A) Income Deduction Order
B) Notice of Settlement
C) Poor Person Order
D) Affidavit in Support of Application to Proceed as a Poor Person

continued

Exhibit 6-15   *continued*

**The instructions for completing each individual form can be found on
pages 13-36 of this Packet.**

A COPY OF EACH COMPLETED FORM SHOULD BE RETAINED FOR YOUR RECORDS.

STARTING THE DIVORCE ACTION

PLEASE NOTE:

1. This packet should be filled out either by typing or printing the information. Printing should be legible and in BLACK ink only.

2. If you need additional space on any form, you may use an addendum sheet. Be sure to note on the particular form that an additional sheet is being attached to that form.

3. Attach to your papers any court orders regarding this marriage and child custody/support.

Please refer to the attached **glossary**, which defines many of the terms and phrases used in this packet.

**IF YOU ARE A SURVIVOR OF DOMESTIC VIOLENCE AND
WISH TO KEEP YOUR ADDRESS CONFIDENTIAL,
PLEASE CHECK WITH THE SUPREME COURT CLERK'S OFFICE
FOR INSTRUCTIONS ON HOW TO OBTAIN CONFIDENTIALITY.
IF CONFIDENTIALITY IS GRANTED BY THE COURT,
YOU SHOULD NOT FILL OUT YOUR ADDRESS ON ANY OF THESE FORMS.**

FOLLOW STEPS 1-7 TO START THE DIVORCE ACTION

STEP 1: Prepare an **original** and **two copies** of the **Summons With Notice (Form UD-1)** *or* the **Summons and Verified Complaint (Form UD-1a and Form UD-2).**

STEP 2: Purchase an **index number** at the County Clerk's Office and file the original of the Summons With Notice *or* the original of the Summons and Verified Complaint with the County Clerk. Unless you are granted a poor person's waiver, you will be required to pay $170 for the index number. Check with the County Clerk regarding acceptable forms of payment. Many County Clerks also will require that you fill out an Index Number Application Form at the time of filing, so be sure to bring with you the names, addresses and telephone numbers of all of the attorneys or, if unrepresented, of the parties themselves.

STEP 3: Put the **index number** and the **date of the filing** on the two copies of the Summons With Notice (or the Summons and Verified Complaint) if this is not done by a clerk upon filing the papers.

STEP 4: Have the Defendant served with one copy of the Summons With Notice or Summons and Verified Complaint by being **personally handed the papers.**

If your spouse lives in New York State:

The server must be a **resident** of New York State, over **eighteen years of age**, and cannot be a party to the action (this means you may not serve your spouse with the Summons).

continued

Exhibit 6-15 *continued*

If your spouse is presently residing outside of New York State:

You must still ensure that he or she is personally served with the summons. If you use a non-New York State resident to serve your spouse outside of New York State, the server must be a person authorized to make service pursuant to the laws of that jurisdiction **or** a duly qualified attorney in that jurisdiction, and you must submit a copy of the authorization that allows that person to serve the summons. You are encouraged to check with the local sheriff and, if necessary, with a country's Consulate or Embassy as to any local requirements for service.

Service upon the Defendant of the Summons With Notice or Summons and Verified Complaint must be made **within 120 days of their filing with the County Clerk's Office**. If you do not know where the Defendant is located, you may wish to delay filing the Summons With Notice or Summons and Verified Complaint until he or she is located, so that the 120-day period does not begin running while you search for your spouse.

IMPORTANT: If there are children under the age of 21, you must also serve a copy of the Child Support Standards Chart on the Defendant. The Chart is available at the Supreme Court Clerk's Office.

STEP 5: Where the Defendant *agrees* to the divorce, he or she will need to sign the **Affidavit of Defendant (Form UD-7)**. The Plaintiff may fill out the form and forward it to the Defendant for signature, or the Plaintiff may send the form to the Defendant with a copy of the instructions on how to fill it out. This may be accomplished by submitting the form to the Defendant together with the Summons With Notice or Summons and Verified Complaint. The Defendant must send the completed form back to the Plaintiff prior to having the case placed on the calendar so that the form can be filed with the other required forms.

STEP 6: Where the Defendant *will not agree* to complete and return the Affidavit of Defendant, the person that served the Defendant must prepare an **"Affidavit of Service" (Form UD-3)**, which attests to the service of the Summons With Notice or Summons and Verified Complaint. This affidavit must be submitted along with the full set of divorce papers when you place your case on the court's calendar. Keep in mind that there is a **40-day** waiting period from when the summons is served to place the matter on the court's calendar. When the Defendant does not sign the Affidavit of Defendant, waiving the 40 days, you must wait the full 40 days before you can place the matter on the court's calendar.

STEP 7: If the parties were married in a religious ceremony, the Defendant must be served with a copy of the **Sworn Statement of Removal of Barriers to Remarriage (Form UD-4)**. The Plaintiff must fill out the original and make a copy of the form. The copy then must be served on the Defendant either by personal service along with the Summons With Notice or the Summons and Verified Complaint, or by mail. If you serve the form by mail, it must be done prior to your placing your action on the court's calendar as described below, because you will need to file the original form with the other required forms. Service by mail must be by someone other than the Plaintiff who is over the age of 18 and not a party to the action. When you file this form, you must attach to the form the Affidavit or Service (Form UD-4a). If the Defendant signs the **Affidavit of Defendant (Form UD-7)**, then you will not have to serve and file this form.

continued

Exhibit 6-15 *continued*

If the Defendant <u>appears and does not consent</u> to this action:

Then your matter **is no longer an uncontested matrimonial** and you will be unable to obtain an uncontested divorce. You may want to consult an attorney at that point.

STEPS FOR PLACING YOUR DIVORCE CASE ON THE COURT CALENDAR

After you have completed **Steps 1-7**, you are ready to place your case on the court's calendar. If the Defendant consents to the action by signing the Affidavit of Defendant (Form UD-7), you may place your case on the court's calendar immediately. Otherwise, you will have to wait until 40 days after the date of the service of the summons.

You must complete the following steps to place your case on the calendar:

STEP 8: You must complete **Forms UD-3 through UD-12** (include UD-7 only if signed by the Defendant). Form UD-3 (Affidavit of Service) and Form UD-4 (Sworn Statement of Removal of Barriers to Remarriage) need not be completed, or filed, if the Defendant has signed Form UD-7 (Affidavit of Defendant). Form UD-8 (Child Support Worksheet), Form UD-8a (Support Collection Unit Information Sheet) and Form UD-8b (Qualified Medical Child Support Order) need not be completed, or filed, if there are no unemancipated children of the marriage.

STEP 9: If you are filing your action <u>outside of the City of New York</u>, you also must complete **Form UD-13 (Request for Judicial Intervention)**.

STEP 10: You also must complete the **Certificate of Dissolution of Marriage, the post-card, and the UCS 113 (Divorce and Child Support Summary Form)**. If a party is requesting child support payable to a person or entity other than a child support collection unit, the party must complete, as well, the **New York State Case Registry Form**.

STEP 11: You must file the completed forms, including a copy of the Summons With Notice or the Summons and Verified Complaint, with the County Clerk's Office. Include three (3) copies of the Note of Issue (Form UD-9).

STEP 12: Unless you are granted a poor person's waiver, you must pay a filing fee for filing the Note of Issue (Form UD-9) and, if outside New York City, the Request for Judicial Intervention (Form UD-13). See page 5 for the schedule of filing fees.

All of the papers filed with the County Clerk's Office will be submitted to the judge. If the papers are approved, the judge will sign the Judgment of Divorce (Form UD-11).

If you are asking for maintenance, custody, visitation, or distribution of property, the court may require a hearing unless you have either a written agreement or prior court order. If you are asking for exclusive occupancy of the marital home, you must assert that your spouse is not living in the marital home; otherwise a hearing may be ordered.

SUPPLEMENTAL FORMS

This packet contains additional forms that you may be required to file depending upon the special requirements in the county where you are bringing the action.

a. Income Deduction Order

In certain circumstances, the court may direct that the payment of maintenance (spousal support) or child support be made by automatically deducting moneys from

continued

Exhibit 6-15 *continued*

the paying spouse's wages through use of an **Income Deduction Order.** This can occur only where the paying spouse is a salaried employee and, in the case of child support, where the support order is not enforced through a local child support collection unit. If the court notifies you that an Income Deduction Order is required, follow the procedure for completing that order set forth in the Supplemental Appendix of Forms at page 33, and submit the order to the Supreme Court Clerk's Office.

  b. Notice of Settlement

  In some instances, the court will not sign the Judgment of Divorce until the Defendant is served with a copy of the unsigned Judgment and any other proposed orders and is permitted an opportunity to object to or comment on them. In that situation, the court will notify you that the Judgment and the proposed orders are to be served upon the Defendant with a **Notice of Settlement** (see Supplemental Appendix of Forms at page 34). Follow the procedure set forth in the Supplemental Appendix of Forms for completing and serving a Notice of Settlement.

AFTER THE PAPERS ARE APPROVED

After your papers have been reviewed and signed by a judge, you will be notified; the papers may need to be re-filed, and the judgment entered, in the County Clerk's Office. The manner in which this filing occurs depends upon the procedure of the county in which you brought the action. Consult the Supreme Court Clerk's Office for information regarding your obligations for the retrieval and/or entry of the signed judgment and supporting papers. *A divorce is not considered final until such time as the signed judgment is entered in the County Clerk's Office.* Should you receive notice that the papers have been filed on your behalf by the court, or if you file the papers, you may go to the County Clerk's Office to obtain a certified copy of the judgment. You must bring identification with you, because matrimonial files are confidential and information will be released only to a party or his or her attorney. The certified copy will cost between <u>$4.00 and $10.00</u>, but the fee will be waived if you obtained a poor person waiver.

A copy of the judgment of divorce must be served on the Defendant. To do this, you must mail to the Defendant a copy of the signed and entered **Judgment of Divorce (Form UD-11),** together with the completed **Notice of Entry (Form UD-14).**

TURN TO PAGES 13-36 FOR INSTRUCTIONS

EXHIBIT 6-16   New York Summons Form UD1A Instructions

Courtesy: http://www.nycourts.gov

1a. SUMMONS (Form UD-1a): (This form must be filed and served simultaneously with the Verified Complaint (Form UD-2)).

Field 1: Put the index number in the space provided.

Field 2: Print the county in which you are bringing this action.

Field 3: Print the date the summons was filed.

Field 4: The same as field 2.

Field 5: Print the Plaintiff's name.

Field 6: You must state the basis of venue, that is, why this case may be heard in the county you select. You have several options: Plaintiff's residence (Plaintiff lives in the county), Defendant's residence (Defendant lives in the county), or CPLR §509 (any other county so long as the Defendant does not object and the court accepts the case). If you choose a county where neither party resides, you must write in CPLR §509. The court must accept the case if it is brought in the county where either the Plaintiff or the Defendant resides. If you choose CPLR §509 and the other side does not challenge the basis for venue, then the action may go forward in that county, but you should be aware that the court may reject your case based on specific venue rules in the county where you are filing.

Field 7: Provide where either the Plaintiff or the Defendant resides depending on which party's residence was chosen as the basis of venue. For example, if the Plaintiff's residence is listed as the basis for venue, place the Plaintiff's address in this space. If Defendant's residence is chosen, list the Defendant's address in this space. If CPLR §509 is chosen, list the Plaintiff's address in this space.

Field 8: Print the Defendant's name.

Field 9: Check the appropriate box.

Field 10: Print the date you prepared the summons.

Field 11: Check the appropriate box.

Field 12: List your attorney's address and telephone number. If you do not have an attorney, list your name, address and telephone number.

EXHIBIT 6-17   New York Summons Form

1   **SUPREME COURT OF THE STATE OF NEW YORK**   Index No.:_____

2 3   **COUNTY OF _____**   Date Summons filed:_____
4   --X   Plaintiff designates ___

5 ____   County as the place of trial
                                                          The basis of venue is:

6   _____

                                         Plaintiff,
              -against-   **SUMMONS**
                                                          Plaintiff/Defendant resides at:
7   _____
8   _____
                                         Defendant.   _____
         --X

ACTION FOR A DIVORCE

To the above named Defendant:

9   **YOU ARE HEREBY SUMMONED** to answer the complaint in this action and to serve
a copy of your answer on the • *Plaintiff* **OR** • *Plaintiff's Attorney(s)* within twenty (20) days
after the service of this summons, exclusive of the day of service, where service is made by delivery
upon you personally within the state, or within thirty (30) days after completion of service where
service is made in any other manner. In case of your failure to appear or answer, judgment will be
taken against you by default for the relief demanded in the complaint.

10, 11 Dated _____   • *Plaintiff*
                                                          • *Attorney(s) for Plaintiff*

EXHIBIT 6-18 New York Instructions for Verified Complaint

Courtesy: **http://www.courts.state.ny.us**

INSTRUCTIONS FOR VERIFIED COMPLAINT (Form UD-2)

Field 1: Fill in the county in which the action is brought. Be consistent with other forms.

Field 2: Print the Plaintiff's name.

Field 3: Write in the index number assigned to this matter.

Field 4: Print the Defendant's name.

Field 5: Write the name of Plaintiff's attorney in the blank space or, if Plaintiff is representing himself or herself, strike the word "by" and leave the space blank.

Field 6: This section informs the court of whether it has the jurisdiction (authority) to hear your case. Check the appropriate box or boxes.

Field 7: Insert the date that you and your spouse were married as listed on a marriage license and the city, town or village; and the state or country of the marriage.

Field 8: Check the appropriate box. If you had a religious ceremony, you must strike the word "not" in the first line and you must check one of the three options below as to your removing barriers to remarriage. If you had a civil ceremony, leave the word "not" in place and do not check any of the three options below. A Barriers to Remarriage Affidavit **(Forms UD-4 and UD-4a)** must be filed with proof of service unless the Defendant waives the filing of the Affidavit.

Field 9: Check the appropriate box. List the number of children either born or adopted during the marriage. List the names, dates of birth and addresses for each.

Field 10: List the Plaintiff's and Defendant's addresses. If child support is not an issue leave this section blank.

Field 11: Fill in the required information about Plaintiff's and Defendant's insurance coverage. Make sure to include the type of coverage. Examples include, but are not limited to, medical, dental and optical coverage. If either party has more than one insurance plan, you must list the additional coverage. Strike this section if child support is not an issue.

Field 12: You must state and describe the grounds for divorce. In addition to selecting the section (be specific as possible) of the Domestic Relations Law that applies, you should fill in the date where appropriate and also give a brief description as to how you meet New York State's grounds requirements. (Refer to **Grounds for Divorce** on pages 2 through 5 of these instructions).

Field 13: This section remains unchanged. If a judgment of divorce was already entered in this state or another state between you and your spouse **and/or** there is another action for divorce pending between you and your spouse, you may not be permitted to maintain this action. You should seek legal assistance as noted in the Foreword.

continued

Exhibit 6-18 *continued*

Field 14: If you are asking for other relief in addition to your request for a divorce, this relief must be listed in this section. Examples include but are not limited to custody, visitation, equitable distribution, maintenance and exclusive occupancy of the marital home. If there are minor children of the marriage, child support must be listed in this section. You should also list any presently existing Family Court orders (with the docket number) that you wish to be continued. (Note: when children reside in New York, custody must be determined).

If you are requesting that an equitable distribution of marital property be made, you must check the appropriate box. Be aware that requests to distribute marital property may require a hearing before a judge or special referee. If you are waiving the distribution of marital property or if marital property is being distributed pursuant to an agreement/stipulation, check the appropriate box.

Field 15: Insert the date that you prepared the document.

Field 16: Check the appropriate box. The attorney for the Plaintiff must sign this line and print his or her name, address and telephone number. If the Plaintiff does not have an attorney, the Plaintiff must sign at that line and put in his or her address and telephone number.

Field 17: The Plaintiff must sign this section in the presence of a notary public, who then must notarize the document. That individual will fill in the remaining information on this page.

EXHIBIT 6-19   New York Verified Complaint Action for Divorce

1   **SUPREME COURT OF THE STATE OF NEW YORK**
COUNTY OF _____
--X

2 3   Index No.:

                                  Plaintiff,

        -against-   **VERIFIED COMPLAINT**

                                                ACTION FOR DIVORCE

4
                                  Defendant.
--X

5   **FIRST:**
        Plaintiff *herein / by* _____, complaining of the Defendant, alleges
that the parties are over the age of 18 years and;

6   **SECOND:**
    •   The Plaintiff has resided in New York State for a continuous period in excess of two
        years immediately preceding the commencement of this action.
                                OR
    •   The Defendant has resided in New York State for a continuous period in excess of two
        years immediately preceding the commencement of this action.
                                OR
    •   The Plaintiff has resided in New York State for a continuous period in excess of one year
        immediately preceding the commencement of this action, and:

            a. •   the parties were married in New York State.
            b. •   the Plaintiff has lived as husband or wife in New York State with the
                    Defendant.
            c. •   the cause of action occurred in New York State.
                                OR
    •   The Defendant has resided in New York State for a continuous period in excess of one
        year immediately preceding the commencement of this action, and:

            a. •   the parties were married in New York State.
            b. •   the Defendant has lived as husband or wife in New York State with the
                    Plaintiff.
            c. •   the cause of action occurred in New York State.
                                OR
    •   The cause of action occurred in New York State and both parties were residents thereof
        at the time of the commencement of this action.

7   **THIRD:** The Plaintiff and the Defendant were married on _____

    in (city, town or village; and state or country) _____.

continued

Exhibit 6-19   *continued*

8   The marriage was   *not*   performed by a clergyman, minister or by a leader of the Society for Ethical Culture.

(If the word "not" is deleted above check the appropriate box below).

•   *To the best of my knowledge I have taken all steps solely within my power to remove any barrier to the Defendant's remarriage.*   **OR**

•   *I will take prior to the entry of final judgment all steps solely within my power to the best of my knowledge to remove any barrier to the Defendant's remarriage.*   **OR**

•   *The Defendant has waived in writing the requirements of DRL §253 (Barriers to Remarriage).*

9   **FOURTH:** • There are no children of the marriage.   **OR**

• There *is (are)* _____ child(ren) of the marriage, namely:

Name	Date of Birth	Address
_____	_____	_____
_____	_____	_____
_____	_____	_____
_____	_____	_____
_____	_____	_____

10   The Plaintiff resides at _____

_. The Defendant resides at _____

___.

11   The parties are covered by the following group health plans:

Plaintiff	**Defendant**
Group Health Plan:_____	Group Health Plan:_____
Address:_____	Address:_____
Identification Number:_____	Identification Number:_____
Plan Administrator:_____	Plan Administrator:_____
Type of Coverage:_____	Type of Coverage:_____

12   **FIFTH:** The grounds for divorce that are alleged as follows:

Cruel and Inhuman Treatment (DRL §170(1)):

•   At the following times, none of which are earlier than (5) years prior to commencement of this action, the Defendant engaged in conduct that so endangered the mental and physical well-being of the Plaintiff, so as to render it unsafe and improper for the parties to cohabit (live together) as husband and wife.

(State the facts that demonstrate cruel and inhuman conduct giving dates, places and specific acts. Conduct may include physical, verbal, sexual or emotional behavior.)

_____

_____

_____

continued

Exhibit 6-19   *continued*

_____

_____

_____

_____

_____

_____

(Attach an additional sheet, if necessary).

Abandonment (DRL 170(2)):

*   That commencing on or about _____, and continuing for a period of more than one (1) year immediately prior to commencement of this action, the Defendant left the marital residence of the parties located at _____, and did not return. Such absence was without cause or justification, and was without Plaintiff's consent.

*   That commencing on or about _____, and continuing for a period of more than one (1) year immediately prior to commencement of this action, the Defendant refused to have sexual relations with the Plaintiff despite Plaintiff's repeated requests to resume such relations. Defendant does not suffer from any disability which would prevent *her / him* from engaging in such sexual relations with Plaintiff. The refusal to engage in sexual relations was without good cause or justification and occurred at the marital residence located at _____.

*   That commencing on or about _____, and continuing for a period of more than one (1) year immediately prior to commencement of this action, the Defendant willfully and without cause or justification abandoned the Plaintiff, who had been a faithful and dutiful *husband / wife*, by depriving Plaintiff of access to the marital residence located at _____. This deprivation of access was without the consent of the Plaintiff and continued for a period of greater than one year.

Confinement to Prison (DRL §170(3)):

*   (a)   That after the marriage of Plaintiff and Defendant, Defendant was confined in prison for a period of three or more consecutive years, to wit: that Defendant was confined in_____ _____ prison on _____, and has remained confined to this date; and

    (b)   not more that five (5) years has elapsed between the end of the third year of imprisonment and the date of commencement of this action.

Adultery (DRL §170(4)):

*   (a)   That on _____, at the premises located at _____ _, the Defendant engaged in sexual intercourse with _____, without the procurement nor the connivance of the Plaintiff, and the Plaintiff ceased to cohabit (live) with the Defendant upon the discovery of the adultery; and

    (b)   not more than five (5) years elapsed between the date of said adultery and the date of commencement of this action.

continued

Exhibit 6-19 *continued*

(Attach a corroborating affidavit of a third party witness or other additional proof).

Living Separate and Apart Pursuant to a Separation Decree or Judgment of Separation (DRL §170(5)):

-    (a)   That the _____ Court, _____ County, _____ (Country or State) rendered a decree or judgment of separation on _____, under Index Number _____; and
  (b)   that the parties have lived separate and apart for a period of one year or longer after the granting of such decree; and
  (c)   that the Plaintiff has substantially complied with all the terms and conditions of such decree or judgment.

Living Separate and Apart Pursuant to a Separation Agreement (DRL §170(6)):

-    (a)   That the Plaintiff and Defendant entered into a written agreement of separation, which they subscribed and acknowledged on _____, in the form required to entitle a deed to be recorded; and
  (b)   that the *agreement / memorandum of said agreement* was filed on _____ in the Office of the Clerk of the County of _____, wherein *Plaintiff / Defendant* resided; and
  (c)   that the parties have lived separate and apart for a period of one year or longer after the execution of said agreement; and
  (d)   that the Plaintiff has substantially complied with all terms and conditions of such agreement.

13   **SIXTH:**   There is no judgment in any court for a divorce and no other matrimonial action between the parties pending in this court or in any other court of competent jurisdiction.

14   **WHEREFORE**, Plaintiff demands judgment against the Defendant as follows: A judgment dissolving the marriage between the parties and

-    _____
   _____
   _____
   _____
   _____

             AND

-    equitable distribution of marital property;
             OR
-    marital property to be distributed pursuant to the annexed separation agreement / stipulation;
             OR
-    I waive equitable distribution of marital property;

and any other relief the court deems fitting and proper.

15   Dated:_____

16   • *Plaintiff*

continued

Exhibit 6-19   *continued*

• *Attorney(s) for Plaintiff*
Address:

Phone No.:

(Form UD-2 - Rev. 5/99)

17   STATE OF NEW YORK, COUNTY OF _____ ss:

        I _____ (Print Name), am the Plaintiff in the within action for
a   divorce. I have read the foregoing complaint and know the contents thereof. The contents are true
    to my own knowledge except as to matters therein stated to be alleged upon information and belief,
    and as to those matters I believe them to be true.

Subscribed and Sworn to
before me on
                                            _____
_____   Plaintiff's Signature

_____
        NOTARY PUBLIC

EXHIBIT 6-20   New York Summons with Notice Instructions
Courtesy: **http://www.courts.state.ny.us.**

INSTRUCTIONS FOR SUMMONS WITH NOTICE (Form UD-1)

This form is used when commencing an action for divorce without a Verified Complaint.

Field 1: Put the index number in the space provided.

Field 2: Print the county in which you are bringing this action.

Field 3: Print the date the summons was filed.

Field 4: The same as field 2.

Field 5: Print the Plaintiff's name.

Field 6: You must state the basis of venue, that is, why this case may be heard in the county you select. You have several options: Plaintiff's residence (Plaintiff lives in the county), Defendant's residence (Defendant lives in the county), or CPLR §509 (any other county so long as the Defendant does not object and the court accepts the case). If you choose a county where neither party resides, you must write in CPLR §509. The court must accept the case if it is brought in the county where either the Plaintiff or the Defendant resides. If you choose CPLR §509 and the other side does not challenge the basis for venue, then the action may go forward in that county, but you should be aware that the court may reject your case based on specific venue rules in the county where you are filing.

Field 7: Provide where either the Plaintiff or the Defendant resides depending on which party's residence was chosen as the basis of venue. For example, if the Plaintiff's residence is listed as the basis for venue, place the Plaintiff's address in this space. If Defendant's residence is chosen, list the Defendant's address in this space. If CPLR §509 is chosen, list the Plaintiff's address in this space.

Field 8: Print Defendant's name.

Field 9: Check the appropriate box.

continued

Exhibit 6-20   *continued*

Field 10: Print the date you prepared the summons.

Field 11: Check the appropriate box.

Field 12: List your attorney's address and telephone number. If you do not have an attorney, list your name, address and telephone number.

Field 13: Fill in the appropriate subdivision number and the grounds for divorce as indicated at the bottom of the form (see pages 3-5 in this booklet). Check with your local clerk's office if you need additional information on where to learn about the grounds for divorce.

Field 14: If you are asking for other relief in addition to your request for a divorce, this relief must be listed in this section. Examples include but are not limited to custody, visitation, child support, equitable distribution, maintenance and exclusive occupancy of the home. If there are minor children of the marriage, child support must be listed in this section. You should also list any presently existing Family Court orders (with the docket number) that you wish to be continued. (Note: when children reside in New York, custody **must** be determined).

continued

EXHIBIT 6-21 New York Summons with Notice

1 **SUPREME COURT OF THE STATE OF NEW YORK**

Index No.:_____

2 3 **COUNTY OF _____**

Date Summons filed:_____

4 --X

Plaintiff designates __

5 ____

County as the place of trial
The basis of venue is:

6

_____

Plaintiff,

-against-

SUMMONS WITH NOTICE
Plaintiff/Defendant resides at:

7
8

_____
_____
_____

Defendant.

--X

ACTION FOR A DIVORCE

To the above named Defendant:

9 **YOU ARE HEREBY SUMMONED** to serve a notice of appearance on the • *Plaintiff* **OR** • *Plaintiff's Attorney(s)* within twenty (20) days after the service of this summons, exclusive of the day of service (or within thirty (30) days after the service is complete if this summons is not personally delivered to you within the State of New York); and in case of your failure to appear, judgment will be taken against you by default for the relief demanded in the notice set forth below.

10, 11 Dated _____

• *Plaintiff*
• *Attorney(s) for Plaintiff*
Address:

12

Phone No.:

13 **NOTICE:** The nature of this action is to dissolve the marriage between the parties, on the grounds: ****DRL §170 subd.____ - _____**
_____

—

The relief sought is a judgment of absolute divorce in favor of the Plaintiff dissolving the marriage between the parties in this action. The nature of any ancillary or additional relief demanded is:

14 _____
_____
_____
_____
_____

_____

**Insert the grounds for the divorce:
DRL §170(1) - cruel and inhuman treatment
DRL §170(2) - abandonment
DRL §170(3) - confinement in prison

DRL §170(4) - adultery
DRL §170(5) - living apart one year after separation decree or judgment of separation
DRL §170(6) - living apart one year after execution of a separation agreement

(Form UD-1 - Rev. 5/99)

Protective/Restraining Orders

COLORADO

The state of Colorado provides a detailed explanation on its Web site for the acquiring of Restraining Orders. The following items are set forth on the following pages:

1. County Court Restraining Orders explanation (Exhibit 6-22).
2. Important Information About Protective Orders (Exhibit 6-23)
3. Return of Service (Exhibit 6-24). The protective order must be served on the adverse party by one who is not a party to the action.
4. The Permanent Civil Protection Order (Exhibit 6-25) that sets forth the protections requested and granted to the Plaintiff by the court. The permanent civil protection order is granted after first obtaining a temporary order from the court.

EXHIBIT 6-22   Colorado County Court Restraining Orders

Courtesy: **http://courts.state.co.us**

Answers to Your Questions About

County Court
Restraining Orders

Excellence in Customer Service
Colorado Judicial Branch

http://www.courts.state.co.us

June 2002

continued

Exhibit 6-22 *continued*

CIVIL LAW

In a civil case, the person seeking the restraining order is the <u>petitioner</u>. The person who is being restrained is the <u>respondent/defendant.</u>

A victim of domestic violence, or any victim of violence or one who is in fear of personal harm, may go to civil court to get a **restraining order,** which is enforceable statewide and nationwide.

There are two stages for getting a restraining order in Colorado:

• <u>First</u>, you must obtain a **temporary restraining order (TRO)**. The TRO lasts up to 14 days. It will state the date and time you must return to make the order permanent (the permanent hearing).

• <u>Second</u>, you must return to court on the date indicated on the TRO for the court to issue a **permanent restraining order (PRO).** If you do not return at this time, the TRO will expire. It will no longer protect you or your child. Once you obtain a PRO, the length of the PRO is at the discretion of the judge (except the part about children, which lasts no more than 120 days). The PRO is enforceable wherever you go.

Advantages of civil court restraining orders:

• **Speedy relief.** A judge usually can decide a TRO on the same day you request it.

• **No attorney necessary.** You do not need an attorney to get a TRO.

• **Personal protection.** A restraining order can do a lot more than order the defendant not to harm you. It can remove the respondent from the home; give you temporary "care & control" of your children; order the defendant to stay away from your work and/or home and order defendant not to call; set parenting time arrangements; deny parenting time if the children are being harmed; and provide safety during the drop-off and pick-up of children.

• **Ease.** A restraining order is relatively easy to obtain. You need only show that violence or threats of violence most likely took place. Filing criminal charges or calling the police is not usually necessary.

Disadvantages of civil court restraining orders:

• The burden of dealing with the legal system is on you. You are the one who goes to court and tells your story to the judge. Be prepared to deal with paperwork. You may decide you need to hire a lawyer to assist you with your case.

• The respondent will not go to jail as a result of the restraining order. However, violation of a restraining order is a crime.

• You will need to arrange for the order to be served on the respondent. You may take the order to the sheriff's department to be served. There is a fee for service only for those who are not a victim of domestic violence, domestic abuse, sexual assault, or stalking.

HOW DO YOU GET A CIVIL RESTRAINING ORDER?

Local law enforcement have procedures to obtain an emergency protective order on your behalf when the courts are not open for regularly scheduled business. Otherwise, during regular business hours, every county court has a time and place for restraining order hearings. Your local domestic violence program can provide this information and can help you fill out the forms. Also, you can call the office of the clerk of court and ask when and where to get a TRO.

continued

Exhibit 6-22 *continued*

There is no fee to file a TRO, nor may the court charge you for certified copies, if you are a victim of domestic violence, domestic abuse, sexual assault, or stalking. The court may charge a fee for filing if it determines you are not seeking the TRO as a victim of domestic violence, domestic assault, sexual assault, or stalking. If you are requested to pay and cannot, you will need to fill out a **motion to waive costs** form. The court must either waive the fee or allow you to pay later.

To get a restraining order:

You must be able to state that the defendant hurt or threatened to hurt you and that you are in imminent (likely) danger of further abuse or threats if the order is not issued.

THE TEMPORARY RESTRAINING ORDER (TRO)

When you go to court, you will fill out a **complaint** and other forms. After you complete the forms, you will have a hearing in person before the judge. This usually happens the same day. The defendant will not be present.

In the complaint, you must give specific information about the abuse—what happened; when it happened; who else, if anyone, was there; and whether any children were there at the time. Include abuse that happened in the past.

The judge can order the defendant to stay a specific distance

• from your residence (even if it is the family residence or if the title/lease is in the defendant's name);

• from your job;
• from your children's day care or school;

• from friends or family places;

• from public places where you go frequently.

> Police officers and deputy sheriffs can serve the defendant with a TRO after a 911 call when the defendant is with you. They will give one copy of the TRO to the defendant and return one to you. Their signature is your Proof of Service, and you must bring the signed TRO with you when you return to court for the PRO.

WHAT CAN YOU DO ABOUT THREATS?

If the defendant does anything prohibited by the TRO after it is served, the defendant has broken the law—**call the police**. When you go to the PRO hearing, **tell the judge what the defendant has done.**

Inform the judge about threats made to stop you from going to court, to take or harm the children, to withhold money for your support, or threats against your family or friends.

The TRO is in effect while you are in the courthouse. The defendant cannot speak to you while waiting for the hearing. If the defendant attempts to do so, immediately tell the bailiff, court clerk, or judge.

continued

Exhibit 6-22 *continued*

THE HEARING

You must return to court on the date ordered by the court. You must be on time. If you cannot arrive at the court on time, call the clerk of court's office.. Give your name and number of your case, and explain why you cannot get to court on time. The court may grant you an extension. However, if the judge calls your name and you are not there and have not made arrangements with the court clerk, the judge will vacate (cancel) your TRO. You will not be able to get another TRO unless the defendant does something new to threaten or harm you.

If the defendant does not make an appearance in court and if you are still afraid, the judge should grant your request for a Permanent Restraining Order (PRO). Bring your Proof of Service.

WHAT HAPPENS AFTER YOU GET THE TEMPORARY RESTRAINING ORDER?

You will need copies of the TRO. You may be required to pay for certified copies to be served on the respondent/defendant if the court determines the TRO is not to prevent domestic violence, domestic assault, sexual assault, or stalking.

You should keep one copy with you always. In addition, you should:

• Leave a copy at any place from which the respondent/defendant is restrained (for example: daycare, work or school).

• Take a copy to your local police or sheriff's department.

• Keep a second copy with you until the defendant is served.

The TRO will contain the date and time that you are scheduled to return to court, so that the order can be made **permanent**. If you do not have the order made permanent, it will be vacated or set aside. (This means the order is no longer in effect.) Therefore, **it will no longer protect you or your children.**

WHAT HAPPENS TO THE ORDER (SERVICE)?

Service

• Service must be done by the sheriff or someone over 18 years of age. **YOU CANNOT SERVE THE TRO**.

• Service is the official word for notifying the respondent that there is a court order in effect.

• The respondent/defendant cannot violate the restraining order <u>until he/she has been served</u>.

• The law requires that a copy of the TRO be given directly to the respondent/ defendant.

• If you cannot get the respondent/defendant served before the return date, go to court on the day and time indicated, and ask the judge for a continuance so that you may continue trying to serve the respondent/ defendant.

WHAT IS A CONTESTED HEARING?

The respondent <u>may</u> choose to appear at the hearing and contest the entire restraining order or part of it. However, the order may be continued (made permanent) without the defendant being present.

continued

Exhibit 6-22   *continued*

- The respondent/defendant can deny that what you said is true but still agree to be restrained. In this case, the judge will make the order permanent, and it will protect you just as if what you said was proven in court.

- If you have children with the respondent/defendant, make sure the TRO specifically identifies parenting time, and it is safe for you and the children.

- You need to prepare carefully for a contested PRO hearing. If you think the respondent will contest the order, contact your local resources (for example: domestic violence shelter, Project Safeguard, legal services) before the PRO hearing. They can give you more information about how to prepare and what to expect.

WHAT IS YOUR ROLE AT THE PRO HEARING?

If you have physical evidence—photos of injuries or damaged property, medical records, 911 or answering machine tapes, etc.—bring these to the court. If you have witnesses who saw what happened and/or saw injuries, heard an argument, or in whom you confided afterward, ask them to come with you to the PRO hearing. By far the most important evidence is what <u>you tell</u> the judge. Make a plan regarding what you want to say. Write your plan down, including a list of the facts you want to tell the judge, and bring it with you to court.

SHOULD YOU GET AN ATTORNEY FOR THE HEARING?

It is not necessary to have an attorney to get a restraining order. Your story of what the defendant did is powerful evidence. Consider consulting with an attorney if the respondent/defendant has an attorney or if you and the defendant have children together. An attorney can assist you in telling your story to the judge and in asking questions of the respondent/defendant and other witnesses. No-cost or low-cost legal help is scarce, but local domestic violence agencies may know of resources.

HOW IS THE RESTRAINING ORDER ENFORCED?

If a respondent/defendant violates any part of the restraining order, **call the police.** Violating a restraining order is a crime in Colorado. If the police have a "probable cause" to believe that the defendant has violated the restraining order, they are required to arrest the defendant and take the defendant to jail. This will start the criminal process. Probable cause means that a reasonable person reasonably believes that a crime has been committed.

If the police tell you that the respondent/defendant cannot be charged, ask for a copy of the incident report, and ask that the officer on duty initial the copy. This documents what happened and can be helpful later.

If the police and prosecutor decide not to file charges, you can file a **motion for contempt** with the court that issued your restraining order. In a contempt proceeding, you (or your lawyer) will need to convince the judge that the defendant did something that the restraining order forbids.

You and the defendant cannot agree to change the PRO without the court's permission. If you want to change the PRO, you will need to have a hearing. During the hearing, the judge will hear from both you and the defendant to determine whether changes should be made. The defendant may request changes, but the judge will not change the PRO without you being present.

continued

Exhibit 6-22 *continued*

YOUR SAFETY

If the defendant is arrested, the defendant may be held in jail overnight, until a bond hearing, or until the defendant posts bond. If the defendant is arrested in the morning, the defendant could be out of jail by the end of the day.

Although the judge will probably issue a no-contact order forbidding the defendant to contact you, you may need to take additional steps to protect yourself after the arrest. **A no-contact order is not the same as a civil restraining order.** It does not last as long and may not give you and your children the same protection.

WHAT ARE VICTIM ADVOCATES AND HOW CAN THEY HELP YOU?

City or district attorneys in Colorado have victim/witness advocates on staff who can give you information about your case. In many cases, they will give you support and accompany you to court. Also, you may be able to get help from advocates at your local domestic violence programs or from law enforcement victim advocates.

WHAT ARE YOUR RIGHTS AS A VICTIM?

• You have a right to know the judgment of the court and whether the defendant is following the conditions of probation.

• If the defendant is sentenced to jail, you have the right to be notified when the defendant is released. You must contact the prosecutor to request notification of the defendant's release.

• If the prosecutor is not going to file charges, if charges are dropped, or if the case is dismissed, you have a right to know why.

HOW DOES THE LAW WORK FOR YOU?

There are two kinds of courts: criminal and civil. Both can act to protect you against a defendant. You may be able to obtain protection from both courts at the same time, but the criminal and civil courts work differently. These differences can be important to you.

CRIMINAL LAW

Because domestic violence is a crime against the community and the victim, a defendant who is arrested is prosecuted in the county where the crime occurred. As the victim of the crime, you will be referred to in legal papers as the **complainant.**

In a criminal case, the person restrained is referred to as the **defendant**. A government lawyer, known as the **prosecutor** or **city/district attorney**, will decide if the case should go to criminal court. If he or she must gather the evidence necessary to bring the case to trial, **only the prosecutor can decide to press or drop** charges. As the **complainant,** your main responsibility in a criminal case is to come to court to **testify—to tell how the defendant harmed you.**

continued

Exhibit 6-22 *continued*

You can also help the prosecution by providing proof of the abuse, such as photographs of injuries, medical records, and the names of any people who witnessed the abuse.

Remember, just because the defendant has an attorney and you do not have an attorney, it does not mean that you will not be able to get a restraining order.

> **This brochure is published as a customer service by the Colorado Judicial Branch. For more information, contact your local county court.**

EXHIBIT 6-23 Colorado Protection Order Information

IMPORTANT INFORMATION ABOUT PROTECTION ORDERS

GENERAL INFORMATION

✓ This order or injunction shall be accorded full faith and credit and be enforced in every civil or criminal court of the United States, Indian Tribe or United States Territory pursuant to 18 USC 2265. This Court has jurisdiction over the parties and the subject matter.

✓ Pursuant to 18 USC § 922(d)(g), it is unlawful for any person to possess or transfer a firearm who is subject to a court order that restrains such person from harassing, stalking or threatening an intimate partner of such person or a child of such intimate partner or person, or engaging in other conduct that would place an intimate partner in reasonable fear of bodily injury to the partner or child.

NOTICE TO DEFENDANT/RESTRAINED PARTY:

✓ A violation of a protection order may be misdemeanor, municipal ordinance violation or a delinquent act (if committed by a juvenile) and is a deportable offense. Anyone over the age of eighteen who violates this order may be subject to fines of up to $5000.00 and up to 18 months in jail. Violation of this order will constitute contempt of court. An adjudicated juvenile may be subject to commitment to the Department of Human Services for up to two years.

✓ You may be arrested or taken into custody without notice if a law enforcement officer has probable cause to believe that you have violated this order.

✓ If you violate this Order thinking that the other party or anyone else has given you permission, **YOU ARE WRONG**, and can be arrested and prosecuted. The terms of this Order cannot be changed by agreement of the parties. Only the Court can change this Order.

✓ Possession of a firearm while this Permanent Protection Order is in effect, may constitute a Felony under the Federal Law, 18 USC §922(g)(8), §924(a)(2).

✓ You may apply to the Court for a modification or dismissal of a protection order after four years from the date of issuance of the permanent protection order, per §13-14-102(17.5)(a - e).

NOTICE TO PLAINTIFF/PROTECTED PARTY:

✓ You are hereby informed that if this Order is violated you may call law enforcement.

✓ You may initiate contempt proceedings against the Defendant/Restrained Person if the Order is issued in a civil action or request the prosecuting attorney to initiate contempt proceedings if the order is issued in a criminal action.

✓ You cannot give the Defendant/Restrained person permission to change or ignore this Order in any way. **ONLY THE COURT CAN CHANGE THIS ORDER.**

✓ You may apply to the Court for a modification or dismissal of a protection order at any time, per §13-14-102(17.5)(a-e).

NOTICE TO LAW ENFORCEMENT OFFICERS:

✓ If the Order has not been personally served, the law enforcement officer responding to a call of assistance shall serve a copy of said order on the person named Defendant/Restrained Person therein and shall write the time, date, and manner of service on the protected person's copy of such order and shall sign such statement. The officer shall provide the Court with a completed return of service form. (§13-14-102(11))

✓ You shall use every reasonable means to enforce this protection order.

✓ You shall arrest or take into custody, or if an arrest would be impractical under the circumstances, seek a warrant for the arrest of the Defendant/Restrained Person when you have information amounting to probable cause that the restrained person has violated or attempted to violate any provision of this order subject to criminal sanctions pursuant to §18-6-803.5, C.R.S. or municipal ordinance and the restrained person has been properly served with a copy of this order or the Defendant/Restrained Person has received actual notice of the existence and substance of such order.

✓ You shall enforce this order even if there is no record of it in the Protection Order Central Registry.

✓ You shall take the Defendant/Restrained Person to the nearest jail or detention facility.

✓ You are authorized to use every reasonable effort to protect the alleged victim and the alleged victim's children to prevent further violence.

✓ You may transport, or arrange transportation to a shelter for the alleged victim and/or the alleged victim's children.

EXHIBIT 6-24   Return of Service

Case Name _____ v. _____   Case Number: _____

RETURN OF SERVICE

I declare under oath that, I am over the age of 18 years and not a party to this case and that, I served this Order on the ❑   Plaintiff/Petitioner ❑   Defendant/Respondent in _____ (County) _____ (State) on _____ (date) at the following location: _____

❑   By handing it to a person identified to me as the ❑   Plaintiff/Petitioner ❑   Defendant/Respondent.

❑   By leaving it with the ❑   Plaintiff/Petitioner ❑   Defendant/Respondent who refused service.

❑   By leaving it with _____ designated to receive service for the ❑   Plaintiff/Petitioner ❑Defendant/Respondent .

❑   I attempted to serve the ❑Plaintiff/Petitioner ❑Defendant/Respondent _____ occasions but have not been able to locate the ❑Plaintiff/Petitioner ❑Defendant/Respondent.   Return   to   the   ❑Plaintiff/Petitioner ❑Defendant/Respondent is made on _____(date).

❑ Private process server
❑ Sheriff, _____County
Fee $ _____ Mileage $ _____

_____
Signature of Process Server

_____
Name (Print or type)

My commission expires: _____

_____
Notary Public /Deputy Clerk   Date

EXHIBIT 6-25   Permanent Civil Protection Order

❑ Municipal Court ❑ County Court ❑ District Court
_____ County, Colorado

Court Address:
_____

Plaintiff(s)/Petitioner(s):
Address: _____

_____

v.

Defendant/Respondent:
Address: _____

_____

The address of the protected party may be omitted from the written order of the Court, including the Register of actions.

COURT USE ONLY

Case Number:

Division   Courtroom

PERMANENT CIVIL PROTECTION ORDER
(This form is subject to the provisions of §§13-14-101 to 13-14-102, C.R.S.

TO: _____, Defendant   Sex ❑ M ❑ F

Race: _____ DOB: _____ Ht: _____ Wt: _____ Hair color: _____ Eye color: _____

THE COURT FINDS that it has jurisdiction over the parties and the subject matter; that the Defendant was personally served and given reasonable notice and opportunity to be heard; that the Defendant constitutes a credible threat to the life and health of the Plaintiff(s); and sufficient cause exists for the issuance of a civil protection order. Unless the box immediately below is checked, the Court finds that the Defendant is/was an intimate partner, as that term is used under 18 USC §922 (d)(8) and (g)(8) of the Brady Handgun Violence Prevention Act.

❑ The Court finds that the Defendant is/was not an intimate partner and is not governed by the Brady Handgun Violence Prevention Act.

THE COURT ORDERS THAT YOU DEFENDANT shall not harass, stalk, injure, threaten, or molest the Plaintiff(s) or otherwise violate this Order. You shall not use, attempt to use, or threaten to use physical force against the Plaintiff(s) that would reasonably be expected to cause bodily injury. You shall not engage in any conduct that would place the Plaintiff(s) in reasonable fear of bodily injury.

> **A violation of a protection order is a crime and may be prosecuted as a misdemeanor, municipal ordinance violation, or a delinquent act (if committed by a juvenile) pursuant to §18-6-803.5, C.R.S. and municipal ordinance.**

1. *No Contact Provisions*
❑ It is ordered that you, the Defendant, **shall have no contact of any kind** with the Plaintiff(s), and you shall not attempt to contact the Plaintiff(s) through any third person, except your attorney, except as follows:
_____

_____

_____

❑ You must keep a distance of at least _____ yards from the Plaintiff(s).

2. *Exclusion from places*
It is ordered that you be excluded, and shall stay at least _____ yards away from the following places: (Please specify the address(es) where the Plaintiff(s) resides, works or attends school.)
❑ Home: _____
❑ Work: _____
❑ School: _____
❑ Other: _____

continued

Exhibit 6-25   *continued*

Case Name _____ **v.** _____ **Case Number:** _____

❑ Exceptions: _____

_____

_____

_____

You may not remain in or return to any of the above locations after you receive this Order. You shall be permitted to return to a shared residence one time to obtain sufficient undisputed personal effects necessary to maintain a normal standard of living ONLY if you are accompanied by a law enforcement officer.

3.   *Care and Control Provisions*

❑   It is in the best interest of the minor child(ren) named below that care and control of these child(ren) be awarded to: _____. This care and control order expires on _____(date a maximum of 120 days from this Order); all other provisions of this Order remain in full force and effect permanently. Any other Court orders regarding the child(ren) must be followed to the extent that the other Orders do not conflict with this Order. This Order governs over any other Orders concerning the care and control of said child(ren).

Name: _____ DOB: _____

Name: _____ DOB: _____

Name: _____ DOB: _____

Name: _____ DOB: _____

LAW ENFORCEMENT SHALL USE REASONABLE MEANS TO EFFECTUATE THIS CARE & CONTROL ORDER.

4.   *Issues Concerning Children*

❑   Parenting time expires on _____(date a maximum of 120 days from this Order) and shall be as follows:

_____

_____

_____

❑   Parenting time shall be as previously ordered by the _____ District Court, Case # _____

❑   You shall have no contact with the following minor child(ren), and shall stay at least _____ yards away from:

Name: _____ DOB: _____

Name: _____ DOB: _____

Name: _____ DOB: _____

Name: _____ DOB: _____

5.   *Other Provisions*

❑   It is further ordered that _____

_____

_____

_____

❑   This permanent protection order is identical to the temporary protection order and does not require service on the Defendant.

❑   This permanent protection order is different from the temporary protection order and requires service on the Defendant before its provisions become effective.

❑   Served Plaintiff/Defendant in Open Court on _____(date).

_____   _____   _____   _____
Plaintiff   Date   ❑ Judge ❑ Magistrate   Date

_____   _____   _____
Defendant   Date   Print Judge/Magistrate Name

continued

MARYLAND

The state of Maryland provides a form on its Web site called "Petition for Protection." The same form is used to seek protection from domestic violence, child abuse, or vulnerable adult abuse. The three-page form (Exhibit 6-26) is included on the following pages. Each numbered item is explained below.

HEADING. Check the appropriate court and fill in the location. Complete the name and address and telephone number for the Petitioner and the Respondent. Do not give an address for the petitioner if doing so risks further abuse. Check whether protection is being sought for domestic violence, child abuse, or vulnerable child abuse.

1. Is the petitioner seeking relief for herself, a minor child, or a vulnerable adult? What is the name of the abuser? Describe the acts of abuse and against whom they were committed? In the box provided, write a narrative description of the details of what happened; describe injuries.

2. If relief is being sought for a child or vulnerable adult, check the appropriate box and fill in the person's name and address. Check the designation of the person completing the form.

3. List the name, birth date, and relationship to the respondent of each person for whom protection is being sought. Complete the heading on page 2.

4. If the person for whom protection is sought has lived with the respondent, complete this section.

5. If other court cases are on file involving the petitioner or individual for whom protection is sought and the respondent, complete this section.

6. Write a detailed description of all past injuries that the respondent has caused the victim and give dates, if known.

7. List any firearms to which the respondent has access.

8. Check all boxes that apply to the orders the petitioner wishes the court to make against the respondent. Do not give an address for petitioner if doing so risks further abuse.

9. Complete if the petitioner wishes child custody and/or use and possession of a jointly-owned vehicle.

10. Complete if the petitioner is seeking emergency family maintenance. The petitioner must date and sign the form. An addendum should be added with a description of the respondent.

Most states provide forms on their Web sites or in the court clerk's office for protective or restraining orders based on physical abuse. Some state courts provide assistance for victims in the completion of these forms. Once the order is granted, a copy should be given to the police department in the city where the victim resides, the police department in the city where the victim works, and with police departments in surrounding communities that are frequented by the victim.

EXHIBIT 6-26   Maryland Petition for Protection

Judge Time _____
Hours   Minutes

MARYLAND JUDICIARY   ☐ **CIRCUIT COURT** ☐ **DISTRICT COURT OF MARYLAND FOR** Allegany County
                                                                                            City/County
Located at...Case No...
                          Court Address

(NOTE: Fill in the following, checking the appropriate boxes. Petitioners *need not give an address* if doing so risks further abuse or reveals the confidential address of a shelter. If this is the case, check here ☐ If you need additional paper, ask the clerk.)

....   vs.   ....
                    Petitioner   Respondent

Street Address, Apt. No.   Home: Street Address, Apt. No.   Home:
                                      Work: Work:
City, State, Zip Code   Telephone Number(s)   City, State, Zip Code   Telephone

PETITION FOR PROTECTION FROM
☐ **DOMESTIC VIOLENCE** ☐ **CHILD ABUSE** ☐ **VULNERABLE ADULT ABUSE**

1. I want relief for ☐ myself ☐ minor child ☐ vulnerable adult, from abuse by ....
                                                                                              Respondent
The Respondent committed the following acts of abuse against...,
                                                                                 Victim

on or about, ...(check all that apply) ☐ kicking   ☐ punching   ☐ choking
                          Date

☐ slapping   ☐ shooting   ☐ rape or other sexual offense (or attempt)   ☐ hitting with object   ☐ stabbing

☐ shoving   ☐ threats of violence   ☐ mental injury of a child   ☐ detaining against will

☐ other ....

The details of what happened are: (Describe injuries. State when and where these acts occurred. Be as specific as you can.):

```



```

2. (If the victim is a child or vulnerable adult, fill in the following.) I am asking for protection for a ☐ child
☐ vulnerable adult whose name is ....
At this time the victim can be found at ....
I am ☐ State's Attorney   ☐ DSS   ☐ a relative   ☐ an adult living in the home.

3. The person(s) I want protected are (include yourself if you are a victim):

Name(s)	Birthdate	Relationship to Respondent
....	....	....
....	....	....
....	....	....
....	....	....
....	....	....

continued

Exhibit 6-26 *continued*

Case No...

.... VS. ....
Petitioner   Respondent

4. The person(s) I want protected now lives, or has lived, with the Respondent for the following period of time during the past year:...

There ☐ are ☐ are not additional persons living in the home.

5. I know of the following court cases involving me, or the person I want protected, and the Respondent. (Examples include: paternity, child support, divorce, custody, domestic violence, juvenile cases, criminal cases)

Court	Kind of Case	Year Filed	Results or Status (if you know)
....	....	....	....
....	....	....	....
....	....	....	....

6. Describe all past injuries the Respondent has caused the victim, and give date, if known............................

7. The Respondent owns or has access to the following firearms:...

8. I want the court to order the Respondent:(NOTE: Petitioner need not give an address if doing so risks further abuse.)

☑ NOT to abuse or threaten to abuse ....
    Name(s)

☐ NOT to contact, attempt to contact, or harass ....
    Name(s)

☐ NOT to go to the residence(s) at ....
    Address

☐ NOT to go to the school(s) at ....
    Name of school and address
    ....

☐ NOT to go to the child care provider(s) ....
    Name of child care provider and address

☐ NOT to go to the work place(s) at ....

☐ To leave the home at ....
    Address
    and give possession of the home to ....
    The name(s) on the deed or lease are: ....

☐ To turn over firearm(s) to a law enforcement agency.

☐ To go to counseling ☐ domestic violence ☐ drug/alcohol ☐ other.............................

☐ To pay money as Emergency Family Maintenance (may be taken from Respondent's paycheck).

continued

Exhibit 6-26 *continued*

Case No...

....
Petitioner   Respondent

9. I also want the Court to order:

☐   Custody of...
Children's names

be granted to ....
Name

☐   Use and possession of the following jointly-owned vehicle be granted to...................................
Name

....
Description of vehicle

10. (Fill in only if you are seeking Emergency Family Maintenance.) The **Respondent** has the following financial resources:

Income from employment in the amount of $... every ☐ week ☐ 2 weeks ☐ month

☐ other ....

Source of employment income ....
Name and address of source and amount(s) received

Income from other source ....
Name and address of source and amount(s) received

The **Respondent** also owns the following property of value: Automobile(s) $ ....
Estimate Value

Home $ .... Bank Account(s) $ ....
Estimate Value   Estimate Value

Other: ....
Estimate Value

I solemnly affirm under the penalties of perjury that the contents of the foregoing Petition are true to the best of my knowledge, information and belief.

....
Date   Petitioner

☐ I have filled in the Addendum (Description of Respondent), CC-DV 1A.

NOTE

If you believe that you have been a victim of abuse and that there is a danger of serious and immediate injury to you, you may request the assistance of a police officer or local law enforcement agency.

The law enforcement officer must protect you from harm when responding to your request for assistance and may, if you ask, accompany you to the family home so that you may remove clothing and medicine, medical devices, and other personal effects required for you and your children, regardless of who paid for them.

The textbook describes the differences between general and limited partners. The format for the Agreement of Limited Partners (Exhibit 7-1) sets forth the rights and responsibilities of the limited partners and general partners of the described partnership. It has been generously provided by Legal Law Forms, whose Web site is available at: **http://www.legallawforms.com**

Most of the required information is provided in the document itself. The items to be completed include names, state, and other identifying material.

EXHIBIT 7-1   Limited Partnership Agreement

Courtesy: Reprinted with permission of **www.LegalLawForms.com**

THE LIMITED PARTNERSHIP INTERESTS EVIDENCED BY THIS AGREEMENT HAVE NOT BEEN REGISTERED WITH THE SECURITIES AND EXCHANGE COMMISSION OR THE _____ SECURITIES COMMISSION, BUT HAVE BEEN ISSUED PURSUANT TO THE PRIVATE OFFERING EXEMPTION UNDER THE SECURITIES ACT OF 1933, AS AMENDED, AND THE _____ SECURITIES ACT. ACCORDINGLY, THE SALE, TRANSFER, PLEDGE, HYPOTHECATION, OR OTHER DISPOSITION OF ANY OF SAID LIMITED PARTNERSHIP INTERESTS IS RESTRICTED AND MAY NOT BE ACCOMPLISHED EXCEPT IN ACCORDANCE WITH ANY INVESTMENT REPRESENTATION, THIS AGREEMENT, AN APPLICABLE REGISTRATION STATEMENT OR AN OPINION OF COUNSEL FOR THE PARTNERSHIP THAT A REGISTRATION STATEMENT IS UNNECESSARY, AND ANY OTHER INSTRUMENTS AND PROCEDURES THAT COUNSEL FOR THE PARTNERSHIP MAY REQUIRE.

AGREEMENT OF LIMITED PARTNERSHIP OF _____ **LTD.**

THIS AGREEMENT OF LIMITED PARTNERSHIP, dated as of _____, 200___, is entered into by those individuals, firms or corporations identified in Exhibit A as the general partner, and the individual or individuals identified in Exhibit "A" as the limited partner or limited partners, upon the following terms and conditions:

RECITALS:

A. The parties desire to form a limited partnership under the laws of the State of _____.

B. The parties wish to set forth their limited partnership agreement in writing.

THEREFORE, in consideration of their mutual promises, and other good and valuable consideration, it is agreed as follows:

ARTICLE 1
DEFINITIONS

When used in this Agreement, the following terms shall have the meanings set forth below:

1.1   Adjusted Capital Contribution.

"Adjusted Capital Contribution" in respect to any partner shall mean the initial investment of such partner increased by the amount of any additional contributions made by such partner to the partnership's capital and decreased by the amount of any capital distributions received by such partner.

1.2   Adjusted Capital Account.

"Adjusted Capital Account" in respect to any partner shall mean: The original capital contribution to the partnership of such partner, increased by (i) additional capital

continued

Exhibit 7-1 *continued*

contributions, if any, and (ii) his distributive share of partnership profits, including gains; and decreased by (a) distributions in reduction of partnership capital and (b) his distributive share of partnership losses.

1.3 Agreement.

"Agreement" shall mean this Agreement of Limited Partnership and any written amendments to it.

1.4 Capital Contribution.

"Capital Contribution" shall mean the total amount contributed to the partnership by any partner or all of the partners.

1.5 Cash Flow.

"Net Cash Flow" for any period shall mean the net income of the partnership for such period as ascertained through generally accepted accounting principles consistently applied, plus depreciation and any other non-cash charges that were deducted in determining such net income, and minus capital expenditures and any other cash expenditures and accrual items which have not been deducted in determining the net income of the partnership. "Distributable Cash Flow" for any period shall mean the net cash flow less any amounts set aside by the general partner to provide a reasonable reserve for the continuing conduct of the business of the partnership and for normal working capital. The amount of such reserve shall be determined by the general partner in his sole discretion and may include cash funds at least equal to the reasonably foreseeable cash requirements of the partnership for repair, replacement and refurbishment of partnership assets and for any other partnership operations for the ensuing 12-month period.

1.6 Internal Revenue Code.

"Code" shall mean the Internal Revenue Code of 1986 and any amendments to it.

1.7 Management Agreement.

"Management Agreement" shall mean the Management Agreement between the partnership and, dated _____, 200___.

1.8 General Partner.

"General Partner" shall mean the corporation identified in Exhibit A. If there is more than one general partner, unless otherwise indicated, the term "General Partner" shall include all general partners.

1.9 Initial Investment.

"Initial Investment" in respect to any partner shall mean the amount set forth opposite his name under the caption "Initial Investment" in Exhibit "A" attached hereto, which exhibit shall indicate the name, residence address, partnership percentage, (subject to the provisions of Article 9) and the initial investment of each partner.

continued

Exhibit 7-1   *continued*

1.10 Limited Partner.

"Limited Partner" shall mean the original limited partner and such other persons who are admitted to the partnership either as additional or substituted limited partners and who are then owners of an interest in the partnership. Reference to a "limited partner" shall mean any of the limited partners. If there is more than one limited partner, the term "Limited Partner" shall include all limited partners.

1.11 Partners.

"Partners" shall mean collectively the general and limited partners. Reference to a partner shall mean anyone of the partners.

1.12 Partnership.

"Partnership" shall mean the limited partnership created under this Agreement.

1.13 Partnership Percentage.

"Partnership Percentage" of any partner shall mean that fraction, expressed as a percentage, which represents each partner's share of the profits of the partnership, as shown on Exhibit "A" attached, and as set forth in Article 9.

1.14 Unit.

"Unit" shall mean the interest of a limited partner attributed to an initial capital contribution of $_____.

ARTICLE 2
ORGANIZATION

2.1 Formation.

The general partner and limited partners agree to form a limited partnership (the "partnership" herein) pursuant to the Uniform Limited Partnership Act ("Act") of the State of _____.

2.2 Name.

The name of the partnership shall be _____.

ARTICLE 3
PRINCIPAL PLACE OF BUSINESS

The principal place of business of the partnership shall be located at _____, or places as the general partner may hereafter determine.

continued

Exhibit 7-1 *continued*

ARTICLE 4
BUSINESS

The character of the business of the partnership shall be the establishment and operation of an enterprise to _____. The partnership may also engage in any other lawful business.

ARTICLE 5
COMMENCEMENT DATE

The partnership shall commence upon the recording of the Certificate of Limited Partnership of the partnership and shall continue until completion of partnership business (unless terminated sooner because of the dissolution and winding up of the partnership in accordance with the provisions of Article 12 hereof or by operation of law) or January 1, 2040, whichever first occurs.

ARTICLE 6
PARTNERS, CAPITAL CONTRIBUTIONS AND STATUS

6.1 Initial Investment.

Each partner shall contribute to the capital of the partnership cash in the amount of his initial investment.

6.2 Additional Contributions.

No partner shall be obligated to contribute additional capital to the partnership.

6.3 Role of Limited Partner.

6.3.1 Limitation on Limited Partner's Liabilities.
A limited partner shall not be bound by, or be personally liable for, the expenses, liabilities or obligations of the partnership or the general partner and the liability of each limited partner shall be limited solely to the amount of his contribution to the capital of the partnership as herein provided.

6.3.2 No Control of Business or Right to Act for Partnership.
A limited partner shall take no part in the management, conduct, or control of the business of the partnership and shall have no right or authority to act for or to bind the partnership.

6.3.3 No Priority.
Except as otherwise specifically set forth herein, no limited partner shall have the right to demand or receive property other than cash in return of his capital contribution or as to distribution of income. No limited partner shall have priority over any other limited partner either as to the return of his original contribution to the capital of the partnership or as to distribution.

continued

Exhibit 7-1 *continued*

ARTICLE 7.1
DUTIES OF AND COMPENSATION TO GENERAL PARTNER

The general partner will be responsible for managing the overall affairs of the partnership.

7.1 Reimbursements.

The partnership shall pay or reimburse the general partner for all reasonable and direct costs and expenses incurred in serving and acting as general partner.

7.2 No Other Compensation.

The general partner shall not be entitled to any salary, fee or other compensation from the partnership except through the provisions of Article 7, Paragraph 7.1 and the Management Agreement.

ARTICLE 8
TAX ELECTION.

The general partner, in its sole discretion, may cause the partnership to make or revoke the elections referred to in Sections 754 and 179 of the Code or any similar provision or provisions enacted in lieu thereof whenever it determines, in the exercise of its reasonable judgment, that the making or revoking thereof would be in the best interests of the partnership.

ARTICLE 9
ALLOCATION OF PROFITS, LOSSES AND CASH DISTRIBUTIONS

9.1 Profits and Losses.

9.1.1 Except as otherwise provided in this Paragraph 9.1, all profits, losses, and credits shall be allocated 90% to the limited partners, in proportion to their respective percentage ownership of the limited partnership interests listed in Exhibit "A" to this agreement, and 10% to the general partner(s) in proportion to their respective percentage ownership of the general partnership interests listed in Exhibit "A" to this agreement.

9.1.2 Notwithstanding Paragraph 9.1.1, if a partner loans funds to the partnership pursuant to Paragraph 9.5, then from and after the date of any such loan, 100% of the interest deductions to which the Partnership is entitled under Section 163(e) of the Code attributable to such loan shall be allocated to the partner or partners making such loan.

9.1.3 Gain arising from the realization of capital proceeds shall be allocated in the following order of priority:
(a) To partners with negative adjusted capital account balances, an amount of gain equal to the sum of the negative adjusted capital account balances, which gain shall be allocated among such partners in proportion to their respective negative balances; and
(b) Any remaining gain shall be allocated to the partners in proportion to the total of their respective distributions which Paragraph 9.3 provides they are entitled to under Paragraphs 12.2.3, 12.2.4 and 12.2.5.

continued

Exhibit 7-1 *continued*

9.1.4 Losses of the partnership arising from an event that would give rise to capital proceeds shall be allocated as follows:

(a) First, to the partners with positive capital accounts, pro rata in accordance with such positive capital accounts, until the positive capital account of each partner is brought to zero, but no losses shall be allocated to a partner under this Paragraph 9.1.4(a) once his positive capital account has been brought to zero; and

(b) Second, the balance to the partners, pro rata in accordance with their interests.

9.1.5 The portion of gain allocated to each partner under Paragraph 9.1.3 that should be treated as ordinary income under Sections 1245 or 1250 of the Code, if any, shall be determined by allocating the total amount to be treated as ordinary income under such section among the partners in proportion to the aggregate amounts of depreciation deductions subject to recapture as ordinary income which were previously allocated to such partners, net of any amount previously allocated under this Paragraph 9.1.5.

9.1.6 Profits and losses for all purposes of this agreement shall be determined in accordance with the accounting method followed by the partnership for federal income tax purposes, except that any adjustments made pursuant to Section 743 of the Code shall not be taken into account. Every item of income, gain, loss, deduction, credit or tax preference entering into the computation of such profit or loss, or applicable to the period during which such profit or loss was realized, shall be considered allocated to each partner in the same proportion as profit and loss are allocated to such partner, except as provided in Paragraph 9.1.2.

9.1.7 Profits, losses and credits allocated to an interest assigned or reissued during a fiscal year, other than gain or loss attributable to the sale of the partnership's capital assets, shall be allocated to the person who was the holder of such interest during such fiscal year, in proportion to the number of days that each such holder was recognized as the owner of such interest during such fiscal year or in any other proportion permitted by the Code and selected by the general partner in accordance with this agreement, which may be without regard to the results of partnership operations during the period in which each such holder was recognized as the owner of such interest during such fiscal year, and without regard to the date, amount or recipient of any distributions that may have been made with respect to such interest. Gain or loss attributable to the sale of the partnership's capital assets shall be allocated to the person who was the holder of such interest on the date the asset was sold.

9.1.8 The general partner may amend this agreement by making appropriate changes if the partnership is advised at any time by its legal counsel that the allocations of profits or losses or interest deductions provided in this agreement, or the allocation of non-recourse liabilities to the partners in accordance with their interests, are unlikely to be respected for federal income tax purposes, either because of the promulgation and adoption of Treasury Regulations under Sections 704 or 752 of the Code or other developments in applicable law. In making any such amendment, the general partner shall use his best efforts to affect as little in the economic and tax arrangements among the partners as he shall determine in his sole discretion to be necessary to provide for allocations of profits, losses, deductions and non-recourse liabilities that will be respected for federal income tax purposes. Notwithstanding any such advice of legal counsel that the allocations provided in this agreement are unlikely to be respected for federal income tax purposes due to developments

continued

Exhibit 7-1 *continued*

in applicable law, the general partner shall be under no obligation to amend this agreement if, in the sole judgment of the general partner, the overall interests of the limited partners would be better served by leaving the economic and tax arrangements among the partners unchanged. Any amendment made by the general partner pursuant hereto, or any decision not to amend, shall be deemed to be made in accordance with the fiduciary obligations of the general partner to the partnership and to the limited partners, and no such amendment or failure to amend shall give rise to any claim or cause of action by any limited partner, if such amendment or decision not to amend, as the case may be, is based upon any reasonable evaluation of the pertinent considerations described by the partnership's accountants or counsel.

9.1.9 Income, gain, loss, and deductions with respect to property contributed to the partnership by a partner shall be allocated among the partners so as to take account of any variation between the basis of the property to the partnership and its fair market value at the time of contribution, in accordance with Section 704(C) of the Code.

9.2 Operating Revenues.

Operating revenues shall be distributed in the following order of priority:

9.2.1 To the payment of (a) operating expenses, (b) principal and interest payments due on partnership obligations, including security interests, mortgages and deeds of trust;

9.2.2 To the payment of expenditures for inventory, equipment, capital constructioh, acquisitions, alterations, improvements, replacements, and other similar capital outlay items deemed reasonably necessary by the general partner;

9.2.3 To the establishment and maintenance of any reserves or escrows that the general partner deems reasonably necessary for anticipated liabilities or obligations of the partnership;

9.2.4 To the repayment of any accrued but unpaid fees due to any partner;

9.2.5 The balance to the partners, pro rata in accordance with their interests.

9.2.6 Notwithstanding any other provision of this Paragraph 9.2, the general partner shall not be required to distribute any portion of the partnership's operating revenues if, in the sole judgment of the general partner, the overall interests of the Partnership would be better served by retaining such operating revenues in the partnership. Any decision made by the general partner pursuant to this Paragraph 9.2.6, shall be deemed to be made in accordance with the iduciary obligations of the general partner to the partnership and to the limited partners, and no such decision shall give rise to any claim or cause of action by any partner.

9.3 Capital Proceeds.

Capital proceeds shall be distributed in accordance with the priority established by Paragraph 12.2.1 through Paragraph 12.2.5.

9.4 Allocation of Distributions.

Except as expressly provided otherwise in this agreement, distributions of operating revenues and capital proceeds allocated to partners shall be made to the partners of record on

continued

Exhibit 7-1 *continued*

the record date of the distribution without regard to the length of time the record holder has been such.

9.5 Loans from Partners.

Any partner may loan the partnership such amounts and upon such terms and conditions as the general partner may determine.

ARTICLE 10
POWERS AND DUTIES OF AND RESTRICTIONS UPON THE GENERAL PARTNER

10.1 Powers.

The management and control of the partnership and its affairs and business rests exclusively with the general partner, which shall have all the rights and powers which may be possessed by a general partner pursuant to the Act, and such rights and powers as are otherwise conferred by law or are necessary, advisable, or convenient to the management of the business and affairs of the partnership. Without limiting the generality of the foregoing, the general partner shall have the following rights and powers:

10.1.1 To spend the capital and net income of the partnership in the exercise of any rights or powers possessed by the general partner hereunder.

10.1.2 To purchase, hold, sell, lease, encumber, mortgage, finance, and manage the partnership's interest in partnership property and to enter into agreements with others, with respect to any such activities, which agreements may contain such terms, provisions, and conditions as the general partner in its sole and absolute discretion shall approve.

10.1.3 To purchase and sell personal property incidental to the operation of the partnership's real property and to borrow money to finance the purchase of such personal property.

10.1.4 To purchase from others, at the expense of the partnership, contracts of liability, casualty, and other insurance, which the general partner deems advisable, appropriate, or convenient for the protection of the properties or affairs of the partnership or for any other purpose convenient or beneficial to the partnership.

10.1.5 To invest partnership funds in government securities, certificates of deposit, ready asset funds or money market accounts, banker's acceptances or similar investments.

10.1.6 To borrow money required for the business and affairs of the partnership from others and, except as hereinafter provided, to secure the repayment of such borrowings by executing mortgages, pledging or otherwise encumbering or subjecting to security interests all or any part of the property of the partnership, and to refund, refinance, increase, modify, consolidate or extend the maturity of any indebtedness created by such borrowing, or any mortgage, pledge, encumbrance, or other security device.

10.1.7 To enter into such agreements, contracts, documents, and instruments with such parties and to give all receipts, releases, and discharges with respect to all of the foregoing and any matters incident thereto as the general partner may deem advisable, appropriate, or convenient.

continued

Exhibit 7-1 *continued*

10.2 Independent Activities.

The general partner and each limited partner may, notwithstanding the existence of this Agreement, engage in whatever other activities they choose, without having or incurring any obligation to offer any interest in such other activities to the partnership or any party hereto. Neither this Agreement nor any activity undertaken pursuant thereto shall prevent the general partner from engaging in such other activities, or require the general partner to permit the partnership or any limited partner to participate in any such other activities and, as a material part of the consideration for the general partner's execution hereof, each limited partner hereby waives, relinquishes, and renounces any such right or claim of participation.

10.3 Duties.

The general partner shall manage and control the partnership, its business and affairs, to the best of its ability and shall use its best efforts to carry out the business of the partnership. The general partner shall devote itself to the business of the partnership to the extent that, in its reasonable judgment, it determines is necessary for the efficient carrying on thereof.

10.4 Certain Limitations.

The general partner shall have no authority to:

10.4.1 Do any act which would make it impossible to carryon the ordinary business of the partnership.

10.4.2 Confess a judgment against the partnership.

10.4.3 Admit a person as a general partner or a limited partner except as otherwise provided in this Agreement.

10.4.4 Do any act in contravention of this Agreement.

10.4.5 Execute or deliver any assignment for the benefit of the creditors of the partnership.

10.4.6 Possess partnership property or assign the rights of the partnership in any partnership property for other than a partnership purpose.

10.4.7 Continue the business of the partnership after its adjudication of bankruptcy or dissolution, except as set forth in Article 12 below.

ARTICLE 11
TRANSFER OF PARTNERSHIP INTEREST

11.1 Substitution of Limited Partner.

No limited partner shall have the right to substitute an assignee as a contributor in his place and no assignee of the whole or any portion of a limited partner's interest in the partnership shall become a substituted limited partner in place of his assignor (other than any other partner or a partner's legal representative or any ancestor, descendant, or spouse of a

continued

Exhibit 7-1 *continued*

partner or any custodian for his or her account) unless all of the following conditions are satisfied:

11.1.1 A duly executed and acknowledged written instrument of assignment which is satisfactory in form and substance to the general partner is filed with the partnership and sets forth the intention of the assignor that the assignee become a substituted limited partner in his place.

11.1.2 The assignor and the assignee execute and acknowledge such other instrument or instruments as the general partner may deem necessary or desirable to effectuate such admission, including the written acceptance and adoption by the assignee of all the terms and conditions of this agreement as the same may have been amended.

11.1.3 The written consent of the general partner to such substitution is obtained, the granting or withholding of which shall be within the sole and absolute discretion of the general partner.

11.1.4 The assignee shall have paid to the partnership a transfer fee which is sufficient, in the reasonable judgment of the general partner, to cover all reasonable expenses connected with such assignment and substitution.

11.1.5 An amended certificate of limited partnership listing the assignee as a limited partner, which amended certificate may be signed by the general partner, the assignor and assignee only and need not be signed by the other members of the partnership, is recorded in accordance with the laws of the State of.

11.2 Substitution of Assignee Failing to Satisfy Conditions.

Should the general partner deem in its sole discretion that such treatment is in the best interests of the partnership, then, at the election of the general partner, an assignee may be substituted as a limited partner, notwithstanding his failure to satisfy the conditions hereinabove set forth.

11.3 Assignment of Income.

The general partner's failure or refusal to grant its consent to the substitution of a limited partner shall not affect the validity or effectiveness of any instrument such as an assignment to an assignee of the right to receive the share of the profits or other compensation by way of income, or the return of his contributions, to which his assignor would be entitled and which was thereby assigned; provided a duly executed and acknowledged written instrument of assignment in form satisfactory to the general partner, the terms of which are not in contravention of any of the provisions of this agreement, is filed with the partnership and the assignee shall have paid to the partnership a transfer fee which is sufficient, in the sole and absolute discretion of the general partner, to cover all reasonable expenses connected with such assignment; provided, however, that except as hereinabove provided, the assignor shall continue to be a limited partner with respect to such interest for all purposes of this partnership.

11.4 Purchase of Interests by General Partner.

In the event the general partner acquires the interest of any limited partner, it shall enjoy all of the rights and be subject to all of the obligations and duties of a limited partner in

continued

Exhibit 7-1   *continued*

respect to that interest. With respect to any interest acquired from any limited partner, the general partner shall become a substituted limited partner within the meaning of the Act.

11.5   Termination of Partnership.

Notwithstanding any other provision of this Agreement, no partner shall have the right to assign all or any portion of his interest in partnership capital or his interest in partnership profits if such assignment together with all prior assignments during the same 12-month period, would result in the sale or exchange of 50% or more of the total interest in partnership capital and profits within a 12-month period and thereby result in termination of the partnership pursuant to Section 708(b) of the Code. Any purported assignment in violation of the terms of this section shall be null and void and of no force or effect.

ARTICLE 12
DISSOLUTION AND WINDING UP OF THE PARTNERSHIP.

12.1   Dissolution of the Partnership.

The partnership shall be dissolved upon the happening of any of the following events:

12.1.1   The resignation, adjudication of bankruptcy or dissolution of the general partner unless within six months after the occurrence of any such event, a successor general partner is elected by unanimous vote of the other partners with the consent of the general partner or its legal representative (which may be granted or denied for any reason), which successor elects to continue the business of the partnership.

12.1.2   Expiration of the term of the partnership as set forth in Article 5 hereof.

12.1.3   One year after the divestiture of all interest of the partnership in all property owned by it (the holding of a security interest or lien only by the partnership in such property being considered a divestiture of all interest for the purposes of this provision).

12.2   Winding Up of the Partnership.

Upon the dissolution of the partnership, the partnership shall be terminated, in which event the general partner shall take full account of the partnership's assets and liabilities and the receivables of the partnership shall be collected and its assets liquidated as promptly as is consistent with obtaining the fair market value thereof; provided, however, that the general partner may, in its sole discretion, distribute all or any portion of the assets of the partnership in kind. Upon dissolution, the partnership shall engage in no further business thereafter other than that necessary to collect its receivables and liquidate its assets. The proceeds from the liquidation of the assets of the partnership and collection of the receivables of the partnership, together with the assets distributed in kind, to the extent sufficient therefor, shall be applied and distributed in the following order:

12.2.1   To the payment and discharge of all of the partnership's debts and liabilities, including all sums due pursuant to Article 7 above and sums due partners on loans to the partnership, and except the claims of secured creditors whose obligations will be assumed or otherwise transferred on the liquidation of the partnership's assets.

continued

Exhibit 7-1 *continued*

12.2.2 To the creation of any reserves which the general partner may deem reasonably necessary.

12.2.3 To the limited partners, a sum equal to the adjusted capital account of each limited partner.

12.2.4 To the general partner, a sum equal to its adjusted capital account.

12.2.5 The balance, if any, shall be distributed and paid to the partners in accordance with their partnership percentages.

ARTICLE 13
BOOKS OF ACCOUNT, ACCOUNTING AND REPORTS

13.1 Books of Account.

The general partner shall keep adequate books of account of the partnership wherein shall be recorded and reflected all of the contributions to the capital of the partnership, and all of the income, expenses, and transactions of the partnership. Such books of account shall be kept at the principal place of business of the partnership and each partner and his authorized representatives shall have at all times, during reasonable business hours, free access to and the right to inspect and copy such books of account, provided that such inspection is made in good faith and without any intent to damage the partnership or any of the partners.

13.2 Accounting and Reports.

At least once a year, within 90 days after the close of the partnership's fiscal year, the general partner shall cause financial statements to be prepared without audit, at the expense of the partnership, by a certified public accountant retained by the general partner, and will transmit to each partner an annual report of the partnership relating to the prior fiscal year.

13.3 Tax Returns.

In addition, the general partner shall cause income tax returns for the partnership to be prepared and filed with the appropriate authorities and, within 90 days after the close of each fiscal year of the partnership, shall furnish copies of the income tax returns for such fiscal year to the limited partners. The cost of said returns and their preparation shall be borne by the partnership.

13.4 Fiscal Year.

The partnership shall adopt a fiscal year which shall begin on January 1 and end on December 31 of each year.

13.5 Banking.

All funds of the partnership shall be deposited in a separate bank account or accounts in the partnership name as shall be determined by the general partner. All withdrawals therefrom shall be made upon checks signed by the general partner or by any other person specifically authorized to do so by the general partner.

continued

Exhibit 7-1 *continued*

ARTICLE 14
POWER OF ATTORNEY

14.1 Appointment.

Each limited partner (including any substituted limited partner) hereby designates and appoints the general partner as his attorney-in-fact with power of substitution to act in his name and on his behalf in the execution, acknowledgment and filing of documents as follows:

14.1.1 Certificates of Limited Partnership, as well as amendments thereto, under the laws of the State of _____ and the laws of any other states in which such a certificate is required to be filed.

14.1.2 Any other instrument which may be required to be filed by the partnership under the laws of any state or by any governmental agency, or which the general partner deems it advisable to file; and

14.1.3 Any documents which may be required to effect the continuation of the partnership, the admission of an additional or substituted limited partner or the dissolution and termination of the partnership, provided any such continuation, admission, or dissolution and termination is in accordance with the terms of this Agreement.

14.2 Powers.

The power of attorney granted by each limited partner to the general partner as hereinabove provided:

14.2.1 Is a special power of attorney coupled with an interest and is irrevocable and shall survive the death, incapacity, insolvency, dissolution, disability or incompetency of a limited partner, or any termination by a limited partner.

14.2.2 May be exercised by the general partner for each limited partner by a facsimile signature of an authorized officer of the general partner or by listing each limited partner and executing any instrument with a facsimile signature of an authorized officer of the general partner acting as attorney-in-fact for all of them; and

14.2.3 Shall survive the delivery of an assignment by a limited partner of the whole or any portion of his interest in the partnership except that, where the assignee thereof has been approved by the general partner for admission to the partnership as a substitute limited partner, the power of attorney shall survive the delivery of such assignment for the sole purpose of enabling the general partner to execute, acknowledge, and file any instrument necessary to effect such substitution.

ARTICLE 15
MISCELLANEOUS

15.1 Exculpation and Indemnification.

15.1.1 The general partner shall not be personally liable for the return of any contribution made to the partnership by a limited partner. No general partner shall be personally

continued

Exhibit 7-1   *continued*

liable to the partnership or to the limited partners for any act or omission performed or omitted by him so long as by acting or omitting to act he is not guilty of fraud, bad faith or gross negligence.

15.1.2   The partnership shall indemnify and hold harmless, to the extent there is cash available after paying or providing for the payment of all other partnership expenses, the general partner and any employee or agent of the general partner, and any partnership employee or agent, (an "indemnified party") from any loss, damage, fine, penalty, expense (including attorneys' fees) judgment or amount paid in settlement incurred by such indemnified party by reason of his performance or non- performance of any act concerning the activities of the partnership or in furtherance of its interests or purposes; provided, however, that there shall be no indemnification in relation to matters as to which such indemnified party is adjudged to have been guilty of fraud, bad faith or gross negligence.

15.1.3   Expenses incurred in defending a civil or criminal action, suit or proceeding may be paid by the partnership in advance of the final disposition of such action, suit or proceeding upon receipt of an undertaking by or on behalf of an indemnified party to repay such amount unless it shall ultimately be determined that he is entitled to be indemnified by the partnership as authorized herein.

15.1.4   The indemnification provided by this Paragraph 15.1 shall not be deemed exclusive of any other rights to which an indemnified party may be entitled under any agreement, vote of limited partners or otherwise, and shall continue as to a person who has ceased to be an indemnified party and shall inure to the benefit of the heirs, executors and administrators of. such a person.

15.1.5   The partnership shall have power to purchase and maintain insurance on behalf of any person who is or was an indemnified party against any liability asserted against him and incurred by him in any such capacity, or arising out of his status as such, whether or not the partnership would have the power to indemnify him against such liability under the provisions of this section.

15.2   Notices.

All notices, demands, and communications of any kind which any partner may be required or desires to serve upon any other partner under the terms of this Agreement shall be in writing and shall be served upon such other partner by personal service upon such other partner or by leaving a copy of such notice, demand, or other communications, addressed to such other partner, at his address set forth in the Certificate of Limited Partnership of the partnership, as amended from time to time, whereupon service shall be deemed complete, or by mailing a copy thereof by certified or registered mail, postage prepaid, with return receipt requested, addressed to such address. In case of service by mail, it shall be deemed complete on the day of actual delivery as shown by the addressee's receipt or at the expiration of the third day after the date of mailing, whichever is earlier in time. The address to which notices, demands and other communications to the general partner shall be delivered or sent may be changed from time to time by notice served as hereinabove provided by the general partner upon the limited partners. The address to which notices, demands, and other communications to any limited partner shall be delivered or

continued

Exhibit 7-1 *continued*

sent may be changed from time to time by notice served as hereinabove provided by any limited partner upon the general who shall notify the other limited partners of such change of address. Any payment required or permitted to be made to any partner under any provision of this Agreement shall be deemed to have been made if delivered or mailed in the manner hereinabove provided to the address to which notices, demands, and other communications to such partners are to be delivered pursuant to the foregoing.

15.3 Article and Section Headings.

Article, section and other headings contained in this Agreement are for reference purposes only and are in no way intended to describe, interpret, define or limit the scope, extent, or intent of this Agreement or any provision hereof.

15.4 Severability.

Every provision of this Agreement is intended to be severable. If any term or provision hereof is illegal or invalid for any reason whatsoever, such illegality or invalidity shall not affect the validity of the remainder of this Agreement.

15.5 Amendments.

Amendments to this Agreement may be proposed by the general partner or by limited partners having an aggregate partnership percentage of at least 40%. Following such proposal, the general partner shall submit to the limited partner a verbatim statement of any proposed amendment provided that counsel for the partnership shall have approved the same in writing as to form, and shall include in any such submission the general partner's recommendation as to the proposed amendment. The general partner shall seek the written vote of the limited partner(s) on the proposed amendment or shall call a meeting to vote thereon and for the purpose of transacting any other business that it may deem appropriate. For purposes of obtaining a written vote, the general partner may require response within a specified time and failure to respond shall constitute a vote which is consistent with the general partner's recommendation with respect thereto. A proposed amendment shall be adopted and effective as an amendment hereto if it receives the vote of the general partner and limited partner(s) having an aggregate partnership percentage of more than 50%.

Notwithstanding anything to the contrary in the preceding paragraph, no amendment shall, without the prior written approval of all partners (a) add to, subtract from or otherwise modify the purpose of the partnership or the character of its business, (b) change the method of determining "partnership percentage", allocating profits or losses or making distributions, (c) enlarge the obligation of any partner to make contributions to the capital of the partnership or change the definition of initial investment, (d) modify the order of distribution, (e) enlarge the liability of the general partner, or affect the role of the limited partners as provided in paragraph 6.3, (f) affect the authority of the general partner to withhold its consent to the substitution of a limited partner, (g) reduce the vote required to elect a successor general partner, or (h) amend this paragraph 15.5.

15.6 Meetings and Means of Voting.

Meetings of the partners may be called by the general partner and shall be called upon written request of the limited partner(s) having an aggregate partnership percentage of at least 40%. The call shall be in writing and shall state the nature of the business to be transacted which shall be limited to those matters upon which the limited partner(s) have the

continued

Exhibit 7-1 *continued*

right to vote pursuant to this Agreement. Notice of any such meeting shall be given to all partners in the manner described in paragraph 15.2 hereof not less than 10 days nor more than 30 days prior to the date of such meeting. Partners may vote in person or by proxy at any such meeting. Notwithstanding anything to the contrary contained herein, anytime that a vote of the limited partner(s) of the partnership is called for by this Agreement, such limited partner(s) may vote by a written instrument or by their failure to respond to the request for such written vote in accordance with the procedure set forth in paragraph 15.5 of this Agreement.

15.7 Right to Rely Upon the Authority of General Partner.

No person dealing with the general partner shall be required to determine its authority to make any commitment or undertaking on behalf of the partnership nor to determine any fact or circumstance bearing upon the existence of its authority. In addition, no purchaser of any property or interest owned by the partnership shall be required to determine the sole and exclusive authority of the general partner to sign and deliver on behalf of the partnership any such instrument or transfer, or to see to the application or distribution of revenues or proceeds paid or credited in connection therewith, unless such purchaser shall have received written notice affecting the same.

15.8 _____ Law.

It is the intention of the parties that the laws of the State of _____ govern the validity of this agreement, the construction of its terms and the interpretation of the rights and duties of the parties.

15.9 Waiver of Action for Partition.

Each of the parties hereto irrevocably waives during the term of the partnership and during any period of winding up and dissolution of the partnership any right that it may have to maintain any action for partition with respect to the property of the partnership.

15.10 Counterpart Execution.

This Agreement may be executed in any number of counterparts with the same effect as if all parties hereto have signed the same document. All counterparts shall be construed together and shall constitute one agreement.

15.11 Parties in Interest.

Subject to the provisions contained in Article 11 hereof, each and all of the covenants, terms, provisions, and agreements herein contained shall be binding upon and inure to the benefit of the heirs, executors, administrators, successors, and assigns of the respective parties hereto.

15.12 Time.

Time is of the essence with respect to this Agreement with respect to payments required to be made by partners to the partnership.

15.13 Integrated Agreement.

This Agreement constitutes the entire understanding and agreement among the parties hereto with respect to the subject matter hereof, and there are no agreements, undertakings,

continued

Exhibit 7-1 *continued*

restrictions, representations, or warranties among the parties other than those set forth herein and provided for. It is the mutual product of the parties, and any rules of construction relating to the preparer of a document shall not apply in any construction or interpretation of this Agreement.

15.14 Meaning of Terms.

Where the context so requires, the use of the neuter gender shall include the masculine and feminine genders and the singular shall include the plural and vice-versa, and the word "person" shall include corporation, firm, partnership, or other form of association.

ARTICLE 16
ACKNOWLEDGMENTS BY LIMITED PARTNERS

16.1 Acknowledgments.

The limited partner, and any additional or substituted limited partner, acknowledges and represents to the partnership, to the general partner, and to its officers and directors that:

16.1.1 He has not been induced to enter into this transaction through any public solicitation or advertising in the State of _____ or elsewhere, and they have no knowledge of any such public solicitation or advertising in _____ or elsewhere.

16.1.2 He has had reasonable access to full and fair disclosure of all material information concerning the partnership, the property, the general partner, the purposes of the partnership, and all other aspects of the partnership.

16.1.3 He is familiar with business transactions of this nature, and he has also retained or had the opportunity to retain counsel of his choice to represent him prior to executing this Agreement, and has received or had the opportunity to receive advice of counsel with respect to this Agreement prior to executing it. He has further obtained or has had adequate opportunity to seek and obtain any other professional advice he may have desired prior to executing this Agreement.

16.1.4 He acknowledges that this is a transaction exempt from the registration requirements of Chapter 517, _____ Statutes, and applicable rules and regulations of the Division of Securities of the State of _____.

16.1.5 He acknowledges that this is a transaction exempt from the registration requirements of federal laws relating to securities and applicable rules and regulations of the Securities Exchange Commission.

IN WITNESS WHEREOF, the undersigned have executed this Agreement as of the day and year first hereinabove written.

GENERAL PARTNER: LIMITED PARTNER(S):

                                                    See signature pages attached

By: _____

continued

Exhibit 7-1 *continued*

EXHIBIT A

NAME AND ADDRESS	FEDERAL ID or SSN	TAX	INITIAL INVESTMENT	PARTNERSHIP PERCENTAGE
General Partner:				
		$		10%
Limited Partners:				
		$		90%
TOTAL		$		100%

FLORIDA PARTNERSHIP FILINGS

The state of Florida requires that a partnership files certain documents with the Division of Corporations. Other states have similar requirements. For the rules in your own state, consult the state's Web page for the secretary of state or the Division of Corporations.

The Partnership Registration Statement form, shown in Exhibit 7-2, requires the following information:

1. Name of partnership
2. State and county of formation
3. Number FEI
4. Street address of chief executive office
5. Principal offices in Florida
6. Either a list of all partners or list the name and street address of the agent in Florida who will maintain the list of all partners.

The document must be signed by two partners and submitted to the Division of Corporations with the filing fee listed.

Florida Statement of Partnership Authority

After the partnership registration is submitted, the statement of partnership authority as shown in Exhibit 7-3 is required. The following items are required:

FIRST: The name of the partnership
SECOND: The date of registration and the number assigned by the state
THIRD: Names and addresses of partners who may transfer real property
FOURTH: Authority or limitations on any partners, along with names and addresses

Two partners must sign this document. It is submitted to the Division of Corporations with the filing fee.

Florida Statement of Partnership Merger

After a partnership merger, the surviving partnership or limited partnership may file this statement that the partnerships or limited partnerships have merged into the surviving entity. See Exhibit 7-4. The items to be completed follow:

1. Name of partnerships or limited partnerships
2. Name of surviving entity
3. Street address of surviving entity (new organization)
4. Check appropriate box.

This document must be signed by two partners and submitted to the state with filing fee.

EXHIBIT 7-2 Florida Partnership Registration Statement

PARTNERSHIP REGISTRATION STATEMENT

1._____
(Name of Partnership)

2._____ 3._____
(State/County of Formation)   (FEI Number)

4._____
(Street Address of Chief Executive Office)

5._____

_____
(Street Address of Principal Office in Florida, if applicable)

6. In accordance with s. 620.8105(1)(c)(1 & 2), Florida Statutes, required partner information is provided in one of the following options:

❑　Attached is a list of the names and mailing addresses of ALL partners and Florida Registration Numbers, if other than individuals, **or:**

❑　The name and street address of the agent in Florida who shall maintain a list of the names and addresses of all partners:

NAME & FLORIDA STREET ADDRESS OF FLORIDA AGENT　　　**IF OTHER THAN INDIVIDUAL, FLORIDA REGISTRATION NUMBER**

_____　　_____

_____

_____

If any of the partners are other than individuals, its entity name and Florida Registration Number must be listed below:

_____　　_____

_____　　_____

_____　　_____
Partner Entity Name　　　　　　　　　Florida Document Number

The execution of this statement as a partner constitutes an affirmation under the penalties of perjury that the facts stated herein are true.

Signed this _____ day of _____, _____.

Signatures of <u>TWO</u> Partners:　　_____

_____

Typed or printed names of partners signing above:_____

_____

Filing Fee:	$50.00
Certified copy:	$52.50 (optional)
Certificate of Status:	$ 8.75 (optional)

CR2E074(1/00)　　**Division of Corporations P.O. Box 6327 Tallahassee, FL 32314**

EXHIBIT 7-3   Florida Statement of Partnership Authority

STATEMENT OF PARTNERSHIP AUTHORITY

Pursuant to section 620.8303, Florida Statutes, this partnership submits the following statement of partnership authority:

(Note: A statement of partnership authority cannot be filed with the Florida Department of State unless a partnership registration was previously filed and is of record with this office.)

FIRST: The name of the partnership is:_____

_____

SECOND: The partnership was registered with the Florida Department of State on _____ and assigned registration number _____ .

THIRD: The names and addresses of the partners authorized to execute an instrument transferring real property held in the name of the partnership are:

_____   _____
_____   _____
_____   _____

_____   _____
_____   _____
_____   _____

(Please list additional partners on attachment, if necessary)

FOURTH: If applicable, state or include the authority, or limitations on the authority, of any of the partners to enter into other transactions on behalf of the partnership, and any other matter:

Names and addresses of Partners: **Statement of Authority or Limitation of Authority:**

_____   _____
_____   _____
_____   _____

_____   _____
_____   _____
_____   _____

(Please list additional partners on attachment, if applicable.)

The execution of this statement as a partner constitutes an affirmation under the penalties of perjury that the facts stated herein are true.

Signed this _____ day of _____, _____ .

Signatures of TWO Partners:_____

_____

Typed or printed names of partners signing above:

_____

_____

NOTE: A FILED STATEMENT OF PARTNERSHIP AUTHORITY IS CANCELED FIVE YEARS AFTER THE DATE ON WHICH THIS STATEMENT, OR THE MOST RECENT AMENDMENT, WAS FILED WITH THE DEPARTMENT OF STATE.

Filing Fee:	$25.00
Certified copy:	$52.50 (optional)
Certificate of Status:	$ 8.75 (optional)

CR2E072(1/00)

Division of Corporations P.O. Box 6327 Tallahassee, FL 32314

EXHIBIT 7-4 Florida Statement of Partnership Merger

STATEMENT OF PARTNERSHIP MERGER

Pursuant to s. 620.8907, Florida Statutes, after a merger, the surviving partnership or limited partnership may file a statement that one or more partnerships or limited partnerships have merged into the surviving entity.

1. The name of each partnership or limited partnership, as identified in the records of the Department of State that is a party to the merger:

_____   _____

_____   _____

_____   _____

_____   _____
                     (Entity name)   (Document number)

2. The name of the surviving entity into which the partnerships or limited partnerships were merged:

_____

3. The street address of the surviving entity's chief executive office and of an office in this state, if any:

_____

_____

4. The surviving entity of the merger is:

   ❑ A partnership

   ❑ A limited partnership

The execution of this statement as a partner constitutes an affirmation under the penalties of perjury that the facts stated herein are true.

Signed this _____day of _____, _____.

Signatures of <u>TWO</u> Partners: _____

                                  _____

Typed or printed names of partners signing above: _____

                                     _____

Filing Fee:	$25.00 per party
Certified copy:	$52.50 (optional)
Certificate of Status:	$ 8.75 (optional)

Make checks payable to Florida Department of State and mail to:
Division of Corporations P.O. Box 6327 Tallahassee, FL 32314

CR2E075(1/00)

DELAWARE PARTNERSHIP

Similar forms are required in the state of Delaware for the formation of a partnership. These forms must be filed with the state:

Delaware Statement of Partnership Existence (Exhibit 7-5)

1. Name of partnership
2. Address and name of partnership's agent in Delaware

Signature of authorized partner.

Delaware Statement of Qualification

This form (Exhibit 7-6) is required for limited liability partnerships.

First: Name of limited liability partnership

Second: Address of agent in Delaware

Third: Number of partners

Fourth: Nothing to be completed

Fifth: Effective date

Signature of authorized partner.

Certificate of Limited Partnership

This form (Exhibit 7-7) is required for limited partnerships in Delaware.

First: Name of limited partnership

Second: Address of office in Delaware and agent

Third: Name and address of each general partner

Signature of general partner.

EXHIBIT 7-5   Delaware Statement of Partnership Existence

STATE OF DELAWARE
STATEMENT OF PARTNERSHIP EXISTENCE
OF

_____

1.   The name of the partnership is _____

_____.

2.   The address of its registered agent in the State of Delaware is_____

_____

in the city of _____.

The name of the registered agent is _____

_____.

IN WITNESS WHEREOF, the undersigned has executed this Statement of

Partnership of _____

this _____ day of _____, _____A.D.

_____
Authorized Partner(s)

_____
Print or Type Name(s)

EXHIBIT 7-6 Delaware Statement of Partnership Authority (Qualification)

STATEMENT OF PARTNERSHIP AUTHORITY

Pursuant to section 620.8303, Florida Statutes, this partnership submits the following statement of partnership authority:

(Note: A statement of partnership authority cannot be filed with the Florida Department of State unless a partnership registration was previously filed and is of record with this office.)

FIRST: The name of the partnership is:_____

_____

SECOND: The partnership was registered with the Florida Department of State on _____
and assigned registration number _____ .

THIRD: The names and addresses of the partners authorized to execute an instrument transferring real property held in the name of the partnership are:

(Please list additional partners on attachment, if necessary)

FOURTH: If applicable, state or include the authority, or limitations on the authority, of any of the partners to enter into other transactions on behalf of the partnership, and any other matter:

Names and addresses of Partners: **Statement of Authority or Limitation of Authority:**

(Please list additional partners on attachment, if applicable.)

The execution of this statement as a partner constitutes an affirmation under the penalties of perjury that the facts stated herein are true.

Signed this _____ day of _____, _____ .

Signatures of TWO Partners:_____

_____

Typed or printed names of partners signing above:

_____

_____

NOTE: A FILED STATEMENT OF PARTNERSHIP AUTHORITY IS CANCELED FIVE YEARS AFTER THE DATE ON WHICH THIS STATEMENT, OR THE MOST RECENT AMENDMENT, WAS FILED WITH THE DEPARTMENT OF STATE.

Filing Fee:	$25.00
Certified copy:	$52.50 (optional)
Certificate of Status:	$ 8.75 (optional)

CR2E072(1/00)

Division of Corporations P.O. Box 6327 Tallahassee, FL 32314

EXHIBIT 7-7 Delaware Certificate of Limited Partnership

STATE OF DELAWARE
CERTIFICATE OF LIMITED PARTNERSHIP

- **The Undersigned,** desiring to form a limited partnership pursuant to the Delaware Revised Uniform Limited Partnership Act, 6 Delaware Code, Chapter 17, do hereby certify as follows:

- **First:** The name of the limited partnership is _____
_____.

- **Second:** The address of its registered office in the State of Delaware is _____
_____ in the city of _____.
The name of the Registered Agent at such address is _____
_____.

- **Third:** The name and mailing address of each general partner is as follows:
_____

_____

_____

_____

- **In Witness Whereof,** the undersigned has executed this Certificate of Limited Partnership of
_____ as of
_____.

By:_____
        General Partner

Name:_____
        (type or print name)

LIMITED LIABILITY COMPANIES

Limited liability companies are described in Chapter 11 of the text-book. Most states require formation documents to be filed with the Department of Corporations or the secretary of state. Forms for your own state may be found either on the web site or from the departments.

DELAWARE

A Certificate of Formation, shown in Exhibit 7-8, is required to form a limited liability company. The format is outlined below as follows:

First: Name of company

Second: Address of registered office in Delaware

Third: Date of dissolution (if appropriate)

Fourth: Any other items the members determine to include

Signature of authorized person.

FLORIDA

The various forms and instructions to form a Florida Limited Liability Corporation are shown in Exhibit 7-9. The instructions are given on the Florida Web site.

EXHIBIT 7-8 Delaware Limited Liability Company Certificate of Formation

STATE *of* DELAWARE
LIMITED LIABILITY COMPANY
CERTIFICATE *of* FORMATION

- **First:** The name of the limited liability company is _____
  _____

- **Second:** The address of its registered office in the State of Delaware is _____
  _____ in the City of _____. The name of its
  Registered agent at such address is _____
  _____

- **Third:** (Use this paragraph only if the company is to have a specific effective date of dissolution: "The
  latest date on which the limited liability company is to dissolve is _____.")
- **Fourth:** (Insert any other matters the members determine to include herein.)
  _____
  _____
  _____
  _____
  _____

In Witness Whereof, the undersigned have executed this Certificate of Formation of
_____this _____ day of _____, 20_____.

By:_____
   Authorized Person(s)

Name:_____
   Typed or Printed

EXHIBIT 7-9 Florida Limited Liability Company

Attached are the forms and instructions to form a *Florida Limited Liability Company* pursuant to Chapter 608, Florida Statutes. All information included in the articles of organization must be in English and must be typewritten or printed legibly. If this requirement is not met, the document will be returned for correction(s). The Division of Corporations suggests using the sample articles merely as a guideline. Pursuant to s. 608.407, Florida Statutes, additional information may be contained in the articles of organization.

Pursuant to section 608.406(2), the name of the limited liability company shall be filed with the Department of State for public notice only and shall not alone create any presumption of ownership beyond that which is created under the common law. The Department of State shall record the name without regard to any other name recorded.

NOTE: This form for filing Articles of Organization is basic. Each limited liability company is a separate entity and as such has specific goals, needs, and requirements. Additionally, the tax consequences arising from the structure of a limited liability company can be significant. The Division of Corporations recommends that all documents be reviewed by your legal counsel. The Division is a filing agency and as such does not render any legal, accounting, or tax advice. The professional advice of your legal counsel to ascertain exact compliance with all statutory requirements is strongly recommended.

Pursuant to s. 608.407, Florida Statutes, the articles of organization must set forth the following:

ARTICLE I:

The name of the limited liability company, which **must** end with the words "limited liability company" or "limited company" or their abbreviation "L.L.C.", "L.C.", "LLC" or "LC". (The word "limited" may be abbreviated as "Ltd." and the word "company" may be abbreviated as "Co".)

ARTICLE II:
The mailing address and the street address of the principal office of the limited liability company.

ARTICLE III:
The name and Florida street address of the limited liability company's registered agent. The registered agent must sign and state that he/she is familiar with and accepts the obligations of the position.

ARTICLE IV: The name and address of each Manager or Managing member. Insert "MGR" for each Manager. Insert "MGRM" for each Managing Member. **IMPORTANT: Most financial institutions require this information to be recorded with the Florida Department of State.**

continued

Exhibit 7-9   *continued*

Articles of organization must be executed by at least one member or authorized representative of a member, and the execution of the document constitutes an affirmation under the penalties of perjury that the facts stated therein are true.

If an effective date is listed, the date must be specific and cannot be more than five business days prior to or 90 days after the date of filing.

FILING FEES:

$ 100.00 Filing Fee for Articles of Organization
$ 25.00 Designation of Registered Agent
$ 30.00 Certified Copy (OPTIONAL)
$ 5.00 Certificate of Status (OPTIONAL)

A letter of acknowledgment will be issued free of charge upon registration. Please submit one check made payable to the Florida Department of State for the total amount of the filing fees and any optional certificate or copy.

A cover letter containing your name, address and daytime telephone number should be submitted along with the articles of organization and the check. The mailing address and courier address are:

Mailing Address	**Street Address**
Registration Section	Registration Section
Division of Corporations	Division of Corporations
Post Office Box 6327	409 E. Gaines St.
Tallahassee, FL 32314	Tallahassee, FL 32399
(850) 245-6051	(850) 245-6051

Any further inquiries concerning this matter should be directed to the Registration Section by calling (850) 245-6051.

continued

Exhibit 7-9 *continued*

TRANSMITTAL LETTER

TO: Registration Section
Division of Corporations

SUBJECT: _____
(Name of Limited Liability Company)

The enclosed Articles of Organization and fee(s) are submitted for filing.

Please return all correspondence concerning this matter to the following:

_____
(Name of Person)

_____
(Firm/Company)

_____
(Address)

_____
(City/State and Zip Code)

For further information concerning this matter, please call:

_____ at (_____) _____
(Name of Person)   (Area Code & Daytime Telephone Number)

STREET ADDRESS: **MAILING ADDRESS:**
Registration Section   Registration Section
Division of Corporations   Division of Corporations
409 E. Gaines Street   P.O. Box 6327
Tallahassee, Florida 32399   Tallahassee, Florida 32314

continued

Exhibit 7-9 *continued*

ARTICLES OF ORGANIZATION FOR FLORIDA LIMITED LIABILITY COMPANY

ARTICLE I - Name:
The name of the Limited Liability Company is:

ARTICLE II - Address:
The mailing address and street address of the principal office of the Limited Liability Company is:

Principal Office Address: **Mailing Address:**

_____   _____

_____   _____

_____   _____

ARTICLE III - Registered Agent, Registered Office, & Registered Agent's Signature:

The name and the Florida street address of the registered agent are:

_____
Name

_____
Florida street address (P.O. Box **NOT** acceptable)

_____FL_____
City, State, and Zip

Having been named as registered agent and to accept service of process for the above stated limited liability company at the place designated in this certificate, I hereby accept the appointment as registered agent and agree to act in this capacity. I further agree to comply with the provisions of all statutes relating to the proper and complete performance of my duties, and I am familiar with and accept the obligations of my position as registered agent as provided for in Chapter 608, F.S..

_____
Registered Agent's Signature

(CONTINUED)

Page 1 of 2

continued

Exhibit 7-9 *continued*

ARTICLE IV- Manager(s) or Managing Member(s):

The name and address of each Manager or Managing Member is as follows:

<u>Title:</u>   **<u>Name and Address:</u>**

"MGR" = Manager
"MGRM" = Managing Member

_____   _____
                                       _____
                                       _____

_____   _____
                                       _____
                                       _____

_____   _____
                                       _____
                                       _____

_____   _____
                                       _____
                                       _____

(Use attachment if necessary)

NOTE: An additional article must be added if an effective date is requested.

REQUIRED SIGNATURE:

_____

Signature of a member or an authorized representative of a member.

(In accordance with section 608.408(3), Florida Statutes, the execution
of this document constitutes an affirmation under the penalties of perjury
that the facts stated herein are true.)

_____

Typed or printed name of signee

<u>Filing Fees:</u>
$100.00 Filing Fee for Articles of Organization
$ 25.00 Designation of Registered Agent
$ 30.00 Certified Copy (Optional)
$ 5.00 Certificate of Status (Optional)

Page 2 of 2

ARTICLES OF INCORPORATION

Most states provide packets for the formation of a corporation. They are usually found on the Web site for the Department of Corporations or thesecretary of state and may be downloaded.

Packets from the following states, along with their instructions, are included herein.

1. Connecticut (Exhibit 7-10)
2. Florida (Exhibit 7-11)
3. Idaho (Exhibit 7-12)
4. Louisiana (Exhibit 7-13)

EXHIBIT 7-10   Connecticut Instructions for Completion

INSTRUCTIONS FOR COMPLETION OF APPLICATION
FOR RESERVATION OF NAME

<u>Instructions correspond with numbered entries on the form</u>

1.   **NAME:** Please provide the name which you intend to reserve. You may reserve for exclusive use the name of one of the following types of business organizations or entities: A corporation (stock & non-stock), limited liability company, limited partnership, limited liability partnership or statutory trust. The name which you reserve <u>must</u> contain the appropriate statutory designation which denotes the type of entity or organization for which the name is intended to be used. Choose a statutory designation from the selection below according to organization type and include it within the name as it appears in block 1 on the form.

CORPORATE DESIGNATIONS
The name of a corporation must contain one of the following designations: corporation, incorporated, company, Societa per Azioni, limited or the abbreviations corp., inc., co., S.p.A. or ltd.

LIMITED LIABILITY COMPANY DESIGNATIONS
The name of a limited liability company must contain one of the following designations: Limited Liability Company, L.L.C., LLC, Limited Liability Co., Ltd. Liability Company or Ltd. Liability Co.

LIMITED PARTNERSHIP DESIGNATIONS
The name of a Limited Partnership must contain, without abbreviation; the words limited partnership.

LIMITED LIABILITY PARTNERSHIP DESIGNATIONS
The name of a limited liability partnership must contain one of the following designations: Registered Limited Liability Partnership, Limited Liability Partnership, L.L.P., or LLP <u>as its last words or letters</u>.

STATUTORY TRUST DESIGNATION
The name of a statutory trust must contain one of the following designations: Statutory Trust, Limited Liability Trust, Limited, LLT, L.L.T., or Ltd.

2.   **NAME OF APPLICANT:** Please print or type the name of the applicant.

3.   **ADDRESS OF APPLICANT:** Please provide the street address of the applicant including street number, street name, city, state and postal code. P.O. box is not acceptable.

4.   **EXECUTION:** Please print or type the complete legal name of the signatory, title (if signing on behalf of an entity) and signature. Note that the execution constitutes a statement made under the penalties of false statement that the information provided in the document is true.

continued

Exhibit 7-10 *continued*

APPLICATION FOR RESERVATION OF NAME
FOR DOMESTIC OR FOREIGN
STOCK & NON-STOCK CORP, LLC, LP, LLP & STATUTORY TRUST
Office of the Secretary of the State
30 Trinity Street / P.O. Box 150470 / Hartford, CT 06115-0470 / Rev. 03/01/2001

Space For Office Use Only   **Filing Fee $30.00**

The undersigned hereby applies for reservation of the following name:

1. **NAME:**

(See instructions for appropriate business/entity designation on the reverse side of this form)

2. **NAME OF APPLICANT:**

3. **ADDRESS OF APPLICANT: (Complete address required. Street name, city, state & zip code.)**

4. **EXECUTION:**

_____

SIGNATURE OF APPLICANT (and title if applicable)

The reservation will be effective for a period of 120 days following filing.

Please type or print all information other than the signature.

See reverse for instruction

continued

Exhibit 7-10 *continued*

SECRETARY OF THE STATE
30 TRINITY STREET
POST OFFICE BOX 150470
HARTFORD, CT 06115-0470

INCORPORATION OF A CONNECTICUT STOCK CORPORATION

We are pleased to enclose forms to incorporate and organize a stock corporation in the State of Connecticut. Enclosed you will find a Certificate of Incorporation form and an Organization and First Report form. The fees for filing these forms are $200.00 to file the Certificate of Incorporation, which includes a $150.00 minimum franchise tax*, and $75.00 to file the Organization and First Report. The Organization and First Report must be filed within 30 days of the date on which the corporation holds its organization meeting. Before filing the forms described above, you may reserve the name you wish for your corporation.** If a name reservation is submitted for filing, it would be prudent to wait until after a confirmation of filing has been issued to file incorporation documents.

The filing of the above referenced documents represent the bare essentials of incorporation in Connecticut. There are many other considerations to take into account when forming a corporation. For this reason, we recommend that an attorney and/or other competent advisor be consulted.

PLEASE MAKE CHECK PAYABLE TO:

CONNECTICUT SECRETARY OF THE STATE

*The minimum franchise tax must be paid by corporations, which authorize 20,000 shares or less upon incorporation. Corporations which authorize more than 20,000 shares must pay a franchise tax calculated on a sliding scale as follows: $.01 per share up to and including 10,000; $.005 per share up to and including 100,000; $.0025 per share up to and including 1,000,000; $.002 per share in excess of 1,000,000.

**The fee to reserve a corporate name for 120 days is $30.00.

See enclosed form instructions for more specifics filing details.

continued

Exhibit 7-10 *continued*

INSTRUCTIONS FOR COMPLETION OF THE CERTIFICATE
OF INCORPORATION STOCK CORPORATION

Instructions correspond with numbered entries on the form

1. NAME OF CORPORATION: Please provide the name of the corporation. The name of the corporation must contain   one of the following designations: "corporation", "incorporated", or "company", or the abbreviation "corp.", "inc." or "co.", or words or abbreviations of like import in another language. The name must also be **distinguishable** from other business names on the records of the Secretary of the State.

2. TOTAL NUMBER OF AUTHORIZED SHARES: Please provide the total number of shares the corporation is authorized to issue. Corporations must pay a <u>minimum</u> franchise tax of $150 dollars for authorizing <u>up to</u> 20,000 shares at the time of incorporation. If the number of shares authorized is greater than 20,000, the franchise tax is calculated based on a sliding scale set forth in section 33-618 as amended. If the corporation seeks authority to issue more than one class of shares, it must clearly designate each class in the block labeled <u>Class</u> and the corresponding number of authorized shares in each class in the block labeled <u>Number of shares per class</u>.

3. TERMS, LIMITATIONS, RELATIVE RIGHTS AND PREFERENCES OF EACH CLASS OF SHARES AND SERIES THEREOF PURSUANT TO CONN. GEN. STAT. SECTION 33-665: Please set forth all information required by section 33-665 as amended for each class of stock authorized in item number 3.

4. APPOINTMENT OF REGISTERED AGENT: The corporation may appoint either a natural person who is a resident of Connecticut, a Connecticut business or a foreign business which has a certificate of authority to transact business in Connecticut, a domestic limited liability company or a foreign limited liability company which has a certificate of authority to transact business in Connecticut. Please note the following: if the agent being appointed is a natural person, that person's business address must be provided under the heading business address. Their residence address under the heading Residence address; if the agent appointed is a business, it must provide its principal office address under the Business address heading; the agent must sign accepting the appointment in the space provided; the signatory must state the capacity under which they sign if signing on behalf of a business; **the corporation may <u>not</u> appoint itself as its registered agent** and; all addresses must include a street number, street name, city, state, postal code.

5. OTHER INFORMATION: Please present in the space provided or on an attachment any information which a stock corporation is permitted but not required to provide.

6. EXECUTION: The document must be executed by one or more incorporators, each of whom must provide an address containing a street and number, city, state and a postal code. The execution constitutes legal statement under the penalties of false statement that the information provided in the document is true.

continued

Exhibit 7-10 *continued*

CERTIFICATE OF INCORPORATION
STOCK CORPORATION
Office of the Secretary of the State
30 Trinity Street / P.O. Box 150470 / Hartford, CT 06115-0470 / Rev. 03/13/2002

Space For Office Use Only	Filing Fee: See cover letter

1. NAME OF CORPORATION:

2. TOTAL NUMBER OF AUTHORIZED SHARES: _____

If the corporation has more than one class of shares, it must designate each class and the number of shares authorized within each class below

Class	Number of shares per class

3. TERMS, LIMITATIONS, RELATIVE RIGHTS AND PREFERENCES OF EACH CLASS OF SHARES AND SERIES THEREOF PURSUANT TO CONN. GEN. STAT. SECTION 33-665:

continued

Exhibit 7-10 *continued*

Space For Office Use Only

4. APPOINTMENT OF REGISTERED AGENT: (Please select only one A. or B.)

Print or type name of agent: **A. Individual's Name:**	Business address: (P.O. Box is unacceptable)
	Residence address: (P.O. Box is unacceptable)
B. Business Entity:	Address: (P.O. Box is unacceptable)

Acceptance of appointment

_____
Signature of agent

5. OTHER PROVISIONS:

6. EXECUTION:

Dated this _____ day of _____, 20_____.

Certificate must be signed by each incorporator.

PRINT OR TYPE NAME OF INCORPORATOR(S)	SIGNATURE(S)	COMPLETE ADDRESS(ES)

continued

Exhibit 7-10 *continued*

INSTRUCTIONS FOR COMPLETION OF THE
ORGANIZATION REPORT CORPORATION

Instructions correspond with numbered entries on the form

1. NAME OF CORPORATION: Please provide the complete name of the corporation as it currently appears on the records of the Secretary of the State.

2. DATE OF ORGANIZATION MEETING: Please provide the month, day and year on which the organization meeting took place.

3. ADDRESS OF PRINCIPAL OFFICE: Please provide a complete address of the corporation's principal office including a number, street, city, state and postal code. **P.O. boxes are only acceptable as additional information.**

4. MAILING ADDRESS: Please provide the address to which the Secretary of the State should mail the corporation's annual report form, if other than its principal office address. A P.O. Box is acceptable for this address.

5. OFFICERS: Please provide the name of all of the corporation's officers, their titles and their residence and business addresses. Complete street addresses including a street number, street name, city, state, postal code and country if other than the United States are required. **Note: P.O. boxes are only acceptable as additional information.**

6. DIRECTORS: Please provide the name of all of the corporation's directors and their residence and business addresses. Complete street addresses including a street number, street name, city, state, postal code and country if other than the United States are required. **Note: P.O. boxes are only acceptable as additional information.**

7. EXECUTION: The document must be executed by an authorized official of the corporation. That person must print or type their name, state the capacity under which they sign and provide a signature. The execution constitutes a legal statement under the penalties of false statement that the information provided in the document is true.

continued

Exhibit 7-10 *continued*

ORGANIZATION AND FIRST REPORT
STOCK OR NON-STOCK CORPORATIONS
Office of the Secretary of the State
30 Trinity Street / P.O. Box 150470 / Hartford, CT 06115-0470 / Rev. 03/01/2001

See reverse for instructions

Space For Office Use Only	Filing Fee: $75.00 Stock
	$25.00 Nonstock

1. Name of Corporation:

2. Date of Organization Meeting: _____ / _____ / _____
Month   Day   Year

3. Address of Principal Office (street address required – P.O. Box is not acceptable):

4. Mailing address (if other than principal office address):

5. OFFICERS:
(Street address required – P.O. Box is not acceptable)

NAME	TITLE	RESIDENCE ADDRESS	BUSINESS ADDRESS

6. DIRECTORS:
(Street address required – P.O. Box is not acceptable)

NAME	RESIDENCE ADDRESS	BUSINESS ADDRESS

Note: If additional space is needed, please reference an 8 1/2 X 11 attachment

7. EXECUTION:

Dated this _____ day of _____, 20_____ .

Print or type name of signatory	Capacity of signatory	Signature

EXHIBIT 7-11 Florida Instructions for a Profit Corporation

INSTRUCTIONS FOR A PROFIT CORPORATION

The following are instructions, a transmittal letter and sample articles of incorporation pursuant to Chapter 607 and 621 Florida Statutes (F.S.).

NOTE: THIS IS A BASIC FORM MEETING MINIMAL REQUIREMENTS FOR FILING ARTICLES OF INCORPORATION.

The Division of Corporations strongly recommends that corporate documents be reviewed by your legal counsel. The Division is a filing agency and as such does not render any legal, accounting, or tax advice.

This office does not provide you with corporate seals, minute books, or stock certificates. It is the responsibility of the corporation to secure these items once the corporation has been filed with this office.

Questions concerning S Corporations should be directed to the Internal Revenue Service by telephoning 1-800-829-1040. This is an IRS designation, which is not determined by this office.

A preliminary search for name availability can be made on the Internet through the Division's records at www.sunbiz.org. Preliminary name searches and name reservations are no longer available from the Division of Corporations. You are responsible for any name infringement that may result from your corporate name selection.

Pursuant to Chapter 607 or 621 F.S., the articles of incorporation **must** set forth the following:

Article I: The name of the corporation **must** include a corporate suffix such as Corporation, Corp., Incorporated, Inc., Company, or Co.

A Professional Association **must** contain the word "chartered" or "professional association" or "P.A.".

Article II: The principal place of business and mailing address of the corporation.

Article III: **Specific Purpose for a "Professional Corporation"**

Article IV: The number of shares of stock that this corporation is authorized to have **must** be stated.

continued

Exhibit 7-11 *continued*

Article V: The names, address and titles of the Directors/Officers **(optional).** The names of officers/directors may be required to apply for a license, open a bank account, etc.

Article VI: The name and **Florida street address** of the initial Registered Agent. The Registered Agent **must** sign in the space provided and type or print his/her name accepting the designation as registered agent.

Article VII: The name and address of the Incorporator. The Incorporator **must** sign in the space provided and type or print his/her name below signature.

An Effective Date: **Add a separate article if applicable or necessary**: An effective date **may** be added to the Articles of Incorporation, otherwise the date of receipt will be the file date. (An effective date can not be more than five (5) business days prior to the date of receipt or ninety (90) days after the date of filing).

****

The fee for filing a profit corporation is:

Filing Fee	$35.00
Designation of Registered Agent	$35.00
Certified Copy (optional)	$ 8.75 (plus $1 per page for each page over 8, not to exceed a maximum of $52.50).
Certificate of Status (optional)	$ 8.75

(Make checks payable to Florida Department of State)

Mailing Address:
Department of State
Division of Corporations
P.O. Box 6327
Tallahassee, FL 32314
(850) 245-6052

Street Address:
Department of State
Division of Corporations
409 E. Gaines St.
Tallahassee, FL 32399
(850) 245-6052

continued

Exhibit 7-11   *continued*

TRANSMITTAL LETTER

Department of State
Division of Corporations
P. O. Box 6327
Tallahassee, FL 32314

SUBJECT: _____

(PROPOSED CORPORATE NAME – <u>MUST INCLUDE SUFFIX</u>)

Enclosed are an original and one (1) copy of the articles of incorporation and a check for:

❏ **$70.00**
Filing Fee

❏ **$78.75**
Filing Fee
& Certificate of Status

❏ **$78.75**
Filing Fee
& Certified Copy

❏ **$87.50**
Filing Fee,
Certified Copy
& Certificate of
Status

ADDITIONAL COPY REQUIRED

FROM: _____

Name (Printed or typed)

_____

Address

_____

City, State & Zip

_____

Daytime Telephone number

NOTE: Please provide the original and one copy of the articles.

continued

Exhibit 7-11 *continued*

ARTICLES OF INCORPORATION
In compliance with Chapter 607 and/or Chapter 621, F.S. (Profit)

ARTICLE I   NAME
The name of the corporation shall be:

ARTICLE II   PRINCIPAL OFFICE
The principal place of business/mailing address is:

ARTICLE III   PURPOSE
The purpose for which the corporation is organized is:

ARTICLE IV   SHARES
The number of shares of stock is:

ARTICLE V   INITIAL OFFICERS AND/OR DIRECTORS
List name(s), address(es) and specific title(s):

ARTICLE VI   REGISTERED AGENT
The **name and Florida street address** of the registered agent is:

ARTICLE VII   INCORPORATOR
The **name and address** of the Incorporator is:

****

Having been named as registered agent to accept service of process for the above stated corporation at the place designated in this certificate, I am familiar with and accept the appointment as registered agent and agree to act in this capacity

_____   _____
Signature/Registered Agent   Date

_____   _____
Signature/Incorporator   Date

EXHIBIT 7-12   Idaho Instructions for Completion

INSTRUCTIONS

Optional: If the document is incorrect where can you be reached for questions? _____

Note: Complete and submit the application in duplicate. It is not necessary to apply for a name reservation if articles of incorporation, organization or other business entity formation are being concurrently filed.

1. Enter the name of the company you would like to reserve for a 4 month period. A name can only be reserved for the name of a corporation or limited liability company.

2. Enter the name and address of the person or company who is applying to reserve the name.

3. The document must be signed by the applicant, or if the applicant is another legal entity, by an officer or agent of the company. Please identify the signer by typing his/her name below the signature and indicating in what capacity they are signing.

4. Enclose the appropriate fee:
    a. The filing fee is $20.00.
    b. If expedited service is requested, add $20.00 to the filing fee.
    c. If the fees are to be paid from the filing party's pre-paid customer account, conspicuously indicate the customer account number in the cover letter or transmittal document. Pursuant to Idaho Code § 67-910(6), the Secretary of State's Office may delete a business entity filing from our database if payment for the filing is not completed.

5. Mail or deliver to:
    Office of the Secretary of State
    700 West Jefferson
    PO Box 83720
    Boise ID 83720-0080

6. If you have any questions for need help, call the Secretary of State's Office at (208) 334-2301.

continued

Exhibit 7-12 *continued*

APPLICATION FOR RESERVATION
OF LEGAL ENTITY NAME

To the Secretary of State of Idaho,
700 W Jefferson, Basement West
PO Box 83720
Boise, Idaho 83720-0080

Pursuant to Idaho Code § 30-1-402 and 53-603, the undersigned applies for reservation
of the following name for a period of four months:

_____

(please print or type)

Dated: _____

Reserved by: _____

Name of applicant (print or type)

_____

Street or P.O. Box

_____

City, State, Zip Code

_____

Signature of applicant or, if applicant is
a corporation, of officer or agent

_____

Typed Name

_____

Capacity

Secretary of State use only

This application must be accompanied by a filing fee of $20.00.
The reservation will be effective for four months from the date of
filing.

[Please note: It is not necessary to apply for a name
reservation if articles of incorporation, organization or other
business entity formation are being concurrently filed.]

g:\corp\forms\misc forms\name
reservation.pmd
Revised 12/2002

continued

Exhibit 7-12 *continued*

INSTRUCTIONS

Optional: If the document is incorrect where can you be reached for corrections?_____

Note: Complete and submit the application in duplicate. Articles of Organization MUST be filed on the form prescribed by the Secretary of State's Office.

1. Line 1 - Enter the name of the limited liability company. Pursuant to Idaho Code § 53-602, the name of the limited liability company must contain the words Limited Liability Company, Limited Company, or the abbreviation L.L.C., L.C., or LLC. The word "Limited" may be abbreviated as Ltd. and the word "Company" may be abbreviated as Co. It is advised that you contact the Secretary of State to check for name availability before filing.

2. Line 2 - Enter the name and street address of the registered agent of the limited liability company. A registered agent is the person designated to receive service of process upon litigation. This person must be located in Idaho at a street address.

3. Line 3 - Enter the mailing address that you would like future reports mailed to.

4. Line 4 - Is the management of the limited liability company to be vested in managers or members? Mark the appropriate box. Note: if you mark the member box you will not have managers (or managing members) until a formal amendment is filed. It is advised you contact an attorney for any legal opinions.

5. Line 5 - If the management is vested in members list the name and address of at least 1 member. If the management is vested in managers list the name and address of at least 1 manager.

6. The articles of organization must be signed by a manager, if the company will be vested in managers, by a member, if management will be vested in members, or by an organizer. Please identify the name of the signer by typing his/her name below the signature.

7. Enclose the appropriate fee:

   a. If the application is typed and there are no attachments, the fee is $100.00.
   b. If the application is not typed or if it has attached pages, the fee is $120.00.
   c. If expedited service is requested, add $20.00 to the filing fee.
   d. If the fees are to be paid from the filing party's pre-paid customer account, conspicuously indicate the customer account number in the cover letter or transmittal document.

   Pursuant to Idaho Code § 67-910(6), the Secretary of State's Office may delete a business entity filing from our database if payment for the filing is not completed.

8. Mail or deliver to:

   Office of the Secretary of State
   700 West Jefferson
   PO Box 83720
   Boise ID 83720-0080

9. If you have questions or need help, call the Secretary of State's office at (208) 334-2301.

continued

Exhibit 7-12   *continued*

ARTICLES OF ORGANIZATION
LIMITED LIABILITY COMPANY

(Instructions on back of application)

1. The name of the limited liability company is:

   _____

2. The street address of the initial registered office is:

   _____

   and the name of the initial registered agent at the above address is:

   _____

3. The mailing address for future correspondence is:

   _____

4. Management of the limited liability company will be vested in:

   Manager(s) ☐ or Member(s) ☐   (please check the appropriate box)

5. If management is to be vested in one or more manager(s), list the name(s) and address(es) or at least one initial manager. If management is to be vested in the member(s), list the name(s) and address(es) of at least one initial member.

Name	Address
_____	_____
_____	_____
_____	_____
_____	_____
_____	_____
_____	_____

6. Signature of at least one person responsible for forming the limited liability company:

   Signature: _____

   Typed Name: _____

   Capacity: _____

   Signature _____

   Typed Name: _____

   Capacity: _____

g:\corp\forms\LLC forms\articlesoforganization.p65
Revised 07/2002

Secretary of State use only

continued

Exhibit 7-12 *continued*

INSTRUCTIONS

Optional: If the document is incorrect where can you be reached for corrections? _____
Note: Complete and submit the application in duplicate.

1. Line 1 - Enter the name of the limited liability company exactly as it is filed with the office of the Secretary of State.

2. Line 2 - Enter the date the articles of organization were filed with this office.

3. Line 3 - List the reason for the dissolution.

4. Line 4 - If you have other comments to make regarding the dissolution of the limited liability company you may do so in this area.

5. The articles of dissolution must be signed by a manager of the LLC, if its articles of organization vested the management in managers, or by a member, if the management is vested in members. Please identify the name of the signer by typing his/her name below the signature and indicate in what capacity he/she signs to the right.

6. Enclose the appropriate fee:

    a. The filing fee is $30.00
    b. If expedited service is requested, add $20.00 to the filing fee.
    c. If the fees are to be paid from the filing party's pre-paid customer account, conspicuously indicate the customer account number in the cover letter or transmittal document.

7. Mail or deliver to:

    Office of the Secretary of State
    700 West Jefferson
    PO Box 83720
    Boise ID 83720-0080

8. If you have questions or need help, call the Secretary of State's office at (208) 334-2301.

continued

Exhibit 7-12 *continued*

ARTICLES OF DISSOLUTION
LIMITED LIABILITY COMPANY
(Instructions on back of application)

The below named limited liability company has been dissolved pursuant to section 53-642, Idaho Code.

1. The name of the dissolved limited liability company is: _____

    _____

2. Its articles of organization were filed with the Secretary of State on: _____

    _____

3. The reason for the dissolution is:

4. Other information concerning the dissolution (optional):

5. Signature of at least 1 manager or member

Signature _____ _____

Typed Name _____ Capacity

Signature _____ _____

Typed Name _____ Capacity

g:\corp\forms\llcforms\arts of dissolution_llc.p65
Revised 01/2001

Secretary of State use only

EXHIBIT 7-13   Louisiana Secretary of State Commercial Division Screen Shot

Louisiana Secretary of State

COMMERCIAL DIVISION

Welcome to the Louisiana Secretary of State's Commercial Division index page. If you are interested in incorporating, need licensing information, are looking for a list of books published by this office, or want information on filing UCC's in Louisiana, you've come to the right place.

Our staff takes pride in being one of the most efficient divisions in state government. If you have any questions that are not answered in this section, please feel free to call (225) 925-4704 for more information.

For your convenience, we accept American Express, Discover, Mastercard and Visa. Be sure to include your account number and expiration date when submitting requests.

Please make your selection from the following index.

Corporations
Information on incorporating, forming a limited liability company, registering a partnership, filing a trade name, including forms in Adobe Portable Document Format (PDF), accessing information on entities already on file, or obtaining certificates and certified copies on existing entities.

Corporations Database
Search the Corporations Database for business names, trademarks, registered agents and individual names.

Direct Computer Access Service
Commercial and high volume users can subscribe to PC dial-up direct access via telephone modem to the Corporations Database and U.C.C. information.   Payment is by check or money order only.

Administrative Services
Service of Process, Authentication of Documents and Distribution of Publications.

First Stop Shop for Business
Cut through the red tape at our licensing information center.

Uniform Commercial Code
UCC Frequently Asked Questions, Clerks of Court List, Fee Schedule, and Direct Access Service.

Read About UCC Revised Article 9 Changes take effect on July 1, 2001. *NEW !*

Other States S.O.S. Offices
Links to other state's Secretary of State web pages.

continued

Exhibit 7-13 *continued*

<u>**Links to Related Sites**</u>
Links to vendors and other sites of interest.

<u>**Send E-mail to the Commercial Division**</u>

<u>**SITE INDEX**</u>

Click for IBM Mark meaning and disclaimers.

IBM and e-business Mark are TM's of IBM Corp.

Download

Acrobat Reader

continued

Exhibit 7-13   *continued*

INSTRUCTIONS

1.   An Initial Report must be completed and filed with the Articles of Incorporation of a Domestic Business Corporation.

2.   If no directors have been selected when the Initial Report and Articles of Incorporation are filed, a Supplemental Report, setting forth their names and addresses must be filed in accordance with R.S. 12:25.

3.   The Affidavit of Acknowledgement and Acceptance contained on the bottom of this form must be signed by each registered agent before a notary public.

   NOTE: Upon filing the Articles of Incorporation and Initial Report with our office, you will receive certified copies of both documents and a Certificate of Incorporation. Within thirty (30) days after filing with the Secretary of State's office, a multiple original of the Articles and the Initial Report (or a copy of the Certificate of Incorporation must be filed with the office of the recorder of mortgages of the parish where the corporation's registered office is located.

continued

Exhibit 7-13 *continued*

W. Fox McKeithen
Secretary of State

DOMESTIC BUSINESS CORPORATION INITIAL REPORT
(R.S. 12:25 AND 12:101)

1. The name of this corporation is: _____

2. The location and municipal address (not a P.O. Box only) of this corporation's registered office:

_____

_____

3. The full name and municipal address (not a P. O. Box only) of each of this corporation's registered agent(s) is/are:

_____

_____

4. The names and municipal address (not a P.O. Box only) of the first directors are:

_____

_____

Incorporator(s) signature(s)

_____

_____

_____

_____

AGENT'S AFFIDAVIT AND ACKNOWLEDGEMENT OF ACCEPTANCE

I hereby acknowledge and accept the appointment of registered agent for and on behalf of the above named corporation.

Registered agent(s) signature(s):

_____

_____

Sworn to and subscribed before me, the undersigned Notary Public, on this date: _____

_____
Notary

341 Rev. 1/01   (See instructions on back)

continued

Exhibit 7-13 *continued*

INSTRUCTIONS

NOTE: A corporation is a complex form of business structure. This form contains only the minimum provisions required by law to be set forth in Articles of Incorporation. Additional provisions may be advisable or necessary, depending on the specific needs of each corporation. Consideration should be given to the advantages and disadvantages of incorporating, and the legal and tax consequences. You are strongly advised to seek legal advice from an attorney and tax and other business advice from an accountant.

1.   File the Articles of Incorporation, and the Domestic Corporation Initial Report (form 341) which contains an agent affidavit and the requisite $60 filing fee with the Secretary of State's office.

2.   The Articles of Incorporation and the Initial Report may be delivered to the Secretary of State's office in advance, for filing as of any specified date (and any given time on such date) within thirty days after the date of delivery. Requests should be made in writing and must be submitted along with the Articles of Incorporation and the Initial Report.

3.   The Articles of Incorporation cannot be accepted for filing unless an Initial Report form (341) is also filed. Upon filing with our office, you will receive a certified copy of the Articles and a Certificate of Incorporation. Within thirty (30) days after filing the Articles of Incorporation with the Secretary of State's office, a multiple original of the Articles and the Initial Report (or a copy of each certified by the Secretary of State), and a copy of the Certificate of Incorporation must be filed with the office of the recorder of mortgages in the parish where the corporation's registered office is located.

4.   Please call the Internal Revenue Service at (901) 546-3920 for information to obtain a corporation's federal tax identification number prior to incorporation.

5.   If the Articles of Incorporation are filed within five (5) working days (exclusive of legal holidays) after acknowledgement, the corporate existence shall begin as of the time of such acknowledgement.

continued

Exhibit 7-13 *continued*

**W. Fox McKeithen
Secretary of State**

ARTICLES OF INCORPORATION
(R.S. 12:24)

Domestic Business Corporation **Enclose $60.00 filing fee** **Make remittance payable to** **Secretary of State** *Do Not Send Cash*	**Return to:** **Commercial Division** P. O. Box 94125 **Baton Rouge, LA 70804-9125** Phone (225) 925-4704 Web Site: www.sec.state.la.us

STATE OF _____

PARISH/COUNTY OF _____

1. The name of this corporation is:_____

2. This corporation is formed for the purpose of : (check one)

       ( )   Engaging in any lawful activity for which corporations may be formed.

       ( )   _____
                           (use for limiting corporate activity)

3. The duration of this corporation is: (may be perpetual) _____

4. The aggregate number of shares which the corporation shall have authority to issue is :_____

5. The shares shall consist of one class only and the par value of each share is _____
(shares may be without par value) per share.

6. The full name and post office address of each incorporator is : _____

    _____

    _____

7. Other provisions: _____

    _____

    _____

8. The corporations's federal tax identification number is: _____

          Incorporator(s) Signature: _____

                               _____

                               _____

On this _____ day of _____200__, before me, personally appeared _____

_____ , to me known to be the person described in and who executed the

foregoing instrument, and acknowledged that he executed it as his free act and deed.

                _____
                            Notary

399 Rev. 03/03   (See instructions on back)

DELAWARE CORPORATION

Delaware provides forms for the following on their Web site:

Certificate of Incorporation—
A Stock Corporation (Exhibit 7-14)

First: Name of corporation

Second: Registered office and agent

Third: Completed

Fourth: Total capital stock authorized

Fifth: Name and mailing address of incorporator

Signature of Incorporator.

Certificate of Incorporation—
A Close Corporation (Exhibit 7-15)

First: Name of corporation

Second: Registered office and agent

Third: Completed

Fourth: Total capital stock authorized

Fifth: Name and mailing address of incorporator

Signature of Incorporator.

EXHIBIT 7-14 Delaware Certificate of Incorporation—A Stock Corporation

STATE *of* DELAWARE
CERTIFICATE *of* INCORPORATION
A STOCK CORPORATION

- **First:** The name of this Corporation is _____
_____.

- **Second:** Its registered office in the State of Delaware is to be located at _____
_____ Street, in the City of _____
County of _____ Zip Code _____. The registered agent in
charge thereof is _____
_____
_____

- **Third:** The purpose of the corporation is to engage in any lawful act or activity for
which corporations may be organized under the General Corporation Law of
Delaware.

- **Fourth:** The amount of the total authorized capital stock of this corporation is
_____ Dollars ($_____) divided into _____ shares of _____
_____ Dollars ($_____) par value each.

- **Fifth:** The name and mailing address of the incorporator are as follows:
Name _____
Mailing Address_____
_____Zip Code_____

- **I, The Undersigned,** for the purpose of forming a corporation under the laws of the State of Delaware,
do make, file and record this Certificate, and do certify that the facts herein stated are true, and I have
accordingly hereunto set my hand this
_____day of _____, A.D. 20_____.

BY:_____
(Incorporator)

NAME:_____
(type or print)

EXHIBIT 7-15   Delaware Certificate of Incorporation—A Close Corporation

CERTIFICATE *of* INCORPORATION
A CLOSE CORPORATION

- **First:** The name of this Corporation is _____
_____.

- **Second:** Its Registered Office in the State of Delaware is to be located at _____
_____._____Street, in the City of _____
County of _____Zip Code_____. The registered agent in charge
thereof is _____
_____
_____

- **Third:** The nature of business and the objects and purposes proposed to be transacted,
promoted and carried on , are to engage in any lawful act of activity for which
corporations may be organized under the General corporation Law of Delaware.

- **Fourth:** The amount of the total authorized capital stock of this corporation is
_____Dollars ($_____) divided into _____shares of _____
_____Dollars ($_____) each.

- **Fifth:** The name and mailing address of the incorporator are as follows:
Name _____
Mailing Address_____
_____Zip Code_____

- **Sixth:** All of the corporation's issued stock, exclusive of treasury shares, shall be held of record by not
more than thirty (30) persons.

- **Seventh:** All of the issued stock of all classes shall be subject to one or more of the restrictions on
transfer permitted by Section 202 of the General Corporation Law.

- **Eighth:** The corporation shall make no offering of any of its stock of any class which would constitute
a "public offering" within the meaning of the United States Securities Act of 1933, as it may be
amended from time to time.

- **I, The Undersigned,** for the purpose of forming a corporation under the laws of the State of Delaware,
do make, file and record this Certificate, and do certify that the facts herein stated are true, and I have
accordingly hereunto set my hand this
_____day of _____, A.D. 20_____.

BY:_____
(Incorporator)
NAME:_____
(type or print)

ILLINOIS

Articles of Incorporation

A two-page form for Articles of Incorporation is included on the Illinois Web site and is shown as Exhibit 7-16. The following information is required:

1. Name of corporation
2. Registered agent and address
3. Purpose for which the corporation is organized
4. Authorized shares, issued shares, and price
5. Number of directors; initial directors' names and addresses
6. Optional section—property value estimate and estimate of gross business
7. Optional provisions
8. Signatures of incorporators with addresses

EXHIBIT 7-16 Illinois Articles of Incorporation

Form **BCA-2.10**	**ARTICLES OF INCORPORATION**	

Form **BCA-2.10**

(Rev. Jan. 1999)

ARTICLES OF INCORPORATION

This space for use by Secretary of State

Jesse White
Secretary of State
Department of Business Services
Springfield, IL 62756
http://www.sos.state.il.us

Payment must be made by certified check, cashier's check, Illinois attorney's check, Illinois C.P.A's check or money order, payable to "Secretary of State."

SUBMIT IN DUPLICATE!

**This space for use by
Secretary of State**

Date

Franchise Tax $
Filing Fee $

Approved:

1. CORPORATE NAME: _____

_____

(The corporate name must contain the word "corporation", "company," "incorporated," "limited" or an abbreviation thereof.)

2. Initial Registered Agent:

First Name	Middle Initial	Last name

Initial Registered Office:

Number	Street	Suite #

IL

City	County	Zip Code

3. Purpose or purposes for which the corporation is organized:
(If not sufficient space to cover this point, add one or more sheets of this size.)

4. Paragraph 1: Authorized Shares, Issued Shares and Consideration Received:

Class	Par Value per Share	Number of Shares Authorized	Number of Shares Proposed to be Issued	Consideration to be Received Therefor
	$			$
				TOTAL = $

Paragraph 2: The preferences, qualifications, limitations, restrictions and special or relative rights in respect of the shares of each class are:
(If not sufficient space to cover this point, add one or more sheets of this size.)

continued

Exhibit 7-16 *continued*

5. *OPTIONAL:*   (a) Number of directors constituting the initial board of directors of the corporation:_____ .
(b) Names and addresses of the persons who are to serve as directors until the first annual meeting of
shareholders or until their successors are elected and qualify:

Name	Residential Address	City, State, ZIP

6. *OPTIONAL:*   (a) It is estimated that the value of all property to be owned by the
corporation for the following year wherever located will be: $_____
(b) It is estimated that the value of the property to be located within
the State of Illinois during the following year will be: $_____
(c) It is estimated that the gross amount of business that will be
transacted by the corporation during the following year will be: $_____
(d) It is estimated that the gross amount of business that will be
transacted from places of business in the State of Illinois during
the following year will be: $_____

7. *OPTIONAL:*   *OTHER PROVISIONS*
Attach a separate sheet of this size for any other provision to be included in the Articles of
Incorporation, e.g., authorizing preemptive rights, denying cumulative voting, regulating internal
affairs, voting majority requirements, fixing a duration other than perpetual, etc.

8.   **NAME(S) & ADDRESS(ES) OF INCORPORATOR(S)**

The undersigned incorporator(s) hereby declare(s), under penalties of perjury, that the statements made in the foregoing
Articles of Incorporation are true.

Dated _____ , _____
                (Month & Day)   Year

Signature and Name	**Address**
1._____	1._____
Signature	Street
_____	_____
(Type or Print Name)	City/Town State ZIP Code
2._____	2._____
Signature	Street
_____	_____
(Type or Print Name)	City/Town State ZIP Code
3._____	3._____
Signature	Street
_____	_____
(Type or Print Name)	City/Town State ZIP Code

(Signatures must be in **BLACK INK** on original document. Carbon copy, photocopy or rubber stamp signatures may only be
used on conformed copies.)
NOTE: If a corporation acts as incorporator, the name of the corporation and the state of incorporation shall be shown and the
execution shall be by its president or vice president and verified by him, and attested by its secretary or assistant secretary.

FEE SCHEDULE

- The initial franchise tax is assessed at the rate of 15/100 of 1 percent ($1.50 per $1,000) on the paid-in capital
represented in this state, with a minimum of $25.
- The filing fee is $75.
- The **minimum total due** (franchise tax + filing fee) is **$100.**
(Applies when the Consideration to be Received as set forth in Item 4 does not exceed $16,667)
- The Department of Business Services in Springfield will provide assistance in calculating the total fees if necessary.
Illinois Secretary of State   Springfield, IL 62756
Department of Business Services   Telephone (217) 782-9522 or 782-9523

                                                                    C-162.20

CONSOLIDATION/MERGER

Packets for consolidation and merger in the states of Florida (Exhibit 7-17) and Massachusetts (Exhibit 7-18) are included herein, along with their explanations.

EXHIBIT 7-17 Florida Articles of Merger

ARTICLES OF MERGER
Sections 607.1101 - 607.1107, F.S.
(Profit Corporations)

The attached form is to be used only when two or more profit corporations merge. This form is basic and may not meet your specific merger needs. The advice of an attorney is recommended.

Please complete only one Plan of Merger form.

Fees:

Filing Fee $35.00 for each merging and surviving corporation (includes a letter of acknowledgment)

Certified Copy (optional) $8.75 (plus $1 per page for each page over 8, not to exceed a maximum of $52.50; **please send an additional copy of your document if a certified copy is requested**)

➤ Send one check in the total amount made payable to the Department of State.

➤ Please include a cover letter containing your telephone number, return address and certification requirements, or complete the attached transmittal letter.

Mailing Address:
Amendment Section
Division of Corporations
P.O. Box 6327
Tallahassee, FL 32314

Street Address:
Amendment Section
Division of Corporations
409 E. Gaines St.
Tallahassee, FL 32399

For further information, you may call (850) 245-6050

continued

Exhibit 7-17   *continued*

TRANSMITTAL LETTER

TO: Amendment Section
Division of Corporations

SUBJECT:_____
(Name of surviving corporation)

The enclosed merger and fee are submitted for filing.

Please return all correspondence concerning this matter to the following:

_____
(Name of person)

_____
(Name of firm/company)

_____
(Address)

_____
(City/state and zip code)

For further information concerning this matter, please call:

_____ at (_____)_____
(Name of person)   (Area code & daytime telephone number)

☐   Certified copy (optional) $8.75 (plus $1 per page for each page over 8, not to exceed a maximum of $52.50; **please send an additional copy of your document if a certified copy is requested**)

<u>Mailing Address:</u>   **<u>Street Address:</u>**
Amendment Section   Amendment Section
Division of Corporations   Division of Corporations
P.O. Box 6327   409 E. Gaines St.
Tallahassee, FL 32314   Tallahassee, FL 32399

continued

Exhibit 7-17 *continued*

ARTICLES OF MERGER
(Profit Corporations)

The following articles of merger are submitted in accordance with the Florida Business Corporation Act, pursuant to section 607.1105, F.S.

First: The name and jurisdiction of the **surviving** corporation:

<u>Name</u>	<u>Jurisdiction</u>	<u>Document Number</u> (If known/ applicable)
_____	_____	_____

Second: The name and jurisdiction of each **merging** corporation:

<u>Name</u>	<u>Jurisdiction</u>	<u>Document Number</u> (If known/ applicable)
_____	_____	_____
_____	_____	_____
_____	_____	_____
_____	_____	_____
_____	_____	_____

Third: The Plan of Merger is attached.

Fourth: The merger shall become effective on the date the Articles of Merger are filed with the Florida Department of State.

OR _____/_____/_____ (Enter a specific date. NOTE: An effective date cannot be prior to the date of filing or more than 90 days in the future.)

Fifth: Adoption of Merger by **surviving** corporation - **(COMPLETE ONLY ONE STATEMENT)**
The Plan of Merger was adopted by the shareholders of the surviving corporation on _____.

The Plan of Merger was adopted by the board of directors of the surviving corporation on _____ and shareholder approval was not required.

Sixth: Adoption of Merger by **merging** corporation(s) **(COMPLETE ONLY ONE STATEMENT)**
The Plan of Merger was adopted by the shareholders of the merging corporation(s) on _____.

The Plan of Merger was adopted by the board of directors of the merging corporation(s) on _____ and shareholder approval was not required.

(Attach additional sheets if necessary)

continued

Exhibit 7-17 *continued*

Seventh: <u>SIGNATURES FOR EACH CORPORATION</u>

<u>Name of Corporation</u>	<u>Signature</u>	<u>Typed or Printed Name of Individual & Title</u>
_____	_____	_____
_____	_____	_____
_____	_____	_____
_____	_____	_____
_____	_____	_____
_____	_____	_____
_____	_____	_____
_____	_____	_____
_____	_____	_____
_____	_____	_____
_____	_____	_____

continued

Exhibit 7-17   *continued*

PLAN OF MERGER
(Non Subsidiaries)

The following plan of merger is submitted in compliance with section 607.1101, F.S. and in accordance with the laws of any other applicable jurisdiction of incorporation.

First: The name and jurisdiction of the **surviving** corporation:

Name   Jurisdiction

_____   _____

Second: The name and jurisdiction of each **merging** corporation:

Name   Jurisdiction

_____   _____

_____   _____

_____   _____

_____   _____

_____   _____

Third: The terms and conditions of the merger are as follows:

Fourth: The manner and basis of converting the shares of each corporation into shares, obligations, or other securities of the surviving corporation or any other corporation or, in whole or in part, into cash or other property and the manner and basis of converting rights to acquire shares of each corporation into rights to acquire shares, obligations, or other securities of the surviving or any other corporation or, in whole or in part, into cash or other property are as follows:

(Attach additional sheets if necessary)

continued

Exhibit 7-17 *continued*

THE FOLLOWING MAY BE SET FORTH IF APPLICABLE:

Amendments to the articles of incorporation of the surviving corporation are indicated below or attached as an exhibit:

OR

Restated articles are attached:

Other provisions relating to the merger are as follows:

continued

Exhibit 7-17   *continued*

PLAN OF MERGER
(Merger of subsidiary corporation(s))

The following plan of merger is submitted in compliance with section 607.1104, F.S. and in accordance with the laws of any other applicable jurisdiction of incorporation.

The name and jurisdiction of the **parent** corporation owning at least 80 percent of the outstanding shares of each class of the subsidiary corporation:

<u>Name</u>   <u>Jurisdiction</u>

_____   _____

The name and jurisdiction of each **subsidiary** corporation:

<u>Name</u>   <u>Jurisdiction</u>

_____   _____

_____   _____

_____   _____

_____   _____

The manner and basis of converting the shares of the subsidiary or parent into shares, obligations, or other securities of the parent or any other corporation or, in whole or in part, into cash or other property, and the manner and basis of converting rights to acquire shares of each corporation into rights to acquire shares, obligations, and other securities of the surviving or any other corporation or, in whole or in part, into cash or other property are as follows:

(Attach additional sheets if necessary)

continued

Exhibit 7-17   *continued*

If the merger is between the parent and a subsidiary corporation and the parent is not the surviving corporation, a provision for the pro rata issuance of shares of the subsidiary to the holders of the shares of the parent corporation upon surrender of any certificates is as follows:

If applicable, shareholders of the subsidiary corporations, who, except for the applicability of section 607.1104, F.S. would be entitled to vote and who dissent from the merger pursuant to section 607.1320, F.S., may be entitled, if they comply with the provisions of chapter 607 regarding the rights of dissenting shareholders, to be paid the fair value of their shares.

Other provisions relating to the merger are as follows:

EXHIBIT 7-18   Massachusetts Articles of Consolidation/Merger

FEDERAL IDENTIFICATION   FEDERAL IDENTIFICATION

NO. _____   NO. _____

Examiner

The Commonwealth of Massachusetts

William Francis Galvin
Secretary of the Commonwealth
One Ashburton Place, Boston, Massachusetts 02108-1512

ARTICLES OF *CONSOLIDATION / *MERGER
(General Laws, Chapter 156B, Section 78)

*Consolidation / *merger of

_____

_____

_____

_____

_____ ,

the constituent corporations, into

_____ ,

*a new corporation / *one of the constituent corporations.

The undersigned officers of each of the constituent corporations certify under the penalties of perjury as follows:

1. An agreement of *consolidation / *merger has been duly adopted in compliance with the requirements of General Laws, Chapter 156B, Section 78, and will be kept as provided by Subsection (d) thereof. The *resulting / *surviving corporation will furnish a copy of said agreement to any of its stockholders, or to any person who was a stockholder of any constituent corporation, upon written request and without charge.

2. The effective date of the *consolidation / *merger determined pursuant to the agreement of *consolidation / *merger shall be the date approved and filed by the Secretary of the Commonwealth. If a *later* effective date is desired, specify such date which shall not be more than *thirty days* after the date of filing:

3. (For a merger)
**The following amendments to the Articles of Organization of the *surviving* corporation have been effected pursuant to the agreement of merger:

C   ☐
P   ☐
M   ☐
R.A. ☐

*Delete the inapplicable word.   **If there are no provisions state "None".
Note: If the space provided under any article or item on this form is insufficient, additions shall be set forth on separate 8 1/2 x 11 sheets of paper with a left margin of at least 1 inch. Additions to more than one article may be made on a single sheet as long as each article requiring each addition is clearly indicated.

P.C.

156b78m 4/4/00

continued

Exhibit 7-18   *continued*

(For a consolidation)

(a) The purpose of the *resulting* corporation is to engage in the following business activities:

(b) State the total number of shares and the par value, if any, of each class of stock which the *resulting* corporation is authorized to issue.

WITHOUT PAR VALUE		WITH PAR VALUE		
TYPE	NUMBER OF SHARES	TYPE	NUMBER OF SHARES	PAR VALUE
Common:		Common:		
Preferred:		Preferred:		

**(c) If more than one class of stock is authorized, state a distinguishing designation for each class and provide a description of the preferences, voting powers, qualifications, and special or relative rights or privileges of each class and of each series then established.

**(d) The restrictions, if any, on the transfer of stock contained in the agreement of consolidation are:

**(e) Other lawful provisions, if any, for the conduct and regulation of the business and affairs of the corporation, for its voluntary dissolution, or for limiting, defining, or regulating the powers of the corporation, or of its directors or stockholders, or of any class of stockholders:

**If there are no provisions state "None".*

continued

Exhibit 7-18 *continued*

4. The information contained in Item 4 is *not* a *permanent* part of the Articles of Organization of the *resulting / *surviving corporation.

(a) The street address of the *resulting / *surviving corporation in Massachusetts is: *(post office boxes are not acceptable)*

(b) The name, residential address, and post office address of each director and officer of the *resulting / *surviving corporation is:

	NAME	**RESIDENTIAL ADDRESS**	**POST OFFICE ADDRESS**
President:			
Treasurer:			
Clerk:			
Directors:			

(c) The fiscal year (i.e. tax year) of the *resulting / *surviving corporation shall end on the last day of the month of:

(d) The name and business address of the resident agent, if any, of the *resulting / *surviving corporation is:

The undersigned officers of the several constituent corporations listed above further state under the penalties of perjury as to their respective corporations that the agreement of *consolidation / *merger has been duly executed on behalf of such corporation and duly approved by the stockholders of such corporation in the manner required by General Laws, Chapter 156B, Section 78.

_____ , *President / *Vice President,

_____ , *Clerk / *Assistant Clerk,

of _____ .
(Name of constituent corporation)

_____ , *President / *Vice President,

_____ , *Clerk / *Assistant Clerk,

of _____ .
(Name of constituent corporation)

Delete the inapplicable words.

continued

Exhibit 7-18 *continued*

THE COMMONWEALTH OF MASSACHUSETTS

ARTICLES OF *CONSOLIDATION / *MERGER
(General Laws, Chapter 156B, Section 78)

I hereby approve the within Articles of *Consolidation / *Merger and, the filing fee in the amount of $ _____ , having been paid, said articles are deemed to have been filed with me this _____ day of _____ , 20 _____ .

Effective date: _____

WILLIAM FRANCIS GALVIN
Secretary of the Commonwealth

TO BE FILLED IN BY CORPORATION
Contact information:

_____

_____

_____

Telephone: _____

Email: _____

A copy this filing will be available on-line at www.state.ma.us/sec/cor once the document is filed.

Corporate Dissolution

Forms and instructions for their completion for the dissolution of a Corporation in the states of Connecticut (Exhibit 7-19), Florida (Exhibit 7-20), and Louisiana (Exhibit 7-21) are included herein. Other states' forms may be found on the state Web sites or by contacting the Department of Corporations or secretary of state.

EXHIBIT 7-19   Connecticut Dissolution of a Stock Corporation

SECRETARY OF THE STATE
30 TRINITY STREET
POST OFFICE BOX 150470
HARTFORD, CT 06115-0470

DISSOLUTION OF A CONNECTICUT STOCK CORPORATION

A Connecticut stock corporation may be dissolved by incorporators, initial directors, shareholders or directors. Please consult The Connecticut Business Corporation Act to determine which of these methods are appropriate, after the necessary corporate action has been taken to authorize the dissolution.

Following dissolution, the affairs of the corporation must be wound up in the manner provided in The Connecticut Business Corporation Act.

Any questions concerning completion of this form or the dissolution process in general should be directed to the Corporation's own legal counsel.

MAKE CHECKS PAYABLE TO THE SECRETARY OF THE STATE

continued

Exhibit 7-19 *continued*

INSTRUCTIONS FOR COMPLETION OF CERTIFICATE OF DISSOLUTION STOCK CORPORATION

Instructions

1. NAME OF CORPORATION: Please provide the complete name of the corporation as it currently appears on the records of the Secretary of the State.

2. DATE DISSOLUTION WAS AUTHORIZED: Please provide the month, day and year on which the directors/shareholders/incorporators authorized the dissolution of the corporation.

3. COMPLETE APPROPRIATE BLOCK (A) OR (B):

    (A) Place a check mark next to 1 or 2 in block (A) if the dissolution was authorized by a majority of the corporation's initial directors or incorporators.

    (B) Place a check in block (B) if the dissolution was approved by shareholders in the manner required by sections 33-600 to 33-998 (inclusive) of the Connecticut General Statutes.

4. EXECUTION: The document must be executed by an authorized official of the corporation. That person must print or type their name, state the capacity under which they sign and provide a signature. The execution constitutes a legal statement under the penalties of false statement that the information provided in the document is true.

A CORPORATION MAY ONLY REVOKE ITS DISSOLUTION WITHIN 120 DAYS FOLLOWING THE EFFECTIVE DATE OF SUCH DISSOLUTION.

continued

Exhibit 7-19 *continued*

CERTIFICATE OF DISSOLUTION
STOCK CORPORATION
Office of the Secretary of the State
30 Trinity Street / P.O. Box 150470 / Hartford, CT 06115-0470 /Rev. 07/01/2003

See reverse for instruction

Space For Office Use Only	Filing Fee $25.00

1. NAME OF CORPORATION

2. DATE ON WHICH DISSOLUTION WAS AUTHORIZED _____/_____/_____

3. Complete Block (A) if Dissolution was authorized by incorporators or initial directors <u>or</u> block (B) if Dissolution was authorized by directors and shareholders.

(A) Place a check mark next to either **1** <u>or</u> **2** as appropriate:

_____**1.** None of the corporation's shares have been issued   _____**2.** The corporation has not commenced business

The undersigned makes the following assertions in connection with the selection made under section (A) of this form: that no debt of the corporation remains unpaid; that if shares were issued, the net assets of the corporation remaining after winding up have been distributed to the shareholders; and that a majority of the incorporators or initial directors authorized the dissolution.

(B) _____The proposal to dissolve was duly approved by the shareholders in the manner required by sections 33-600 to 33-998 (inclusive) of the Connecticut General Statutes, and by the Certificate of Incorporation.

4. EXECUTION

Dated this _____ day of _____, 20_____.

Print or type name of signatory	Capacity of signatory	Signature

**<u>NOTE: A corporation may only revoke its dissolution within 120 days
following the effective date of such dissolution.</u>**

EXHIBIT 7-20   Florida Dissolution of a Profit Corporation

Attached is the information concerning the dissolution of a Florida profit corporation.

A corporation can voluntarily dissolve by filing articles of dissolution with the Division of Corporations in accordance with section 607.1401 or 607.1403, Florida Statutes. Section 607.1401, Florida Statutes, provides for the dissolution of a corporation that has not issued shares or commenced business. Section 607.1403, Florida Statutes, provides for the dissolution of a corporation that has commenced business and issued shares.

For your convenience, attached to this letter are sample forms for dissolution. Please choose the appropriate form. Section 607.0120, Florida Statutes, requires that the document be typed or printed, and must be legible.

Pursuant to section 607.0123, Florida Statutes, a delayed effective date may be specified but may not be later than the 90th day after the date on which the document is filed.

The filing fee for the articles of dissolution is $35. Certified copies of the dissolution are $8.75 each (plus $1 per page for each page over 8, not to exceed a maximum of $52.50). A certificate of status is $8.75. Submit one check for the correct amount made payable to Florida Department of State. Please include a cover letter containing your telephone number and return address.

Any further inquiries on this matter should be directed to the Amendment Section by calling (850) 245-6050, or by writing: Division of Corporations, P. O. Box 6327, Tallahassee, FL 32314.

Note: These forms for filing articles of dissolution are basic. Each corporation is a separate entity and as such has specific goals, needs and requirements. Additional sheets may be attached as required. The Division of Corporations recommends that corporate documents be reviewed by your legal counsel. The division is a filing agency and as such does not render any legal, accounting, or tax advice. The professional advice of your legal counsel to ascertain exact compliance with all statutory requirements is strongly recommended.

continued

Exhibit 7-20 *continued*

ARTICLES OF DISSOLUTION

Pursuant to 607.1401, Florida Statutes, this Florida profit corporation submits the following articles of dissolution:

FIRST: The name of the corporation is:_____

_____

SECOND: The filing date of the articles of incorporation was:_____

THIRD: (CHECK ONE)

❑ None of the corporation's shares have been issued.

❑ The corporation has not commenced business.

FOURTH: No debt of the corporation remains unpaid.

FIFTH: The net assets of the corporation remaining after winding up have been distributed to the shareholders, if shares were issued.

SIXTH: Adoption of Dissolution (CHECK ONE)

❑ A majority of the incorporators authorized the dissolution.

❑ A majority of the directors authorized the dissolution.

Signed this _____ day of _____, _____.

Signature _____
(By the chairman or vice chairman of the board, president, or other officer - if there are no officers or directors, by an incorporator.)

_____
(Typed or printed name)

_____
(Title)

continued

Exhibit 7-20   *continued*

ARTICLES OF DISSOLUTION

Pursuant to section 607.1403, Florida Statutes, this Florida profit corporation submits the following articles of dissolution:

FIRST: The name of the corporation is:_____

_____

SECOND: The date dissolution was authorized:_____

THIRD: Adoption of Dissolution   (CHECK ONE)

❑ Dissolution was approved by the shareholders. The number of votes cast for dissolution was sufficient for approval.

❑ Dissolution was approved by vote of the shareholders through voting groups.

The following statement must be separately provided for each voting group entitled to vote separately on the plan to dissolve:

The number of votes cast for dissolution was sufficient for approval by

_____
(voting group)

Signed this _____ day of _____, _____.

Signature _____
(By the Chairman or Vice Chairman of the Board, President, or other officer)

_____
(Typed or printed name)

_____
(Title)

EXHIBIT 7-21 Louisiana Dissolution

INSTRUCTIONS

1. File this form, along with the appropriate filing fee with the Secretary of State's office.

2. You will receive two Certificates of Dissolution, one copy of which should be filed with the Clerk of Court where the corporation maintains its registered office. If the corporation's registered office is located in Orleans Parish, a Certificate of Dissolution must be filed with the recorder of mortgages.

continued

Exhibit 7-21 *continued*

W. Fox McKeithen
Secretary of State

AFFIDAVIT TO DISSOLVE CORPORATION
(R.S. 12:142.1 & 12:250.1)

Domestic Corporation (Business or Non-Profit) Enclose $60.00 filing fee Make remittance payable to Secretary of State *Do Not Send Cash*	Return to:	Commercial Division P. O. Box 94125 Baton Rouge, LA 70804-9125 Phone (225) 925-4704 Web Site: www.sec.state.la.us

STATE OF _____

PARISH/COUNTY OF _____

BEFORE ME, the undersigned Notary Public in and for the parish/county herein above shown, personally came and appeared the undersigned who, after being duly sworn, did depose and say that:

_____
Corporation Name

_____

is no longer doing business, owes no debts and is dissolved by filing this affidavit with the Secretary of State, executed by the shareholder(s), or incorporator(s) if no shares have been issued, attesting to such facts.

The undersigned further declared that they are: (check one)

( )   The shareholders of the above named corporation.

( )   The incorporators of the above named corporation and no shares have been issued.

_____

_____

_____

_____
Incorporator(s) or Shareholder(s)

Sworn to and subscribed before me, the undersigned Notary Public, on this date: _____

_____
Notary

339 Rev. 5/00   (See instructions on back)

A complete packet of forms for a Chapter 11 or Chapter 7 bankruptcy, along with instructions for their completion, is included herein. They were obtained from the Bankruptcy Court Web site for the Southern District of California.

Each state has its own Federal Bankruptcy Court. Except for the caption, all forms should be almost identical. Check your own state's Federal Bankruptcy Court Web site to be sure you are using the latest and most accurate forms.

The following forms are included:

Exhibit 8-1   Notice of Commencement of Case
Exhibit 8-2   United States Bankruptcy Court Form
Exhibit 8-3   Voluntary Petition
Exhibit 8-4   Notice of Chapter 11 Bankruptcy Case
Exhibit 8-5   Notice of Chapter 7 Bankruptcy Case
              (Corporation/Partnership Asset Case)
Exhibit 8-6   Notice of Chapter 7 Bankruptcy Case
              (Individual or Joint Debtor Asset Case)
Exhibit 8-7   Application for the Appointment for an Appraiser
Exhibit 8-8   Declaration on Behalf of a Corporation or Partnership

EXHIBIT 8-1 Notice of Commencement of Case

FORM 9. NOTICE OF COMMENCEMENT OF CASE UNDER THE
BANKRUPTCY CODE, MEETING OF CREDITORS,
AND DEADLINES

9A...........Chapter	7, Individual/Joint, No-Asset Case
9B...........Chapter	7, Corporation/Partnership, No-Asset Case
9C...........Chapter	7, Individual/Joint, Asset Case
9D...........Chapter	7, Corporation/Partnership, Asset Case
9E...........Chapter	11, Individual/Joint Case
9E(Alt.)..Chapter	11, Individual/Joint Case
9F...........Chapter	11, Corporation/Partnership Case
9F(Alt.)..Chapter	11, Corporation/Partnership Case
9G...........Chapter	12, Individual/Joint Case
9H...........Chapter	12, Corporation/Partnership Case
9I...........Chapter	13, Individual/Joint Case

EXHIBIT 8-2 United States Bankruptcy Court Form

CSD 1000 [04/28/96]
Name, Address, Telephone No. & I.D. No.

UNITED STATES BANKRUPTCY COURT
SOUTHERN DISTRICT OF CALIFORNIA
325 West F Street, San Diego, California 92101-6991

In Re

BANKRUPTCY NO.

[add in filing in response to hearing
Date of Hearing:
Tax I.D. #:   Time of Hearing:
Social Security #:   Debtor.   Name of Judge:

EXHIBIT 8-3 Voluntary Petition

(Official Form 1) (12/02)

FORM B1	United States Bankruptcy Court _____District of_____	Voluntary Petition

Name of Debtor (if individual, enter Last, First, Middle):	Name of Joint Debtor (Spouse) (Last, First, Middle):
All Other Names used by the Debtor in the last 6 years (include married, maiden, and trade names):	All Other Names used by the Joint Debtor in the last 6 years (include married, maiden, and trade names):
Soc. Sec./Tax I.D. No. (if more than one, state all):	Soc. Sec./Tax I.D. No. (if more than one, state all):
Street Address of Debtor (No. & Street, City, State & Zip Code):	Street Address of Joint Debtor (No. & Street, City, State & Zip Code):
County of Residence or of the Principal Place of Business:	County of Residence or of the Principal Place of Business:
Mailing Address of Debtor (if different from street address):	Mailing Address of Joint Debtor (if different from street address):

Location of Principal Assets of Business Debtor
(if different from street address above):

Information Regarding the Debtor (Check the Applicable Boxes)

Venue (Check any applicable box)

☐ Debtor has been domiciled or has had a residence, principal place of business, or principal assets in this District for 180 days immediately preceding the date of this petition or for a longer part of such 180 days than in any other District.

☐ There is a bankruptcy case concerning debtor's affiliate, general partner, or partnership pending in this District.

Type of Debtor (Check all boxes that apply)	**Chapter or Section of Bankruptcy Code Under Which the Petition is Filed** (Check one box)
☐ Individual(s) ☐ Railroad ☐ Corporation ☐ Stockbroker ☐ Partnership ☐ Commodity Broker ☐ Other_____ ☐ Clearing Bank	☐ Chapter 7 ☐ Chapter 11 ☐ Chapter 13 ☐ Chapter 9 ☐ Chapter 12 ☐ Sec. 304 - Case ancillary to foreign proceeding
Nature of Debts (Check one box) ☐ Consumer/Non-Business ☐ Business	**Filing Fee** (Check one box) ☐ Full Filing Fee attached
Chapter 11 Small Business (Check all boxes that apply) ☐ Debtor is a small business as defined in 11 U.S.C. § 101 ☐ Debtor is and elects to be considered a small business under 11 U.S.C. § 1121(e) (Optional)	☐ Filing Fee to be paid in installments (Applicable to individuals only) Must attach signed application for the court's consideration certifying that the debtor is unable to pay fee except in installments. Rule 1006(b). See Official Form No. 3.

Statistical/Administrative Information (Estimates only)	THIS SPACE IS FOR COURT USE ONLY

☐ Debtor estimates that funds will be available for distribution to unsecured creditors.

☐ Debtor estimates that, after any exempt property is excluded and administrative expenses paid, there will be no funds available for distribution to unsecured creditors.

Estimated Number of Creditors	1-15	16-49	50-99	100-199	200-999	1000-over
	☐	☐	☐	☐	☐	☐

Estimated Assets

$0 to $50,000	$50,001 to $100,000	$100,001 to $500,000	$500,001 to $1 million	$1,000,001 to $10 million	$10,000,001 to $50 million	$50,000,001 to $100 million	More than $100 million
☐	☐	☐	☐	☐	☐	☐	☐

Estimated Debts

$0 to $50,000	$50,001 to $100,000	$100,001 to $500,000	$500,001 to $1 million	$1,000,001 to $10 million	$10,000,001 to $50 million	$50,000,001 to $100 million	More than $100 million
☐	☐	☐	☐	☐	☐	☐	☐

continued

Exhibit 8-3   *continued*

| (Official Form 1) (12/02) | FORM B1, Page 2 |

| **Voluntary Petition**
(This page must be completed and filed in every case) | Name of Debtor(s): |

Prior Bankruptcy Case Filed Within Last 6 Years (If more than one, attach additional sheet)

| Location
Where Filed: | Case Number: | Date Filed: |

Pending Bankruptcy Case Filed by any Spouse, Partner or Affiliate of this Debtor (If more than one, attach additional sheet)

| Name of Debtor: | Case Number: | Date Filed: |
| District: | Relationship: | Judge: |

Signatures

Signature(s) of Debtor(s) (Individual/Joint)

I declare under penalty of perjury that the information provided in this petition is true and correct.
[If petitioner is an individual whose debts are primarily consumer debts and has chosen to file under chapter 7] I am aware that I may proceed under chapter 7, 11, 12 or 13 of title 11, United States Code, understand the relief available under each such chapter, and choose to proceed under chapter 7.
I request relief in accordance with the chapter of title 11, United States Code, specified in this petition.

X _____
Signature of Debtor

X _____
Signature of Joint Debtor

_____
Telephone Number (If not represented by attorney)

_____
Date

Signature of Attorney

X _____
Signature of Attorney for Debtor(s)

_____
Printed Name of Attorney for Debtor(s)

_____
Firm Name

_____
Address

_____
Telephone Number

_____
Date

Signature of Debtor (Corporation/Partnership)

I declare under penalty of perjury that the information provided in this petition is true and correct, and that I have been authorized to file this petition on behalf of the debtor.

The debtor requests relief in accordance with the chapter of title 11, United States Code, specified in this petition.

X _____
Signature of Authorized Individual

_____
Printed Name of Authorized Individual

_____
Title of Authorized Individual

_____
Date

Exhibit A

(To be completed if debtor is required to file periodic reports (e.g., forms 10K and 10Q) with the Securities and Exchange Commission pursuant to Section 13 or 15(d) of the Securities Exchange Act of 1934 and is requesting relief under chapter 11)

☐   Exhibit A is attached and made a part of this petition.

Exhibit B

(To be completed if debtor is an individual whose debts are primarily consumer debts)

I, the attorney for the petitioner named in the foregoing petition, declare that I have informed the petitioner that [he or she] may proceed under chapter 7, 11, 12, or 13 of title 11, United States Code, and have explained the relief available under each such chapter.

X _____
Signature of Attorney for Debtor(s)   Date

Exhibit C

Does the debtor own or have possession of any property that poses a threat of imminent and identifiable harm to public health or safety?

☐   Yes, and Exhibit C is attached and made a part of this petition.
☐   No

Signature of Non-Attorney Petition Preparer

I certify that I am a bankruptcy petition preparer as defined in 11 U.S.C. § 110, that I prepared this document for compensation, and that I have provided the debtor with a copy of this document.

_____
Printed Name of Bankruptcy Petition Preparer

_____
Social Security Number

_____
Address

Names and Social Security numbers of all other individuals who prepared or assisted in preparing this document:

If more than one person prepared this document, attach additional sheets conforming to the appropriate official form for each person.

X _____
Signature of Bankruptcy Petition Preparer

_____
Date

A bankruptcy petition preparer's failure to comply with the provisions of title 11 and the Federal Rules of Bankruptcy Procedure may result in fines or imprisonment or both 11 U.S.C. §110; 18 U.S.C. §156.

EXHIBIT 8-4 Notice of Chapter 11 Bankruptcy Case

FORM B9E (Chapter 11 Individual or Joint Debtor Case) (9/97)

UNITED STATES BANKRUPTCY COURT	_____ District of _____

Notice of
Chapter 11 Bankruptcy Case, Meeting of Creditors, & Deadlines

[A chapter 11 bankruptcy case concerning the debtor(s) listed below was filed on _____ (date).]

or [A bankruptcy case concerning the debtor(s) listed below was originally filed under chapter _____ on _____ (date) and was converted to a case under chapter 11 on_____ .]

You may be a creditor of the debtor. **This notice lists important deadlines.** You may want to consult an attorney to protect your rights. All documents filed in the case may be inspected at the bankruptcy clerk's office at the address listed below. NOTE: The staff of the bankruptcy clerk's office cannot give legal advice.

See Reverse Side For Important Explanations.

Debtor(s) (name(s) and address):	Case Number:
	Social Security/Taxpayer ID Nos.:
Attorney for Debtor(s) (name and address):	Telephone number:

Meeting of Creditors:

Date: / /	Time: ( ) A.M. ( ) P.M.	Location:

Deadlines:

Papers must be *received* by the bankruptcy clerk's office by the following deadlines:

Deadline to File a Proof of Claim:

Notice of deadline will be sent at a later time.

Deadline to File a Complaint to Determine Dischargeability of Certain Debts:

Deadline to File a Complaint Objecting to Discharge of the Debtor:

First date set for hearing on confirmation of plan.
Notice of that date will be sent at a later time.

Deadline to Object to Exemptions:

Thirty (30) days after the *conclusion* of the meeting of creditors.

Creditors May Not Take Certain Actions:

The filing of the bankruptcy case automatically stays certain collection and other actions against the debtor and the debtor's property. If you attempt to collect a debt or take other action in violation of the Bankruptcy Code, you may be penalized.

Address of the Bankruptcy Clerk's Office:	**For the Court:**
	Clerk of the Bankruptcy Court:
Telephone number:	
Hours Open:	Date:

continued

Exhibit 8-4 *continued*

EXPLANATIONS	FORM B9E (9/97)

Filing of Chapter 11 Bankruptcy Case	A bankruptcy case under chapter 11 of the Bankruptcy Code (title 11, United States Code) has been filed in this court by or against the debtor(s) listed on the front side, and an order for relief has been entered. Chapter 11 allows a debtor to reorganize or liquidate pursuant to a plan. A plan is not effective unless confirmed by the court. You may be sent a copy of the plan and a disclosure statement telling you about the plan, and you might have the opportunity to vote on the plan. You will be sent notice of the date of the confirmation hearing, and you may object to confirmation of the plan and attend the confirmation hearing. Unless a trustee is serving, the debtor will remain in possession of the debtor's property and may continue to operate any business.
Creditors May Not Take Certain Actions	Prohibited collection actions are listed in Bankruptcy Code § 362. Common examples of prohibited actions include contacting the debtor by telephone, mail or otherwise to demand repayment; taking actions to collect money or obtain property from the debtor; repossessing the debtor's property; starting or continuing lawsuits or foreclosures; and garnishing or deducting from the debtor's wages.
Meeting of Creditors	A meeting of creditors is scheduled for the date, time and location listed on the front side. *The debtor (both spouses in a joint case) must be present at the meeting to be questioned under oath by the trustee and by creditors.* Creditors are welcome to attend, but are not required to do so. The meeting may be continued and concluded at a later date without further notice.
Claims	A Proof of Claim is a signed statement describing a creditor's claim. If a Proof of Claim form is not included with this notice, you can obtain one at any bankruptcy clerk's office. You may look at the schedules that have been or will be filed at the bankruptcy clerk's office. If your claim is scheduled and is *not* listed as disputed, contingent, or unliquidated, it will be allowed in the amount scheduled unless you file a Proof of Claim or you are sent further notice about the claim. Whether or not your claim is scheduled, you are permitted to file a Proof of Claim. If your claim is not listed at all *or* if your claim is listed as disputed, contingent, or unliquidated, then you must file a Proof of Claim or you might not be paid any money on your claim against the debtor in the bankruptcy case. The court has not yet set a deadline to file a Proof of Claim. If a deadline is set, you will be sent another notice.
Discharge of Debts	Confirmation of a chapter 11 plan may result in a discharge of debts, which may include all or part of your debt. See Bankruptcy Code § 1141(d). A discharge means that you may never try to collect the debt from the debtor except as provided in the plan. If you believe that a debt owed to you is not dischargeable under Bankruptcy Code § 523(a)(2), (4), (6), or (15), you must start a lawsuit by filing a complaint in the bankruptcy clerk's office by the "Deadline to File a Complaint to Determine Dischargeability of Certain Debts" listed on the front side. The bankruptcy clerk's office must receive the complaint and the required filing fee by that Deadline. If you believe that the debtor is not entitled to receive a discharge under Bankruptcy Code § 1141(d)(3), you must file a complaint with the required filing fee in the bankruptcy clerk's office not later than the first date set for the hearing on confirmation of the plan. You will be sent another notice informing you of that date.
Exempt Property	The debtor is permitted by law to keep certain property as exempt. Exempt property will not be sold and distributed to creditors, even if the debtor's case is converted to chapter 7. The debtor must file a list of all property claimed as exempt. You may inspect that list at the bankruptcy clerk's office. If you believe that an exemption claimed by the debtor is not authorized by law, you may file an objection to that exemption. The bankruptcy clerk's office must receive the objection by the "Deadline to Object to Exemptions" listed on the front side.
Bankruptcy Clerk's Office	Any paper that you file in this bankruptcy case should be filed at the bankruptcy clerk's office at the address listed on the front side. You may inspect all papers filed, including the list of the debtor's property and debts and the list of the property claimed as exempt, at the bankruptcy clerk's office.
Legal Advice	The staff of the bankruptcy clerk's office cannot give legal advice. You may want to consult an attorney to protect your rights.

—Refer To Other Side For Important Deadlines and Notices—

EXHIBIT 8-5 Notice of Chapter 7 Bankruptcy Case (Corporation/Partnership Asset Case)

FORM B9D (Chapter 7 Corporation/Partnership Asset Case) (9/97)

UNITED STATES BANKRUPTCY COURT _____ District of _____

Notice of
Chapter 7 Bankruptcy Case, Meeting of Creditors, & Deadlines

[A chapter 7 bankruptcy case concerning the debtor [corporation] *or* [partnership] listed below was filed on _____ (date).]

or [A bankruptcy case concerning the debtor [corporation] *or* [partnership] listed below was originally filed under chapter ____

on

_____ (date) and was converted to a case under chapter 7 on_____.]

You may be a creditor of the debtor. **This notice lists important deadlines.** You may want to consult an attorney to protect your rights. All documents filed in the case may be inspected at the bankruptcy clerk's office at the address listed below. NOTE: The staff of the bankruptcy clerk's office cannot give legal advice.

See Reverse Side For Important Explanations.

Debtor (name(s) and address):	Case Number:
	Taxpayer ID Nos.:
Attorney for Debtor (name and address):	Bankruptcy Trustee (name and address):
Telephone number:	Telephone number:

Meeting of Creditors:

Date: /   /   Time: (   ) A.M.   Location: _____
                           (   ) P.M.

Deadline to File a Proof of Claim

Proof of Claim must be *received* by the bankruptcy clerk's office by the following deadline:

For all creditors (except a governmental unit):   For a governmental unit:

Creditors May Not Take Certain Actions:

The filing of the bankruptcy case automatically stays certain collection and other actions against the debtor and the debtor's property. If you attempt to collect a debt or take other action in violation of the Bankruptcy Code, you may be penalized.

Address of the Bankruptcy Clerk's Office:	**For the Court:**
	Clerk of the Bankruptcy Court:
Telephone number:	
Hours Open:	Date:

continued

Exhibit 8-5   *continued*

	EXPLANATIONS	FORM B9D (9/97)

Filing of Chapter 7 Bankruptcy Case	A bankruptcy case under chapter 7 of the Bankruptcy Code (title 11, United States Code) has been filed in this court by or against the debtor listed on the front side, and an order for relief has been entered.
Creditors May Not Take Certain Actions	Prohibited collection actions are listed in Bankruptcy Code § 362. Common examples of prohibited actions include contacting the debtor by telephone, mail or otherwise to demand repayment; taking actions to collect money or obtain property from the debtor; repossessing the debtor's property; and starting or continuing lawsuits or foreclosures.
Meeting of Creditors	A meeting of creditors is scheduled for the date, time and location listed on the front side. *The debtor's representative must be present at the meeting to be questioned under oath by the trustee and by creditors.* Creditors are welcome to attend, but are not required to do so. The meeting may be continued and concluded at a later date without further notice.
Claims	A Proof of Claim is a signed statement describing a creditor's claim. If a Proof of Claim form is not included with this notice, you can obtain one at any bankruptcy clerk's office. If you do not file a Proof of Claim by the "Deadline to File a Proof of Claim" listed on the front side, you might not be paid any money on your claim against the debtor in the bankruptcy case. To be paid you must file a Proof of Claim even if your claim is listed in the schedules filed by the debtor.
Liquidation of the Debtor's Property and Payment of Creditors' Claims	The bankruptcy trustee listed on the front of this notice will collect and sell the debtor's property. If the trustee can collect enough money, creditors may be paid some or all of the debts owed to them, in the order specified by the Bankruptcy Code. To make sure you receive any share of that money, you must file a Proof of Claim, as described above.
Bankruptcy Clerk's Office	Any paper that you file in this bankruptcy case should be filed at the bankruptcy clerk's office at the address listed on the front side. You may inspect all papers filed, including the list of the debtor's property and debts, at the bankruptcy clerk's office.
Legal Advice	The staff of the bankruptcy clerk's office cannot give legal advice. You may want to consult an attorney to protect your rights.

—Refer To Other Side For Important Deadlines and Notices—

EXHIBIT 8-6 Notice of Chapter 7 Bankruptcy Case (Individual or Joint Debtor Asset Case)

FORM B9C (Chapter 7 Individual or Joint Debtor Asset Case) (9/97)

UNITED STATES BANKRUPTCY COURT _____ District of _____

Notice of
Chapter 7 Bankruptcy Case, Meeting of Creditors, & Deadlines

[A chapter 7 bankruptcy case concerning the debtor(s) listed below was filed on _____ (date).]

or [A bankruptcy case concerning the debtor(s) listed below was originally filed under chapter _____ on _____ (date) and was converted to a case under chapter 7 on_____.]

You may be a creditor of the debtor. **This notice lists important deadlines.** You may want to consult an attorney to protect your rights. All documents filed in the case may be inspected at the bankruptcy clerk's office at the address listed below. NOTE: The staff of the bankruptcy clerk's office cannot give legal advice.

See Reverse Side For Important Explanations.

Debtor(s) (name(s) and address):	Case Number:
	Social Security/Taxpayer ID Nos.:
Attorney for Debtor(s) (name and address):	Bankruptcy Trustee (name and address):
Telephone number:	Telephone number:

Meeting of Creditors:

Date: /   /   Time: (   ) A.M.   Location:
                                       (   ) P.M.

Deadlines:

Papers must be *received* by the bankruptcy clerk's office by the following deadlines:
Deadline to File a Proof of Claim:

For all creditors (except a governmental unit):	For a governmental unit:

Deadline to File a Complaint Objecting to Discharge of the Debtor or to Determine Dischargeability of Certain Debts:

Deadline to Object to Exemptions:
Thirty (30) days after the *conclusion* of the meeting of creditors.

Creditors May Not Take Certain Actions:

The filing of the bankruptcy case automatically stays certain collection and other actions against the debtor and the debtor's property. If you attempt to collect a debt or take other action in violation of the Bankruptcy Code, you may be penalized.

Address of the Bankruptcy Clerk's Office:	**For the Court:**
	Clerk of the Bankruptcy Court:
Telephone number:	
Hours Open:	Date:

continued

Exhibit 8-6 *continued*

EXPLANATIONS		FORM B9C (9/97)
Filing of Chapter 7 Bankruptcy Case	A bankruptcy case under chapter 7 of the Bankruptcy Code (title 11, United States Code) has been filed in this court by or against the debtor(s) listed on the front side, and an order for relief has been entered.	
Creditors May Not Take Certain Actions	Prohibited collection actions are listed in Bankruptcy Code § 362. Common examples of prohibited actions include contacting the debtor by telephone, mail or otherwise to demand repayment; taking actions to collect money or obtain property from the debtor; repossessing the debtor's property; starting or continuing lawsuits or foreclosures; and garnishing or deducting from the debtor's wages.	
Meeting of Creditors	A meeting of creditors is scheduled for the date, time and location listed on the front side. *The debtor (both spouses in a joint case) must be present at the meeting to be questioned under oath by the trustee and by creditors.* Creditors are welcome to attend, but are not required to do so. The meeting may be continued and concluded at a later date without further notice.	
Claims	A Proof of Claim is a signed statement describing a creditor's claim. If a Proof of Claim form is not included with this notice, you can obtain one at any bankruptcy clerk's office. If you do not file a Proof of Claim by the "Deadline to File a Proof of Claim" listed on the front side, you might not be paid any money on your claim against the debtor in the bankruptcy case. To be paid you must file a Proof of Claim even if your claim is listed in the schedules filed by the debtor.	
Discharge of Debts	The debtor is seeking a discharge of most debts, which may include your debt. A discharge means that you may never try to collect the debt from the debtor. If you believe that the debtor is not entitled to receive a discharge under Bankruptcy Code § 727(a) *or* that a debt owed to you is not dischargeable under Bankruptcy Code § 523(a)(2), (4), (6), or (15), you must start a lawsuit by filing a complaint in the bankruptcy clerk's office by the "Deadline to File a Complaint Objecting to Discharge of the Debtor or to Determine Dischargeability of Certain Debts" listed on the front side. The bankruptcy clerk's office must receive the complaint and the required filing fee by that Deadline.	
Exempt Property	The debtor is permitted by law to keep certain property as exempt. Exempt property will not be sold and distributed to creditors. The debtor must file a list of all property claimed as exempt. You may inspect that list at the bankruptcy clerk's office. If you believe that an exemption claimed by the debtor is not authorized by law, you may file an objection to that exemption. The bankruptcy clerk's office must receive the objection by the "Deadline to Object to Exemptions" listed on the front side.	
Liquidation of the Debtor's Property and Payment of Creditors' Claims	The bankruptcy trustee listed on the front of this notice will collect and sell the debtor's property that is not exempt. If the trustee can collect enough money, creditors may be paid some or all of the debts owed to them, in the order specified by the Bankruptcy Code. To make sure you receive any share of that money, you must file a Proof of Claim, as described above.	
Bankruptcy Clerk's Office	Any paper that you file in this bankruptcy case should be filed at the bankruptcy clerk's office at the address listed on the front side. You may inspect all papers filed, including the list of the debtor's property and debts and the list of the property claimed as exempt, at the bankruptcy clerk's office.	
Legal Advice	The staff of the bankruptcy clerk's office cannot give legal advice. You may want to consult an attorney to protect your rights.	
—Refer To Other Side For Important Deadlines and Notices—		

EXHIBIT 8-7 Application for the Appointment of an Appraiser

CSD 2048 [04/28/96]
Name, Address, Telephone No. & I.D. No.

UNITED STATES BANKRUPTCY COURT
SOUTHERN DISTRICT OF CALIFORNIA
325 West F Street, San Diego, California 92101-6991

In Re

BANKRUPTCY NO.

Debtor.

APPLICATION FOR THE APPOINTMENT OF AN APPRAISER

The undersigned respectfully represents that:

1.   Your applicant is the duly appointed and qualified Trustee for the estate of the above-named debtor.

2.   Certain assets of this estate require an appraisal, consisting of:
        <u>General Description</u>   <u>Location</u>

3.   No previous application for appraisal of these assets has been made.

4.   It is necessary and in the best interests of creditors that said assets be appraised.

5.   The following disinterested person has agreed to serve as appraiser in this case, namely:

[Name and Address]   _____

                      _____

                      _____

6.   The recommended appraiser has agreed to perform an appraisal of the above-described property for a fee not to exceed the sum of $_____, plus necessary expenses.

7.   The attached is the verified statement required of the proposed Appraiser by Federal Rule of Bankruptcy Procedure 2014(a) and 2016(a).

DATED: _____   _____
                                             Trustee in Bankruptcy

EXHIBIT 8-8   Declaration on Behalf of a Corporation or Partnership

Form 2. DECLARATION UNDER PENALTY OF PERJURY ON BEHALF OF A CORPORATION OR PARTNERSHIP

   I, [the president *or* other officer *or* an authorized agent of the corporation] [*or* a member *or* an authorized agent of the partnership] named as the debtor in this case, declare under penalty of perjury that I have read the foregoing [list *or* schedule *or* amendment *or* other document (describe)] and that it is true and correct to the best of my information and belief.

Date _____

             Signature _____

             _____

             (Print Name and Title)

Forms for the purchase or real property are available from the Department of Real Estate for each state. Local real estate offices may also provide copies of these forms.

Unlawful detainer or eviction actions are instituted against tenants by landlords. The appropriate forms for these cases are found in the textbook in Chapter 13.

If a civil action is commenced where the relief sought affects title to or interests in real property, a Notice of Lis Pendens is filed with the Superior Court. A sample Notice of Lis Pendens for Arizona is shown in Exhibit 9-10. The format for other states is either similar or identical.

EXHIBIT 9-1   Arizona Notice of Lis Pendens

```
 1   JEFFREY B. GOOD
     2433 Yavapai Boulevard
 2   Scottsdale, AZ 23456
     Telephone:  (480) 123-4567
 3
                              ARIZONA SUPERIOR COURT
 4                              COUNTY OF MARIPOSA

 5

 6
     ROBERT R. MILLER,                  ) Case No.: No. 12-3-456789-1
 7                                      )
                 Plaintiff,             ) NOTICE OF LIS PENDENS
 8                                      )
            vs.                         )
 9                                      )
     JOHN GAGLIO,                       )
10                                      )
                 Defendant              )
11   _____   )

12
     PLEASE TAKE NOTICE that a civil action, captioned as noted above, has been
13
     instituted in the above-named Court. The relief sought in this action affects
14
     title to or interests in real property.
15
          1. The names of the parties to the action are:  ROBERT R. MILLER,
16
     Plaintiff, vs. JOHN GAGLIO, Defendant.
17
          2. The object of the action is vacant land located in the City of
18
     Tempe, County of Mariposa, State of Arizona, commonly known as 4444 East
19
     Pendens Lane.
20
21        3. The relief demanded in the action is the sum of $15,000 for the
22   grading and clearing of the above-named land.
23
          4. The real property affected by the action is described as follows:
24
25
                              SUMMARY - 1
```

continued

Exhibit 9-1 *continued*

1 Lot 125 of Tract 2345 in the City of Tempe, County of Mariposa, State of

2 Arizona, commonly known as 4444 East Pendens Lane.

3

4 DATED this _____ day of _____, 2004.

5

6

7

8   JEFFREY B. GOOD

9   Attorney for Plaintiff

10   2433 Yavapai Boulevard
                                           Scottsdale, AZ 23456
11   (480) 123-4567

12

13

14

15

16

17

18

19

20

21

22

23

24

25

                          SUMMARY - 2

A formal written contract may be one paragraph or several pages in length. Items that must be included in all contracts are:

1. Names of the parties
2. Consideration of both parties
3. Signatures of parties
4. Date

The simple contract shown in Exhibit 10-1 illustrates the items listed above. The names and addresses of the parties are given. Consideration is the truck that Ms. Bishop is selling and also the $12,000 that Mr. Yardley is paying. The date is given before the signature line. The date the contract is effective is also given: "payable upon receipt of the truck."

EXHIBIT 10-1 Formal Written Contract

FORMAL WRITTEN CONTRACT

This contract entered into this 20th day of September, 2002, between LENORE

BISHOP of 24222 Poplar Avenue, in the City of Memphis, County of Shelby, and State

of Tennessee and JOSEPH M. YARDLEY of 111 Electric Avenue, in the City of

Cordova, County of Shelby, and State of Tennessee, consists of the following terms:

LENORE BISHOP agrees to sell JOSEPH M. YARDLEY her 2002 Toyota truck,

Tennessee license number "XBB111" for the sum of $12,000, payable upon receipt of the

truck.

IN WITNESS WHEREOF, the parties have hereby executed this contract on the

20th day of September, 2002, at Memphis, Tennessee.

_____

LENORE BISHOP, Seller

_____

JOSEPH M. YARDLEY, Buyer

California Contract Action

A breach of contract suit is commenced by the filing of a Contract Complaint. California provides a Judicial Council form for this purpose. Other states may require that a formal typed pleading be prepared with similar information contained therein.

A complaint form for a contract action in California and a form for an Answer in this type of action are shown in Exhibits 10-2 and 10-6, respectively.

The following forms are also included in this section:

Exhibit 10-3 California Cause of Action—Breach of Contract
Exhibit 10-4 California Cause of Action—Common Counts
Exhibit 10-5 California Cause of Action—Fraud
Exhibit 10-6 California Cause of Action—Form Answer

EXHIBIT 10-2   California Contract Action—Complaint

982.1(20)

ATTORNEY OR PARTY WITHOUT ATTORNEY *(Name, state bar number, and address):*	FOR COURT USE ONLY

TELEPHONE NO: FAX NO. *(Optional):*

E–MAIL ADDRESS *(Optional):*

ATTORNEY FOR *(Name):*

SUPERIOR COURT OF CALIFORNIA, COUNTY OF

STREET ADDRESS:

MAILING ADDRESS:

CITY AND ZIP CODE:

BRANCH NAME:

PLAINTIFF:

DEFENDANT:

☐   DOES 1 TO _____

CONTRACT

☐ **COMPLAINT**   ☐ **AMENDED COMPLAINT** *(Number):*

☐ **CROSS–COMPLAINT** ☐ **AMENDED CROSS–COMPLAINT** *(Number):*

Jurisdiction *(check all that apply):*	CASE NUMBER:

Jurisdiction *(check all that apply):*
☐ **ACTION IS A LIMITED CIVIL CASE**
    Amount demanded ☐ **does not exceed $10,000**
                         ☐ **exceeds $10,000, but does not exceed $25,000**
☐ **ACTION IS AN UNLIMITED CIVIL CASE (exceeds $25,000)**
☐ **ACTION IS RECLASSIFIED by this amended complaint or cross-complaint**
        ☐ **from limited to unlimited**
        ☐ **from unlimited to limited**

1. PLAINTIFF* *(names):*

   alleges causes of action against DEFENDANT* *(names):*

2. This pleading, including attachments and exhibits, consists of the following number of pages:

3. a. Each plaintiff named above is a competent adult
      ☐ **except** plaintiff *(name):*
            ☐ a corporation qualified to do business in California
            ☐ an unincorporated entity *(describe):*
            ☐ other *(specify):*

   b. ☐ Plaintiff *(name):*
            ☐ has complied with the fictitious business name laws and is doing business under the fictitious name of *(specify):*

            ☐ has complied with all licensing requirements as a licensed *(specify):*
   c. ☐ Information about additional plaintiffs who are not competent adults is shown in Complaint—Attachment 3c.

4. a. Each defendant named above is a natural person
      ☐ **except** defendant *(name):*   ☐ **except** defendant *(name):*
            ☐ a business organization, form unknown   ☐ a business organization, form unknown
            ☐ a corporation   ☐ a corporation
            ☐ an unincorporated entity *(describe):*   ☐ an unincorporated entity *(describe):*

            ☐ a public entity *(describe):*   ☐ a public entity *(describe):*

            ☐ other *(specify):*   ☐ other *(specify):*

Page 1 of 2

* If this form is used as a cross-complaint, plaintiff means cross-complainant and defendant means cross-defendant.

Form Approved for Optional Use
Judicial Council of California

COMPLAINT—Contract

Code of Civ. Proc., § 425.12

continued

Exhibit 10-2 *continued*

SHORT TITLE:	CASE NUMBER:

COMPLAINT—Contract

4. *(Continued)*
  b. The true names and capacities of defendants sued as Does are unknown to plaintiff.
  c. ☐ Information about additional defendants who are not natural persons is contained in Complaint—Attachment 4c.
  d. ☐ Defendants who are joined pursuant to Code of Civil Procedure section 382 are *(names):*

5. ☐ Plaintiff is required to comply with a claims statute, **and**
  a. ☐ plaintiff has complied with applicable claims statutes, or
  b. ☐ plaintiff is excused from complying because *(specify):*

6. ☐ This action is subject to   ☐ Civil Code section 1812.10   ☐ Civil Code section 2984.4.

7. This court is the proper court because
  a. ☐ a defendant entered into the contract here.
  b. ☐ a defendant lived here when the contract was entered into.
  c. ☐ a defendant lives here now.
  d. ☐ the contract was to be performed here.
  e. ☐ a defendant is a corporation or unincorporated association and its principal place of business is here.
  f. ☐ real property that is the subject of this action is located here.
  g. ☐ other *(specify):*

8. The following causes of action are attached and the statements above apply to each *(each complaint must have one or more causes of action attached):*
  ☐ Breach of Contract   ☐ Common Counts
  ☐ Other *(specify):*

9. ☐ Other:

10. **PLAINTIFF PRAYS** for judgment for costs of suit; for such relief as is fair, just, and equitable; and for
  a. ☐ damages of: $
  b. ☐ interest on the damages
      (1) ☐ according to proof
      (2) ☐ at the rate of   percent per year from *(date):*
  c. ☐ attorney's fees
      (1) ☐ of: $
      (2) ☐ according to proof.
  d. ☐ other *(specify):*

11. ☐ The following paragraphs of this pleading are alleged on information and belief *(specify paragraph numbers):*

Date:

▶

_____   _____
(TYPE OR PRINT NAME)   (SIGNATURE OF PLAINTIFF OR ATTORNEY)

(If you wish to verify this pleading, affix a verification.)

982.1(20) [Rev. July 1, 2002]   **COMPLAINT—Contract**   Page 2 of 2

EXHIBIT 10-3   California Cause of Action—Breach of Contract

982.1(21)

SHORT TITLE:	CASE NUMBER:

_____   **CAUSE OF ACTION**—Breach of Contract   Page _____
(number)

ATTACHMENT TO ☐ Complaint ☐ Cross-Complaint

(Use a separate cause of action form for each cause of action.)

BC-1. Plaintiff *(name)*:

alleges that on or about *(date)*:
a ☐ written ☐ oral ☐ other *(specify)*:
agreement was made between *(name parties to agreement)*:

☐ A copy of the agreement is attached as Exhibit A, **or**
☐ The essential terms of the agreement ☐ are stated in Attachment BC-1 ☐ are as follows *(specify)*:

BC-2. On or about *(dates)*:
defendant breached the agreement by ☐ the acts specified in Attachment BC-2 ☐ the following acts
(specify):

BC-3. Plaintiff has performed all obligations to defendant except those obligations plaintiff was prevented or excused from performing.

BC-4. Plaintiff suffered damages legally (proximately) caused by defendant's breach of the agreement
☐ as stated in Attachment BC-4 ☐ as follows *(specify)*:

BC-5. ☐ Plaintiff is entitled to attorney fees by an agreement or a statute
☐ of $
☐ according to proof.

BC-6. ☐ Other:

CAUSE OF ACTION—Breach of Contract

EXHIBIT 10-4 California Cause of Action—Common Counts

982.1(22)

SHORT TITLE:

CASE NUMBER:

_____ **CAUSE OF ACTION—Common Counts** Page _____
(number)

ATTACHMENT TO ☐ Complaint ☐ Cross-Complaint

(Use a separate cause of action form for each cause of action.)

CC-1. Plaintiff *(name)*:

alleges that defendant *(name)*:

became indebted to ☐ plaintiff ☐ other *(name)*:

a. ☐ within the last four years
(1) ☐ on an open book account for money due.
(2) ☐ because an account was stated in writing by and between plaintiff and defendant in which it was agreed that defendant was indebted to plaintiff.

b. ☐ within the last ☐ two years ☐ four years
(1) ☐ for money had and received by defendant for the use and benefit of plaintiff.
(2) ☐ for work, labor, services and materials rendered at the special instance and request of defendant and for which defendant promised to pay plaintiff
☐ the sum of $
☐ the reasonable value.
(3) ☐ for goods, wares, and merchandise sold and delivered to defendant and for which defendant promised to pay plaintiff
☐ the sum of $
☐ the reasonable value.
(4) ☐ for money lent by plaintiff to defendant at defendant's request.
(5) ☐ for money paid, laid out, and expended to or for defendant at defendant's special instance and request.
(6) ☐ *other (specify)*:

CC-2. $ _____ , which is the reasonable value, is due and unpaid despite plaintiff's demand,
plus prejudgment interest ☐ according to proof ☐ at the rate of _____ percent per year
from *(date)*:

CC-3. ☐ Plaintiff is entitled to attorney fees by an agreement or a statute
☐ of $
☐ according to proof.

CC-4. ☐ Other:

CAUSE OF ACTION—Common Counts

EXHIBIT 10-5   California Cause of Action—Fraud

982.1(23)

SHORT TITLE:

CASE NUMBER:

_____ **CAUSE OF ACTION**—Fraud   Page _____
(number)

ATTACHMENT TO ☐ Complaint ☐ Cross-Complaint

(Use a separate cause of action form for each cause of action.)

FR-1.   Plaintiff *(name)*:

alleges that defendant *(name)*:

on or about *(date)*:   defrauded plaintiff as follows:

FR-2.   ☐ **Intentional or Negligent Misrepresentation**
a. Defendant made representations of material fact   ☐ as stated in Attachment FR-2.a   ☐ as follows:

b. These representations were in fact false. The truth was   ☐ as stated in Attachment FR-2.b   ☐ as follows:

c. When defendant made the representations,
☐ defendant knew they were false, **or**
☐ defendant had no reasonable ground for believing the representations were true.

d. Defendant made the representations with the intent to defraud and induce plaintiff to act as described
in item FR-5. At the time plaintiff acted, plaintiff did not know the representations were false and believed they
were true. Plaintiff acted in justifiable reliance upon the truth of the representations.

FR-3.   ☐ **Concealment**
a. Defendant concealed or suppressed material facts   ☐ as stated in Attachment FR-3.a   ☐ as follows:

b. Defendant concealed or suppressed material facts
☐ defendant was bound to disclose.
☐ by telling plaintiff other facts to mislead plaintiff and prevent plaintiff from discovering the concealed
or suppressed facts.

c. Defendant concealed or suppressed these facts with the intent to defraud and induce plaintiff to act
as described in item FR-5. At the time plaintiff acted, plaintiff was unaware of the concealed or suppressed
facts and would not have taken the action if plaintiff had known the facts.

(Continued)

Form Approved by the
Judicial Council of California
Effective January 1, 1982
Rule 982.1(23)   **CAUSE OF ACTION**—Fraud

continued

Exhibit 10-5 *continued*

SHORT TITLE:	CASE NUMBER:

_____ **CAUSE OF ACTION—Fraud (Continued)**   Page _____
(number)

FR-4. ☐ **Promise Without Intent to Perform**
   a. Defendant made a promise about a material matter without any intention of performing it ☐ as stated
      in Attachment FR-4.a ☐ as follows:

   b. Defendant's promise without any intention of perfomance was made with the intent to defraud and induce
      plaintiff to rely upon it and to act as described in item FR-5. At the time plaintiff acted, plaintiff was unaware of
      defendant's intention not to perform the promise. Plaintiff acted in justifiable reliance upon the promise.

FR-5. In justifiable reliance upon defendant's conduct, plaintiff was induced to act ☐ as stated in Attachment FR-5
      ☐ as follows:

FR-6. Because of plaintiff's reliance upon defendant's conduct, plaintiff has been damaged ☐ as stated in
      Attachment FR-6 ☐ as follows:

FR-7. Other:

[982.1(23)]

EXHIBIT 10-6   California Contract Action—Form Answer

982.1(35)

ATTORNEY OR PARTY WITHOUT ATTORNEY (NAME AND ADDRESS)	TELEPHONE:	FOR COURT USE ONLY

ATTORNEY FOR (NAME):

Insert name of court, judicial district or branch court, if any, and post office and street address:

PLAINTIFF:

DEFENDANT:

ANSWER—Contract

☐ **TO COMPLAINT OF** *(name):*
☐ **TO CROSS-COMPLAINT OF** *(name):*

CASE NUMBER:

1. This pleading, including attachments and exhibits, consists of the following number of pages: _____
2. DEFENDANT *(name):*

   answers the complaint or cross-complaint as follows:
3. ***Check ONLY ONE of the next two boxes:***
   a. ☐ Defendant generally denies each statement of the complaint or cross-complaint. *(Do not check this box if the verified complaint or cross-complaint demands more than $1,000.)*
   b. ☐ Defendant admits that all of the statements of the complaint or cross-complaint are true EXCEPT:
      (1) Defendant claims the following statements are false *(use paragraph numbers or explain):*

      ☐ Continued on Attachment 3.b.(1).
      (2) Defendant has no information or belief that the following statements are true, so defendant denies them *(use paragraph numbers or explain):*

      ☐ Continued on Attachment 3.b.(2)
                                        (Continued)

If this form is used to answer a cross-complaint, plaintiff means cross-complainant and defendant means cross-defendant.

Form Approved by the
Judicial Council of California
Effective January 1, 1982
Rule 982.1(35)

ANSWER—Contract

continued

Exhibit 10-6   *continued*

SHORT TITLE:	CASE NUMBER:

ANSWER—Contract

4. ☐ AFFIRMATIVE DEFENSES
    Defendant alleges the following additional reasons that plaintiff is not entitled to recover anything:

☐ Continued on Attachment 4.

5. ☐ Other:

6. DEFENDANT PRAYS
   a. that plaintiff take nothing.
   b. ☐ for costs of suit.
   c. ☐ other *(specify)*:

....
                (Type or print name)

[982.1(35)]

_____
      (Signature of party or attorney)

USEFUL WEB SITES

Federal Government Agencies/Organizations

Central Intelligence Agency (CIA)   **http://www.odci.gov/cia/**

Department of Justice   **http://www.usdoj.gov**

Department of Transportation   **http://www.dot.gov/**

Federal Aviation Administration   **http://www.faa.gov/**

Federal Bureau of Investigation (FBI)   **http://www.fbi.gov/**

National Transportation Safety Board   **http://www.ntsb.gov/aviation/aviation.htm**

Securities and Exchange Commission (SEC)   **http://www.sec.gov/**

State Department   **http://www.state.gov/index.html**

Finding Law Firms or Legal Organizations

FindLaw   **http://www.findlaw.com**

West Legal Directory   **http://www.lawoffice.com/**

Attorney Locator Service   **http://www.attorneyfind.com/**

Martindale-Hubbell Legal Directory of Attorneys   **http://www.martindale.com**

Legal Employment Center

Hieros Gamos   **http://www.hg.org/employment.html**

Professional Organizations

American Bar Association   **http://www.abanet.org/**

National Association of Legal Assistants   **http://www.nala.org**

National Association of Legal Professionals   **http://www.nals.org**

National Federation of Paralegal Associations   **http://www.paralegals.org**

State Government Offices   **http://www.findlaw.com/**

INDEX OF FORMS BY STATE

Alaska

Arizona

California

Colorado

Connecticut

Delaware

Florida

Hawaii